*Dedicated to* John Manos *and all of the other inventors, whose ideas made this book possible.*

# Ice Cream Dippers

An Illustrated History and Collector's Guide to Early Ice Cream Dippers

Wayne Smith

Front cover photo: Gem Spoon Company catalog (ca. 1900)
Back cover photo: Gilchrist Co. display at the 1917
Association of Ice Cream Supply Men
Convention, in Boston, Mass.
Courtesy Dairy and Food Industries Supply Association


Printed in the United States of America
2nd printing, 1991

For additional copies of this book, send $19.95 + $1.50 shipping to:
Wayne Smith
P.O. Box 418
Walkersville, MD 21793

# Contents

# Introduction

The early ice cream dipper . . . a link to a bygone era. An era that many of us are too young to remember. Those who can, usually have fond memories of the old soda fountain. After all, it was a place where hard working fathers took their families for a Sunday afternoon treat. The soda fountain was the place where one took that special girl after the latest "moving picture." Many a romance bloomed in the ice cream parlor, over sundaes with names such as, "Dreamland", "Peg O'My Heart", and "Bridal Path". These were the happy times, the carefree times of youth, that tend to be remembered long after anything else.

The soda fountain is also the place where the main topic of this book, the ice cream scoop or disher, was found in constant use. The last decade has seen an increased interest in the collecting of early soda fountain memorabilia, particularly these ice cream dishers. With the number of collectors growing weekly, there is, obviously, a growing demand for the dishers. It is no wonder, because they are useful, unique to display, and just plain fun to collect.

What is evident, to both old and new collectors, is the obvious lack of written information on the subject of ice cream dishers. That is a situation that this book will attempt to remedy. It would take more than a lifetime of research to uncover everything there is to know, about every disher ever produced. This is not the purpose, nor the claim of this book. This book is designed to be a handy reference guide for collectors, dealers, and anyone interested in ice cream history. The information in it can be used to identify, date, and evaluate most of the ice cream dishers, both common and rare, found in collections today. It can, and hopefully will, be used as a basis for further research into this fascinating hobby.

The ice cream disher went through periods of developments and changes, as did the ice cream industry and the entire country. Technological advances contributed to some of these changes. From the simple tin dishers of the late 19th century, to the complex models of the 1920's, the ice cream disher showed a definite pattern of evolution. I will attempt to relate this evolution to developments in the ice cream industry, and other historical events.

In this book, I have tried to accomplish a number of things. First, concerning the dishers, I have given information to identify, date, and determine their rarity. Next, various magazine and catalog ads were reproduced to show the features that the manufacturers thought were important. Manufacturers were listed with the address, if known, and the approximate dates in business. Patent records are also included, as a prime source of information. They provide much valuable material. Inventor information is given, because it is important to remember, that behind each scoop, there was a person with an idea. The stories of some of these men are interesting insights into the early ice cream industry. Finally, other practical information is given to the collector, such as cleaning, displaying, and terminology.

I hope that this book will serve as a useful reference guide to collectors, for years to come. If it motivates just one person to delve deeper into the history of the ice cream industry, it was well worth the effort.

# Acknowledgments

So many people have assisted in the preparation of this book, that it is hard to know how to thank them all. I'll begin with the most important person, my wife, Joy. Without her great patience, understanding, encouragement and cooperation, this book would never have been written. Besides, it was the Benedict Indestructo that I gave *her* as a birthday gift, 12 years ago, that started *my* collection.

I would like to give credit to Fred Smith, for his contribution to the finished product. He has spent many hours helping with the tedious process of searching through the available records. His photographic skills and advice were also greatly appreciated. Thanks, Dad!

Two fine friends, to whom I am indebted, in my research and writing are, Ed Marks, of Lancaster, Pa., and Allan Mellis, of Chicago, Ill. Ed and Allan both provided me with much valuable information, from their vast ice cream collections. Just as important, were the suggestions and the encouragement they offered. Allan has one of the finest ice cream collections in the country. Ed, along with Bob Bruce, of Eagle Point, Ore., founded the Ice Screamers collector organization.

I'd like to thank Fred Greiner and the wonderful people at the Dairy and Food Industries Supply Assoc., for allowing me access to their early photo files. This early photographic history was an invaluable research tool. Also, well deserved credit goes to Gary Hedges, of Walkersville, Md., for his fine photos of most of the collection. I'd also like to thank Diana Mallette for her pen and ink illustrations. A special thanks goes to Bob and Phyllis Roberts for their support and confidence in my project.

I'd also like to thank Bob Bruce, Carl Abel, Bill Thunell, Bill Burg, Barbara Hadden, Morton Burness, Harold Screen and Joanne Gaylord, who generously loaned material, or scoops, from their collections. I'd like to thank Bob Cahn, the "Primitive Man", for his enthusiasm and his knack for finding the rare ones. Also, John McColley, whose encouragement prompted me to begin my research.

A good part of the biographical section couldn't have been written without the help of the following people: James Denaro (Automatic Cone Co.), Thomas Funka (Zeroll Co.), John Manos, and Edward C. Walker.

There have been numerous others who have offered bits of information and encouragement. To them, I say thanks! Without their help, the road would have been much longer.

# Chapter 1

# Ice Cream—From Creation to Consumption

I Scream– You Scream– We all Scream for ICE CREAM. The title of this popular 1927 song reflects the passion and love affair that Americans had for this delicious frozen treat. This visual tour will give you a flavor for the ice cream industry, during the first quarter of the twentieth century. The fact that 150 million gallons of ice cream were produced in 1919, helps to show that these years were "boom" years for the early ice cream manufacturer and retailer. In fact, the entire time scope of this book, 1876–1940, was characterized by rapid growth and change.

The photos in this chapter are primarily taken from turn of the century postcards and factory photos. They help to illustrate the life of ice cream, from creation to consumption. Much of the commercially produced ice cream was made in ice cream factories, as well as soda fountains and confectionaries. There were thousands of manufacturers around the country, ranging from one person operations, to large plants, employing hundreds of people. The delivery systems were also diverse, ranging from simple wagons, to electric and motor trucks. The consumption of ice cream occurred almost everywhere; soda fountains, confectionaries, drug stores, bowling alleys, picnics, ballgames, fairs, and the home, just to name a few. A look at these photos will help impart a sense of nostalgia for the early days of ice cream, and set the tone for the rest of the book.

The Best Ice Cream Co., of Syracuse, N.Y., in 1914. The company, founded in 1912, was a medium size ice cream plant, serving retailers in the local Syracuse area. The office and loading area are in the foreground.

Plant of the Walker Creamery Products Co., ca. 1915. This large producer of Walker's Celebrated IXL ice cream was located in Warren, Pa.

Semi-solid ice cream being emptied into cans for hardening, at the Best Ice Cream Co., in 1914. The horizontal, circulating brine freezer was introduced in 1904, to increase production.

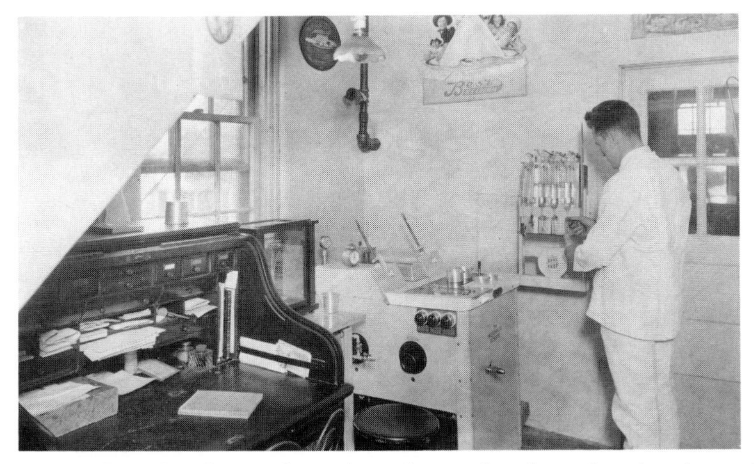

The lab at the Best Ice Cream Co., where the product is analyzed and tested. The Mojonnier overrun tester, introduced in 1914, was the first machine developed to test the ice cream mix.

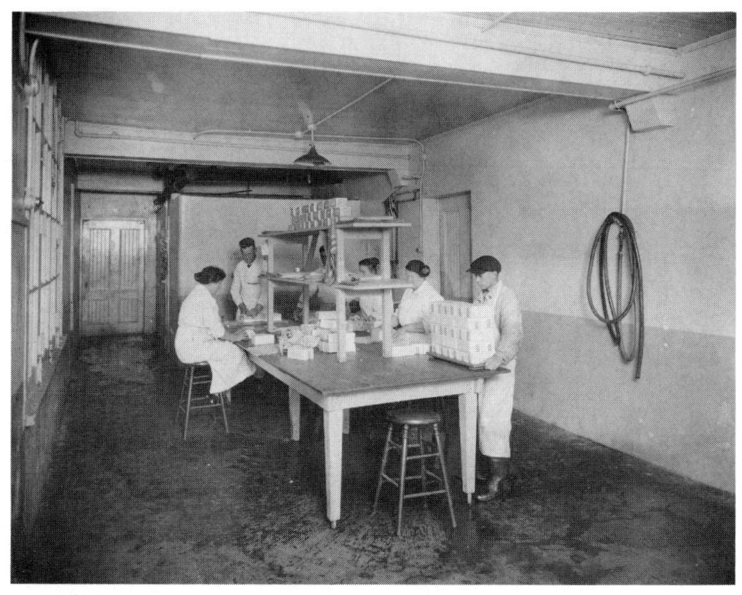

Ice cream bricks were cut and wrapped in this room, at the Best Ice Cream Co. These pre-cut bricks were a popular form of ice cream, each having two or three flavors, in one piece.

The ice room at the Best Ice Cream Co., where ice was cut and crushed. In the 1890's, one of the larger factories in New York City, used upwards of 100,000 lbs. of ice *per day,* during the peak summer season.

This is the workshop at the Hendler Ice Cream plant, in Baltimore, Md., where wooden ice cream cabinets were made, ca. 1927.

A finished product, ready for shipment to a soda fountain or drug store. These were later replaced by electric cabinets.

*Allan Mellis*

Loading time at Gray's Lake (Ill.) Ice Cream Factory, ca. 1910. The ice cream was packed in tubs with salt and ice, for the trip. Of necessity, the delivery area was local, until the advent of dry ice and the mechanically refrigerated truck, in the 1920's.

Tags such as this, were attached to the filled ice cream cans, before delivery to the retailer. The reverse states, "All shipments of Ice Cream are carefully packed and inspected before leaving our factory, and should withstand the warm weather for several hours, but should be repacked as soon as received . . ."

An early horse drawn delivery wagon belonging to A. C. Mencke, "Manufacturer of Ice Cream and Confectionery". The company, located on Chesapeake St., in Baltimore, Md., was bought by Hendler Ice Cream. Photo ca. 1897.

These electric delivery trucks, in front of the Hendler plant, represented a great improvement in the delivery system. Mr. Hendler introduced his fleet in 1919. Two advantages of these trucks were the greatly expanded delivery territory, and the fact that the ice cream could be unloaded by the driver, from the outside, at ground level.

Ice cream parlors and soda fountains were a common sight in almost every city and town. Some of the larger cities had 500 or more. Chicago, in 1906, had at least 3500. Competition was keen, as you can see by the proximity of these two ice cream parlors, in Northville, N.Y., ca. 1910.

*Allan Mellis*

This 1912 photo shows an early marble soda fountain. Note the syrup bottles on top, which were mixed to flavor the soda water. The carbonator, used to charge the soda water, was usually located in the basement.

*Allan Mellis*

The drugstore at Norris, Texas, contained this small soda fountain, around 1905. Notice the Hires Mettlach dispenser sitting on the backbar. It is an extremely collectable piece.

*Allan Mellis*

Ladies gathering for cold refreshments, at Stewart's Drug Store, in Union City, Ind.

The William's Cafe, in Toronto, Canada, ca. 1910. Notice the ornamental umbrella shade on the marble draftstand.

Smyser's Drug Store, in York, Pa., also had a marble soda fountain on the backbar. The ice cream dippers were usually kept in a container of water, behind the front bar.

Elaborate backbars such as this one, at Boldt's, in Dubuque, Iowa, in 1906, were a drawing attraction for customers.

Besides the soda fountain, ice cream was served in numerous places. This carnival in Savige, Co., on Sept. 9, 1909, featured a 5¢ ice cream cone stand. Judging from the number of people at the stand, they were doing a good business. The ice cream cone was only 5 years old, but was becoming, very rapidly, the most popular way to eat ice cream.

Fairs and ballgames were other places that people could be found enjoying ice cream. This young couple was obviously enjoying their ice cream cone.

Fred, the ice cream man, of Montandon, Pa. posed for the photographer, in this ca. 1910 photo. He was probably one of the area's most popular businessmen.

# Chapter 2

# The Scoop on Scoops

## Disher, Dipper or Scoop?

Disher, dipper, or scoop . . . which term is most appropriate to describe the subject of this book? In our present terminology the work *scoop* is the most widely used term for this ice cream serving device. This was not always so, however. In order to determine the most popular contemporary term, we must go back in the records to find out what the inventors and manufacturers called them. Early patent records and magazine ads are the prime source for this information.

241 patent records of ice cream scoops, between 1878 and 1940, were analyzed for nomenclature and the results were as follows:

| | |
|---|---|
| disher | 77 |
| dipper | 67 |
| scoop | 27 |
| spoon | 19 |
| other | 51 |
| total | 241 |

We can see here that the term, *disher,* was used slightly more often, in the patent records, than the term, *dipper*. The term, *scoop,* was hardly used at all. It didn't really start to appear in the records, until the 1920's. Other terms used included, *mold, ladle, measuring device,* and *dispenser*.

A second survey, this time of 31 different trade magazine ads, appearing between 1900 and 1940, was also taken. The result: *disher* was the overwhelming favorite. It was used in 24 ads, as compared to 5 for *dipper,* 1 *scoop,* and 1 *spoon*. The ads, since they were read by almost everyone in the business, reflected the term most widely used.

If we take the results of both of these surveys, we see that *disher* was the clearly preferred term. The term *scoop* may have gradually evolved into present day use, because it is a concise, one syllable word that is easy to pronounce. So, for the benefit of historical accuracy, I'll primarily use the term *disher* throughout the book, although any are perfectly acceptable.

## Dating an Ice Cream Disher

Determining the approximate date an ice cream disher was manufactured, using the information in this book, can be done fairly accurately. By accurate, I mean within a five year period, generally. Since almost all of the manufacturers have long been out of business, very few, if any, production records survive. Without these records, we do not know the exact dates the dishers were made. We do, however, have several means to approximate the date of manufacture. These sources are: patent records, trade magazine ads, dates the manufacturer was in business, and the characteristics of the dishers themselves. We will look at each one individually to see how they can be used for dating.

### Patent Records

Probably the most accurate dating source we have, is contained in the U.S. Patent Office records. Each record has two dates. The first one is the date the patent application was *filed*. After this date, the inventor could start production of his disher, if he so desired, and still have his rights protected. Patent attorneys generally tried to discourage this practice. Any public knowledge of this invention, before the patent actually was issued, could invalidate any chance of obtaining a foreign patent. However, if the inventor or manufacturer did choose to commence production after the filing date, the disher had to be marked either *Patent Pending* or *Patent Applied For*. A number of dishers produced were marked as such. It is possible that a disher marked in this manner was never granted a patent for one or more reasons. If the application was rejected, they could no longer be made. So, if a disher is marked *Pat. Pend.* or *Pat. Apld. For,* it was manufactured between the filing date and the issue date.

The *issue date* is the second date on the patent record. After a patent was approved and issued, it was assigned a number. A patent was good for seventeen years from the date of issue. A disher could then be marked with the patent date, patent number, or just *Patented*. Probably, most of the dishers produced were done so for only a very short period after the patent date, several years at the most. They were then replaced with newer models or just discontinued. One notable exception was the Gilchrist #31. It was the *Model T* of the ice cream dishers. In fact, production was probably started after the filing date, in 1908, the same year that Henry Ford introduced his fabulous Model T, the Universal Car. Ford's car was the most popular car ever made, until it was discontinued, in 1927. The Gilchrist #31 surpassed that feat by retaining its popularity until the company merged with Hamilton Beach, in 1931.

## Trade Magazine Ads

A second method for dating ice cream dishers, is through the use of early ice cream trade journals and catalogs. Since the dishers were sold primarily for soda fountain use, and not for home use, these are the magazines that contain the information. Publications such as, *The Soda Fountain, Ice Cream Review, Pharmaceutical Era,* and others have numerous ads for the latest dishers. They are fascinating to read and contain a wealth of information. The one disadvantage of this source, is that the magazines are hard to locate. Major libraries, such as the Library of Congress and the National Library of Medicine, have some, but none, to my knowledge, has a large collection. One source not to be overlooked, are the collectors of ice cream memorabilia. They seem to have a knack for finding the treasured pieces at flea markets and giving them a good home.

## Manufacturers

Another approximate way of dating dishers is to determine when the company was in business. City records and local city directories often yield this information. This will only give us a rough estimate, because some companies were in business for a long period of time. For example, the Automatic Cone Co., of Cambridge, Mass., began business around 1903, and still continues in business at the present time. Their IcyPi ice cream dipper, however, was made circa 1924–1930. On the other hand, some companies probably only existed to produce one dipper, and were in business a very short period. The list of manufacturers, included in this book, will give the approximate dates, or periods, that they were in business.

## Characteristics

If there wasn't any written information available, on a particular disher, one could still make a reasonable guess as to it's age by looking at it's physical characteristics. The four main points to take into account are: handle construction, shank construction, working mechanism, and shape of bowl.

HANDLE. The earliest handles were made of steel and tin. They were probably used as late as 1930, but the vast majority of these were made prior to 1910. Various types of metal handles began to appear on dishers around 1900. Nickel-plated brass was the most common, but other metals were also used. The nickel plating gave a sanitary appearance. The Kingery Co. and the Gem Spoon Co., were probably the first companies to use metal, other than tin and steel, for their handles.

Wood handles came into use around 1900, and continued until the late 1930's. This was generally the most popular type of handle. In the late 1920's, bakelite, a hard rubber, was introduced as a handle material. Hamilton Beach and the Benedict Mfg. Co. used bakelite on many of their dishers throughout the 1930's.

SHANK. Shank construction is the next characteristic to consider when dating an ice cream disher. This is the area between the handle and the bowl. Again, the first type of metal used was steel or tin. Brass or bronze followed after 1900. This was always nickel-plated, and enjoyed great popularity through the 1930's. Around 1910, aluminum was used by several companies, most notably the Erie Specialty Co. It's use was much more widespread after 1930, though.

MECHANISM. The first type of mechanism used on an ice cream disher was the key type. This dispenser was required to hold the disher with one hand, while twisting a key connected to a scraper, to release the ice cream. The spring action mechanism was a welcome development, after 1900. This left one hand free to hold the dish or cone. There are almost as many different types of springs, as there are ice cream dishers. The 1930's showed an increase in the non-mechanical, one piece dippers, such as the Zeroll.

SHAPE. The shape of the "bowl" on an ice cream disher, is also helpful in determining it's age. It's shape varied with the function of the disher. The very earliest ones were cone, or pyramid, shaped. Their use was limited to serving ice cream in bowls or on plates. Generally, the cone shape dissappeared by 1920, although, several companies did use it throughout the 1930's.

The round shape was, by far, the most practical for a disher bowl. The Gem Spoon Co. and the H. S. Geer Co. were among the first to use this style, beginning around the turn of the century, when the ice cream cone became popular. Round bowls were made in a variety of sizes ranging from size 6 (scoops to the quart), all the way down to size 60. Each size had different uses. Size 16, for example, was recommended for ice cream sodas.

During the 1920's, the ice cream sandwich was a popular novelty. They could be made by two methods. The slab of ice cream could be either cut from a brick, or dispensed directly from a tub of ice cream, using a square or rectangular dipper. Since the latter was probably more appealing to the customer, a number of these ice cream sandwich dippers were invented. At least 15 different ones were produced.

The novelty era of the 1920's gave birth to a number of unusual shaped bowls. The oval one, for banana splits, is very popular among collectors. A

## Dating an Ice Cream Disher

| CHARACTERISTICS | 1876 to 1900 | 1900–1910 | 1910–1920 | 1920–1930 | 1930–1940 |
|---|---|---|---|---|---|
| **Handle** | | | | | |
| steel | —X— | —X— | —X— | | |
| brass or bronze | | —X— | —X— | —X— | |
| wood | | —X— | —X— | —X— | —X— |
| bakelite | | | | | —X— |
| **Shank** | | | | | |
| steel | —X— | —X— | —X— | | |
| brass or bronze | | —X— | —X— | —X— | —X— |
| aluminum | | —X— | —X— | —X— | —X— |
| **Mechanism** | | | | | |
| key | —X— | —X— | —X— | | |
| spring | | —X— | —X— | —X— | —X— |
| push type | | | | —X— | |
| none | | | | | —X— |
| **Shape** | | | | | |
| conical | —X— | —X— | —X— | | |
| round | | —X— | —X— | —X— | —X— |
| square or rectangular | | | | —X— | —X— |
| cylindrical | | | | —X— | |
| oval | | | | —X— | —X— |

cylindrical, or tubular, dipper was designed for filling edible containers. A flat, disk shaped disher was used for filling paper cups. The Pi-Alamoder Co. made a triangular one, the shape of a piece of pie. Finally, the most unusual shaped disher, the heart disher, was used to fill beautiful heart shaped dishes.

## Values of Ice Cream Dishers

Determining the value of an ice cream disher can be a very controversial topic among collectors. Each collector seems to have his or her own opinion as to the worth of particular dishers. Sometimes it's not an easy task to arrive at a consensus that will please everyone. The values that I have listed in this book are my *opinion,* based on more than ten years of collecting experience and many conversations with both dealers and fellow collectors. They are also based on several variables, upon which I will elaborate further.

### Unusual Features

This is undoubtedly the most important factor in determining value. Is the bowl round, or is it oval, square, cylindrical or some other odd shape? If the shape is unusual, it is probably worth more than if it were just round. Also, look at the working mechanism, the unusual ones might flip the bowl upside down or divide it in half, to use two examples. In other words, unusual features generally indicate a higher value.

### Rarity

Some dishers were so unique and specialized, that there was very little demand for them at the time they were produced. Consequently, very few were sold and production numbers were low. These are some of the ones that command a higher price. The ice cream sandwich was very popular in the 1920's, so the square style dipper isn't that rare, but some models are scarcer than others. The IcyPi is probably the most common of these, due to it's huge success.

### Condition

Condition is an important variable in determining value. Mint condition is unusual in an ice cream disher, because they were bought as functional tools for the soda fountain, and most were well used. On the other hand, some are so damaged that they are only useable for parts. A scoop in mint condition, especially one in the original box, will always bring a higher price.

The springs were usually the first part to break, and they are almost always impossible to replace now. Sometimes the bowl would come loose and would require soldering, which decreases the value. Some collectors have the nickel plated dishers stripped and polished. The original condition is much preferable, but if the plating is badly flaking, stripping won't affect the value.

## Age

In general, the age has little affect on the value of the disher. The oldest dishers aren't necessarily the most valuable ones. Many dishers from the 1920's are more valuable that the ones made 40–50 years earier.

## Location

With the recent influx of collectors in this field, and better communication between collectors, location isn't as much of a factor as it once was. However, prices do tend to be slightly higher on the West and East Coasts. The same seems to hold true for the big city antique shows, as compared with the small country flea markets. Generally, the closer the scoop is to the original source, the lower the price. Each successive transaction usually increases the price.

With these variables in mind, I have assigned each disher a guide number, that corresponds to a price range in the following chart. As I have said before, these prices are only my educated *opinion,* and I assume no responsibility for their accuracy. They reflect what collectors have paid and what dealers have recently sold them for. Even though the prices only reflect recent transactions, the guide numbers should always give you a relative pricing scale, regardless of the actual figures.

## Guide Numbers

| | |
|---|---|
| 1—common | $20–40 |
| 2—relatively easy to find, but possibly has an unusual feature | $40–75 |
| 3—not too easy to find, but some still available | $75–125 |
| 4—few produced, has unusual features | $125–200 |
| 5—rare, few known | $200 up |

# Chapter 3

# Inventors

It is difficult to believe that a tool as simple as an ice cream disher, has been produced in well over 100 variations. Each of these variations is the end result of much effort on the part of one person, the inventor. At least 200 inventors, between 1876 and 1940, saw a way to improve the serving of ice cream, and resolved to do something about it.

These inventors came from all walks of life. Some were connected with the ice cream industry, and some were not. One early inventor, Martin Bohlig, was in the printing business. Another, George Parr, worked as a jeweler, engineer, and a salesman, before he invented his pie-ala-mode scoop. Henry A. Keiner, of the Keiner-Williams Stamping Co., went on to

*Dairy and Food Industries Supply Association*

Henry A. Keiner, President of Dairy and Ice Cream Machinery Supplies Association (1935) and Keiner-Williams Stamping Co. He obtained pat. #803,906 for an ice cream disher.

become the president of the Dairy and Food Industries Supply Association, in 1935.

Most inventors held but one patent. A few, however, were very prolific in their ideas. Edwin Walker, of Erie, Pa., was one of the busier inventors. He held at least 9 patents on ice cream dippers, and many others, on items such as cork screws and lemon squeezers. Rasmus Nielsen, of Troy, N.Y., claimed at least 10 patents. Dosier Mosteller, of Chicago, is credited with at least 5 patents on ice cream dishers.

In the following brief biographical sketches, I have tried to select key inventors, who were important in the history and development of the ice cream disher. The first, William Clewell, was one of the true pioneers. His patent was a model for others, for many years. Edwin Walker contributed many different types of dishers to the industry. Raymond Gilchrist was an inventor whose company produced more dishers than any other. James Denaro had one of the more successful novelty scoops of the 1920's. John Manos was responsible for one of the most unique dishers ever made. Last, but not least, was Sherman Kelly, who revolutionized the design of ice cream dippers, with his famous Zeroll.

Each of these inventors had something in common. They saw a need in the growing ice cream industry, for more efficient and novel dishers. It is their ideas that make the collecting of early ice cream dishers so fascinating.

## William Clewell

George William Clewell, a confectioner from Reading, Pa., can be considered the originator of the ice cream disher. His novel serving device was the very first to be patented and commercially manufactured. This gives him the distinct honor of being the pioneer, in a field that included several hundred variations, over the next century. To get a glimpse of the life and times of this ingenious man, we have to turn back the hands of time to the mid-19th century.

William Clewell was born in Pa., probably in the Reading area, on Oct. 14, 1835. We have no record of his parents, other than they were Pa. natives. Records of his childhood are also elusive. When he was 21 years of

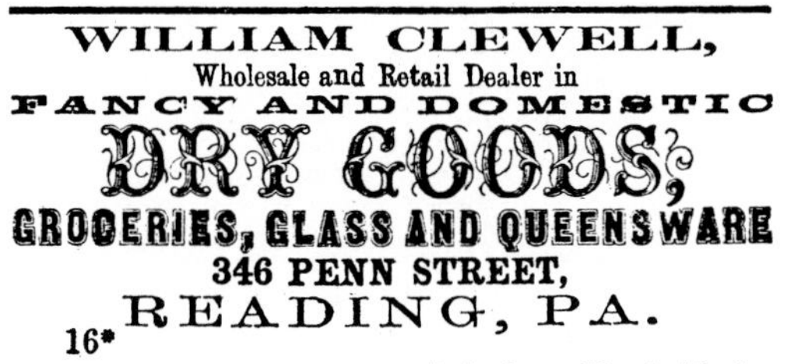


*Berks County Historical Society*

William Clewell's 1866 ad for his Dry Goods Store.

age, in 1856, he was working as a salesman and living at 48 W. Penn St., in Reading.

Reading was the 5th largest city in Pa., with a population close to 23,000, in 1860. Penn St. was the busiest thoroughfare in the city, and Penn Square, the 400–500 blocks of Penn St., was the heart of trade. It was called Market Square before 1870, because of the public farmer's markets in the center. I mention these facts because Clewell lived and worked, his entire adult life, within two blocks of the square.

William Clewell and his wife, Ellen, were married sometime around 1860, and their first child, Lucy, was born about 1861. The 1866 *Boyd's Reading Directory* listed him as owning a dry goods store at 346 Penn St. Interestingly enough, the business next door was Alfred M. Souders' Confectionary, Bakery, and Ice Cream Saloon. Clewell must have been impressed by Souder's business, because he gave up dry goods and opened a similar confectionary and ice cream establishment just three blocks away, at 607 Penn St., in 1867. At the time, there were around 15 other confectioners in the city.

The country was beginning to return to normal, after the Civil War, when Clewell embarked on his new venture. The location he chose, next to the square, was certainly a good one for ice cream and candy. His shop was across the street from the Keystone Hotel and Hall, which hosted such famous visitors as Mark Twain and General Tom Thumb. It's entirely possible that these two well known figures sampled some of Clewell's confections. Only half a block down the street, was Mishler's Academy of Music, the first modern theater in Pa., outside of Philadelphia and Pittsburgh. The 1000 seat theater featured Henry Ward Beecher's talent, among others.

By the mid-1870's, Clewell was probably one of the leading confectioners in the city. Business must have flourished, because in 1870, his personal assets were valued at $5,000, well above average for the period in which he

Reading's Penn Square (ca. 1905). Clewell's confectionary and ice cream parlor was located 2 doors up from building on far left, 30 years earlier.

lived. His second daughter, Bertha, was born in 1873. In 1876, the year Tufts exhibited his famous soda fountain at the Centennial, he took on a partner, Jacob Addis. The partnership was known as Clewell and Addis.

It was around this time that Clewell came up with his novel idea of a device to serve ice cream. Previously, spoons were used, but Clewell invented a device with a handle that would mold ice cream into a conical form, then release it onto a plate by means of a key operated scraper. The result would be more appealing to the customer and more efficient for the server. His device was originally conceived to be used as a mold, but within a short period of time, was used as a disher. He had his idea patented.

Clewell had his disher manufactured by Valentine Clad, a tinsmith located at 117–23 S. 11th St., in Philadelphia. Clad's shop was only a 45 mile trip by rail or stage, from Reading. Tin and steel were used to make the dishers. Over the next 20–30 years the same basic design, that is, a conical mold with key release and a handle, was used by a number of different companies, thus attesting to it's popularity.

There does appear to be a slight discrepancy as to the first patent date on his invention. The first patent record available lists the patent date as Nov. 12, 1878. However, there were dishers produced that bear this date, and dishers produced bearing the dates May 3, 1876 and May 3, 1878. The mystery concerns the two latter dates. There were *no* patents issued on those dates. Patents were only issued on Tuesday's, and neither of the dates fell on a Tuesday. Also, no records of a similar patent could be found anywhere close to these dates. The question remains, why then would these dates be stamped on the dishers? We may never know the answer. One possible con-

*Allan Mellis*

Valentine Clad, manufacturer of Clewell's disher.

*Allan Mellis*

Clewell's first disher was manufactured here, at 117–123 S. 11th St., in Philadelphia, Pa.

nection for the May 3, 1878 date, was that a Patent Office circular was issued for the Nov. 12 patent, on May 3. The May 3, 1876 date offers no clues. An interesting coincidence though, is that the Centennial celebration in Phila., where the disher was made, opened exactly one week later!

After 1878, Clewell and Addis' business may have fallen on hard times, because they sold the store to a competitor, Christian M. Groff. Clewell went to work as a clerk for the American House Hotel, and Addis became an insurance agent. Clewell remained at the hotel for ten years until 1888, when he took over his old neighbor, Alfred Souder's confectionary for a brief period. In 1890 he became the proprietor of a Turkish and Russian bath, on Court St., and operated that establishment until 1903.

On Nov. 23, 1903, at the age of 69, Clewell died of a heart attack, while at the Court House, just across the street from his home. He was laid to rest in the Charles Evans Cemetary.

William Clewell was a pioneer. His shop is no longer standing, replaced instead by the modern Penn Square Center. Examples of his invention still exist, in collections around the country, as a reminder of the early development of the ice cream industry. William Clewell's ice cream disher was an important contribution to this development.

## Edwin Walker

If any one person can claim credit for the most varieties of ice cream dishers produced, it would be Edwin Walker, of Erie, Pa. He held at least nine patents on dishers, all manufactured by the Erie Specialty Co.

Edwin Walker was born in Aug., of 1847, at Sheshequin, Pa., a tiny town in the north-central section of the state. He was one of three children, born to George and Mary Walker. George, his father, was a mechanical engineer, who built a number of bridges and flouring mills, in that section of Pa. and neighboring New York. Edwin received his education at the academy in Springville, N.Y., south of Buffalo. At an early age he showed an aptitude for mechanics by building one of the first bicycles in the area, from only a design!

Around 1868, Edwin Walker left home for his first job, at a plant manufacturing flour milling machinery, in Silver Creek, N.Y. It was there, at

*Bob Bruce*

Edwin Walker, in 1909.

Silver Creek, that he met Edith May Wright, and married her in 1871. Their first of six children, Clarence, was born that same year.

In 1880, Walker moved south, to Erie, Pa., a growing industrial city of 28,000 people. He was employed as a draughtsman and pattern maker for several manufacturing companies. Three years later, he formed the Edwin Walker Tool Co. They manufactured, among other things, planes, chisels, and Walker's own patented cork extractors. He sold the company in 1888.

The Erie Specialty Manufacturing Co. was founded in 1889, with Edwin Walker, Thomas Thomas, and Benjamin Brown as equal partners. The original location was at 345–51 W. 12th St. Approximately twenty people were employed. Most, if not all, of the products made were patented by Edwin Walker. These included cork screws, ice shavers, lemon squeezers, and milk shake machines.

On Feb. 12, 1892, Walker Bought out his two partners, added a new one, Z. T. Brindley, and changed the name to Erie Specialty Co. Around 1896, the company was moved to larger quarters, a three story, brick building, located at 520 W. 12th St. Walker's son, Clarence, joined the business in 1902. At this time, they employed 67 people.

Edwin Walker applied for his first ice cream disher patent in 1905, shortly after the ice cream cone was introduced. This first model was an unusual looking, cone shaped device, with a brass loop handle. The Erie Specialty Co. manufactured them, and at least several thousand were sold, by 1909.

Between 1905 and 1915, Walker patented at least nine different dishers, possibly more. Eight were featured in his 1908 catalog alone. He advertised his line of ice cream dishers as "Quick and Easy".

One of the novel features used by Walker, was a cone insert attached to the scraper in the bowl. It's purpose was to make "sundae creams", as it left an indentation in the top of the ice cream for a cherry. He was also one of the first to use aluminum in the production of some of his dishers.

Erie, Pa., in 1905, the year that Edwin Walker applied for his first ice cream disher patent.

Edwin Walker was a well known and respected man in Erie. For a period, he served on the Chamber of Commerce and the Board of Trade. In addition to his other achievements, Walker was responsible for at least 50 other patents.

The Erie Specialty Co. went out of business in the mid-1920's, after more than 30 years in operation. Thanks to Edwin Walker, they produced more different models of ice cream dishers than any other company, past or present. Walker undoubtedly left his mark on the ice cream industry.

## Raymond B. Gilchrist

Gilchrist . . . a name recognized by every collector of early ice cream dishers. Who was this person, and why were his scoops such a success? Unfortunately, an abundance of information is not available, but with the facts we have, we can arrive at some answers to these questions.

Raymond Gilchrist was born in New Jersey, around 1866. His parents were also natives of this country. He was married to his Canadian born wife, Agnes, around 1891. His father probably worked as a screwmaker, in Newark. This is possibly where Raymond received the necessary background to open his own hardware business, in 1902.

The Gilchrist Co. was originally located at 133 Lafayette St., in Newark, a large industrial center, just outside of New York City. By 1905, the company had grown, listing a capital of $200,000 and Charles D. Halsey, of New York City, as it's president. Gilchrist was the vice-president. Halsey was probably the financial backer. In 1906, they moved to a building at 236 Bank St., in Newark, where they would conduct business for the next 25 years.

The Gilchrist Co. manufactured hardware specialty items such as cork pullers, ice picks, and lemon squeezers, as did their competitor, the Erie

Newark, N.J. (ca. 1910), home of the Gilchrist Co.

Specialty Co., during the same period. These were all tools used in the soda fountain of the day. In 1907, Gilchrist applied for a patent for his #30 squeeze handled ice cream disher. The following year, he did the same for his well known #31 disher, and added them to his line of goods. By the end of the decade, Gilchrist employed 38 people in the business.

In 1910, the company was incorporated and began an era of ice cream scoop manufacturing that was unparalleled, up to that time. Even without production records, I think it is safe to say that the Gilchrist Co. produced more dishers, than any other single company, in previous history. The company employed 75–85 workers during it's peak production period, from 1910–1920.

One key to Raymond Gilchrist's great success was marketing. Almost all of the soda fountain trade journals carried his advertising. Full page, colored ads praised his "better than need be" goods. He was so confident of their quality and success, that he actually advertised the fact that they cost *more* than other dishers! Also, the booth that he set up at the 1917 Association of Ice Cream Supply Men convention, in Boston, for example, provided good exposure and a nice showcase for his wares. Many major soda fountain equipment suppliers contracted to carry his line of dishers.

*Dairy and Food Industries Supply Association*

Gilchrist Co. display at the 1917 Association of Ice Cream Supply Men convention.

The company produced basically four different types of dishers. The #30 was a round, squeeze handled model with a variety of uses. It was convenient for left-handed users. The #31 was the most popular, and was also a universal one. It had a wooden handle. The #33, a pyramid shaped disher, was for those who preferred to have their ice cream served on a plate. The #44 was a tin, key type pyramid disher reminiscent of the earliest ones. All of Gilchrist's dishers were simple, well made, and easy to disassemble for cleaning. Very few changes were made to the designs in 25 years of production.

The banana split disher is one of the favorites among collectors. It is a variation of the Gilchrist #31, with an oval, instead of a round bowl. This shape of ice cream fit perfectly between a sliced banana. The model number marked on most of them is #31, with the exception of some of the later ones, which were marked #34. These later dishers, ca. 1930, also had a slightly shorter shank.

After W.W.I, the capital of the Gilchrist Co., had decreased to $125,000, signifying a slower production period. Around 1926, Raymond Gilchrist left the company, possibly having passed away this year.

It was about this time, 1926, that the Scoville Mfg. Co., of Waterbury, Conn., probably acquired the Gilchrist Co. as it's subsidiary. A long time employee of the company, Thomas Jameson, replaced Gilchrist and became the treasurer and general manager. Jameson began his career with the Gilchrist Co. around 1911, as a clerk, eventually holding positions as a book keeper and purchasing agent. He also secured a patent for an ice cream disher in 1930.

After the takeover, the capital of the Gilchrist Co. quadrupled, to $500,000, and production increased once again. It was during this period, the novelty era of the 1920's, that the banana split disher was probably introduced. What the company lacked in variety, it compensated for in volume.

In 1931, the Great Depression was probably the influencing factor in the merger of the Gilchrist Co. with the Hamilton Beach Co., of Racine, Wisc., also a Scoville subsidiary. Hamilton Beach carried Gilchrist's line of dishers, under their own name, for several years.

When Raymond Gilchrist introduced his first disher, I wonder if he knew just how successful they would become? Marketing, advertising, and good simple designs were all keys to his success. They were as popular then, with the early soda fountain operators, as they are today with collectors.

## James Denaro

One of the most successful 5¢ ice cream novelties of the 1920's, was the IcyPi (pronounced I-C-Pie). The man responsible for it's creation and suc-

*James Denaro*

James Denaro, founder of the Automatic Cone Co. and inventor of the IcyPi.

cess was Giacomo Denaro, an Italian immigrant, who was a success story himself.

Giacomo, or James, Denaro was born April 19, 1883, to Domenic and Rosaria Denaro, in Faro Superiore, Sicily. He received no formal education past the second grade. At the age of twenty, in 1903, Denaro sailed for the United States, in search of new opportunities. As a stowaway on a ship, he was caught and made to shovel coal to pay his passage. After landing in New York City, with only $5 in his pocket, he worked his way up to Boston, doing a variety of odd jobs, such as busboy and laborer.

Denaro was a very enterprising young man. Shortly after he arrived, with the help of his brothers, he began a business baking ice cream cones. It was located on Broadway, in South Boston, until 1911, when he moved to Oakland, Ca., for a brief period. Gradually, his four brothers left the business, leaving James the sole owner. In 1915, he returned to Mass. to set up shop on River St., in Cambridge.

Denaro's company, the Automatic Cone Co., was named after his patented automatic cone maker. His machine was a much improved system for baking cones, than the old hand baking method. It was a circular machine that sat on the floor. This was such a success, that Denaro spent quite a lot of time and expense protecting his patent rights from infringers, who tried to profit from his idea.

In 1921, the Automatic Cone Co. was moved once again to 83 Clark St., in Cambridge. On one hot summer day, while walking in the Cambridge Square, Denaro's wife Margaret, noticed that people eating ice cream sandwiches, literally had a mess on their hands. Upon returning home, she made the suggestion to James, that he develop an ice cream sandwich that didn't drip. Well, that suggestion was the catalyst, which resulted in six years of phenomenal success, for a novelty called the IcyPi, and the Automatic Cone Co., beginning around 1924.

The IcyPi was an ice cream sandwich-like wafer, that was enclosed on three sides and open on the top. It was filled with ice cream by means of a square, flat dipper. The cake wafers were made by the Automatic Cone Co., but the dippers were not. Denaro applied for a patent on the dipper and contracted it's manufacture to the Philadelphia Ice Cream Cone Machinery Co.

At the height of the IcyPi's popularity, the Automatic Cone Co. employed 100–125 people. As a measure of it's success, their advertising bro-

Window decal advertising the IcyPi.

chure stated that just ten dealers sold 6,750,000 IcyPi and nearly 3,000 scoops in one five month period. Their display at the 1927 and 1928 Dairy Industries Expositions undoubtedly helped sales. Orders came from all over the country and around the world. By 1929, the Automatic Cone Co. licensed other bakers to help supply the demand, among them, the United Products Co., of Chelsea, Mass., and the McLaren Cone Co., of Dayton, Ohio.

The stock market crash, in 1929, triggered the beginning of the Depression, and the end of the IcyPi's popularity. Even though the IcyPi was still being made, its production never reached the levels of the mid-1920's.

After the war, in the late 1940's or early 1950's, Denaro tried to re-introduce the IcyPi to a new generation of ice cream lovers. This time he was not nearly as successful. The ever cost-conscious soda fountain operator realized that the IcyPi scoop compressed the ice cream, thus resulting in a loss of profits.

The scoop Denaro used this time was not exactly the same as his original model. The basic design was the same, but the body was made of stainless steel and the handle was a yellow plastic one, instead of wood. It was manufactured by Peter Gray and Co., in Cambridge.

James Denaro was active in the business until he retired, in the 1950's, and passed it on to his son. Even in his retirement he was very active, always keeping in touch with the company. It is a credit to this man, that with little formal education, he proved to be such a talented inventor, promoter, and businessman. He once said that his success could only have been achieved in this country.

On December 22, 1977, James Denaro passed away, at the age of 95. He was one of the last links to the early ice cream industry and truly a remarkable man.

## John Manos

The story of John Manos, is the story of an inventor whose unique idea never quite caught on. Born July 22, 1896, in Spartan, Greece, Manos came to this country at the age of sixteen, in 1912. He eventually settled in the little town of Toronto, Ohio, on the banks of the Ohio River.

John Manos opened a confectionary called Candyland, with another brother, Nicholas, on Clark St. in Toronto. A second brother, George, owned two moving picture theaters in town. Around 1921, the Manos' moved Candyland adjacent to George's Washington Theater, on N. 4th St. No doubt, after the latest movie, many theater patrons stopped in at Candyland to enjoy refreshments. For a while, Candyland was the "in" place to go in town. Many young children received their first Easter basket of goodies from Candyland.

The phenomenal success of Christian Nelson's Eskimo Pie, inspired

*Joanne Gaylord and James Welshman*

Mr. and Mrs. John A. Manos.

Manos to search for an idea of his own. He wanted an ice cream novelty that could be made right at the soda fountain, without the trouble of packaging and shipping. The idea he conceived was a heart shaped block of ice cream, formed with a special disher, that could be served in a heart shaped dish.

*Jefferson County Historical Association*

George Manos' Washington Theater, in Toronto. Candyland was the entrance on the left side of the theater.

Manos took his idea to J. E. Parker, an engineer in one of the local mills. Parker designed the actual scoop, in exchange for ⅕ of the patent rights. Manos then applied for a patent on Sept. 17, 1924. It was granted on Mar. 10, 1925. Another patent for a slightly improved and simplified scoop was granted on Nov. 17, 1925. The patent for the dish was issued May 12, 1925.

To sell his idea, John Manos travelled over 400 miles, quite a journey in those days, to Troy, N.Y. Troy was the home of at least three companies that manufactured ice cream dishers, the F.S. Co., H. S. Geer Co. and the Gem Spoon Co. There he met with a gentleman experienced in the business.

This person was very candid and told him that the reason he wouldn't buy his design was that it was done too well. If there were no breakable parts, then there would be no re-order business. This meeting was a discouraging one to Manos, who thought his idea was a good one.

Manos returned to Ohio and contracted with a machinist in Cincinnati, Mr. Drexler, to produce 500 of his scoops. He planned to market them himself. The disher was made in two different sizes, nos. 10 and 12 scoops to the quart.

The dishes were heart shaped, on a pedestal, with a heart shaped base. They were made with two different designs on the clear glass, a bird motif and a Greek motif. The reason for the latter design, was that Manos hoped to sell quite a few to other Greek confectioners, which numbered around 40,000 in the country at the time. The molds for these dishes were made in Wheeling, W.Va., at a cost of $500 each. The dishes were made in New Cumberland, W.Va. They are marked on the bottom, "J M Pat. Pend."

His advertising appeared in the *Soda Fountain* magazine, under the name of the Manos Novelty Co. Scoops sold for $3.25 each and dishes were $2.50 a dozen. A set, for $8.25, consisted of two dozen dishes and one scoop. As each order came in, he would first send a photo to the prospective customer. And orders did come in, from all over the U.S. and Canada. His

*Joanne Gaylord and James Welshman*

John Manos' heart shaped dishes with bird motif.

largest single order, for $300 worth of goods, he packed in a barrel and shipped to Australia. His first supply sold out and he ordered another 500 scoops. These eventually sold out, and that was all that he ever had made.

In 1928, Manos left the confectionary business and opened the Jeddo restaurant in Toronto. That same year, he married Amelia Poulos and their first child was born. The Depression forced him to close his restaurant, and in 1935 he packed his belongings and moved to another state to begin again. He opened another confectionary and successfully ran that business, until he retired, in the late 1950's.

John Manos, even though a sucessful businessman, considered his invention a failure. It had not sold nearly as well as he had planned, and in this, he was disappointed. Financially, his venture may have been a failure, but from a collector's standpoint, it was not. His heart shaped disher is recognized as one of the most unique and certainly the most beautiful disher ever made.

## Sherman Kelly

Zeroll . . . the ultimate in durability, practicality, and simplicity. As it's name implies, it is the easiest to use of any ice cream dipper ever invented. That is why it is still on the market, a full half century after it was introduced, in 1935. This can be considered the first *modern* ice cream dipper, and was a major reason for the demise of the earlier ice cream dippers.

The man responsible for it's development was Sherman Kelly, of Toledo, Ohio. Kelly had earned his wealth in the early stock and commodities market. He owned a large home in Toledo, and a winter home in West Palm Beach, Fla. As the story goes, Kelly was vacationing in West Palm Beach, when he had the occasion to watch a young lady dipping ice cream. He also noticed the blisters on her hand from the constant use of the ice cream dipper, in the hard ice cream. He thought, there must be a better way of doing it, and he resolved to find it. The end result was the Zeroll.

The Zeroll was a non-mechanical ice cream dipper, made of cast aluminum, with fluid inside the handle. It was unique, because, as you used it, the heat from your hand warmed the fluid, which in turn defrosted the ice cream dipper. There was no need to rinse the device in water, between servings. The lack of breakable parts was also an advantage. Another advantage, was that it *rolled* the ice cream into a ball, instead of squeezing it. Without the resulting shrinkage, it allowed the dispenser to get 10–20% more servings per gallon. This was one of it's key selling points, and understandably so, in the middle of the Depression. Kelly applied for a patent on May 23, 1935.

Sherman Kelly set up the Zeroll Company offices above his three car garage, at his home, at 2410 Robinwood Ave. His first business check was dated June 7, 1935. His wife, Hazel, worked for him at an hourly wage of

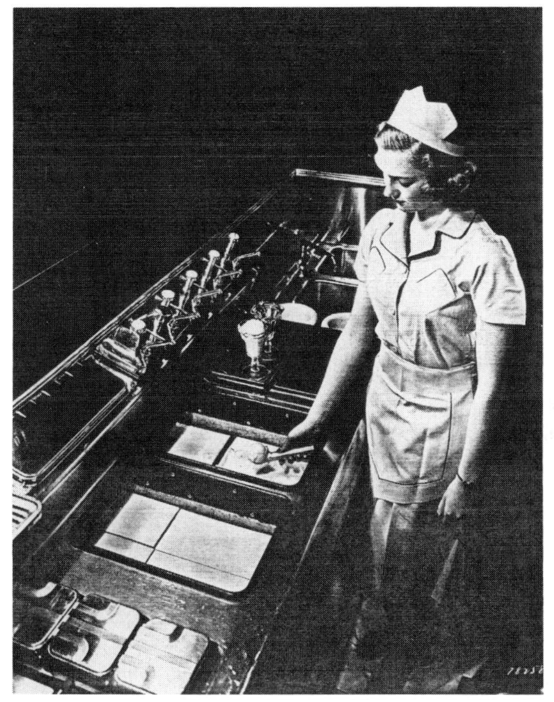

Carl Abel

This shows how easy the Zeroll was to use.

50¢. His first ad, a full page one, was published in the July, 1935 issue of the *Ice Cream Review,* at a cost of $200.

The actual dipper was made to Kelly's specifications by ALCOA, the Aluminum Co. of America. They handled all of the manufacturing processes, from the die-casting, to the finished product. Kelly did all the advertising and marketing. An engineer, Estal O. Weaton, worked for him, in the design end of the business.

The Zeroll was priced at $2.25 each, in five different sizes. They were sold directly to the soda fountains, as well as the larger distributors. A five day, money back guarantee came with each one. Given all of it's advantages, it is no wonder that it became a great success. In the first year of production, thousands were sold.

The early success of the Zeroll Company was halted by W.W.II. The aluminum needed for the dippers, was diverted to wartime use. The business was virtually dormant for several years. After the war, Ralph Kelly, Sherman's son, and Noel Dowling were credited with reviving the company. According to an article in the Wall Street Journal, the Zeroll Co. was one of the first to obtain aluminum, after the war. It was during this period, the

*Dairy and Food Industries Supply Association*

Zeroll Co. display, in the background, at the 1940 dairy convention. Notice how busy the stand was.

1940's, that the Nuroll and Roldip lines were introduced, to capitalize on the increasing home market. These lacked the fluid filled handles of the Zeroll. Around 1950, Sherman Kelly passed away, at the age of 83.

In 1953, Ralph Kelly moved the company to Maumee, Ohio, and changed it's name to Roll Dippers, Inc. It was the beginning of a slow period for the company, until they were purchased by the Funka brothers, in 1968. The year 1981 marked another turning point, when Thomas Funka purchased his brother's stock, moved back to Toledo, and most importantly, changed the name back to Zeroll Co. Presently employing 10 people, the Zeroll Co. continues to produce the same fine product, virtually unchanged in 50 years.

Sherman Kelly did find a better way. His classic dipper is honored in the Museum of Modern Art design collection. Kelly had created what hundreds of inventors before him had attempted . . . the perfect ice cream scoop!

## The Pittsburgh Mystery

Pittsburgh, Pa., in 1896, was the world's largest steel manufacturing center. Located in Western Pa., at the forks of the Monongahela and the Allegheny Rivers, it boasted a population of over one half million, in the 1890's. The famous Andrew Carnegie was one of the city's most influential citizens. His steel mill, the world's largest, employed 30,000 men.

Living conditions at the time were far from ideal. Men labored 12 hours a day, in the hot mills, to earn a wage of only 15¢ an hour. The Depression of 1893 was a recent memory. A typhoid out-break plagued the city that was constantly clouded in smoke, from the steel mills. The 550 confectionaries around the city provided a brief escape for the people, when they had the luxury of enjoying their favorite ice cream and candy treats.

Something very interesting happened, in Pittsburgh, in 1896, relating to the ice cream industry. The fact is, that between March and November of that year, at least 11 patent applications were filed, for ice cream dippers, by

Pittsburgh, Pa. around the turn of the century.

local inventors. This occurance was extremely unusual. Only 7 other similar patents were issued, in the *entire country,* in the previous *18 years.* What is even more unusual, is that each inventor employed the same patent attorney, the same draftsman, and were all for, with the exception of one, conical, one handed dippers. It is also interesting to note, that I have *never* seen any of these dishers, in any collection. Strange coincidences, to say the least! What was the story behind these similarities? The patent numbers involved are as follows: 561727, 568274, 571118, 571170, 572987, 573681, 574185, 576395, 578195, 586181, 599157. See the patent list for further information.

In searching for clues to this mystery, we have to consider the little information that is available. For example, city directories of the period, list the addresses and occupations of the inventors. They all lived in Pittsburgh, or in one of the surrounding communities. Their occupations were varied, including jobs such as, architect, tinner, patternmaker, machinist, grocer, porter, shipping clerk, roller, and printer. Some of these occupations can obviously be related to the manufacture of ice cream dishers, while others cannot. The wide variety of occupations doesn't suggest that they may have known each other, either. These clues, therefore, do not offer us a distinct pattern for answering out question.

The attorney, Henry C. Evert, was a prominent lawyer and patent solicitor in the Pittsburgh area. He also had an office in Washington, D.C., opposite the Patent Office, with his associate, Alfred M. Wilson. Given his status, it is logical to assume that he probably handled most of the patent applications in the Pittsburgh area. His office was located in the Park Bldg., at the corner of 5th Ave. and Smithfield St.

A. Roy Appleman was the draftsman, who put each of the inventor's ideas into drawing form. His drawings accompanied all of the patent applications. His office was located in the 1800 block of 5th Ave.

None of this information really gives us a motive for such a large number

Henry C. Evert, patent attorney.

of disher applications, from the same general area, in such a short period of time. There is one theory, however, that I will advance for consideration.

Located in the heart of Pittsburgh, was the S.L. McFarland Co. They were a large wholesale and retail dealer in ice cream and soda fountain supplies. They most likely provided many of the city's 550 confectionaries and ice cream establishments with their dishers and other supplies. Just having become a recent successor to the Horner and Co., they were probably very responsive to the needs of their new customers. After a number of years of using the two handed, key release type disher, the soda fountain dispenser, was probably ready for an easier to use, one handed model. The McFarland Co. was a logical one to fill this need, and Pittsburgh was a logical manufacturing site.

Now, it is very possible that Mr. McFarland took the initiative to locate inventors for this type of disher, in order to satisfy his customer's needs. He could have, for example, sponsored some type of a contest, through the local newspapers or other advertising, that would encourage local inventors to come up with a better idea for an ice cream disher. This would have provided the needed incentive for such a large number of patents, in a short period.

Whether this theory is a valid one, or not, still remains to be proven. There is one thing for certain, however, that some connection exists between all of these ice cream disher patents. Possibly some day, the answer will be found in a more thorough study of the early ice cream industry, in Pittsburgh.

# Chapter 4

# Manufacturers

The following list of manufacturers is the result of a compilation of information from a number of different sources. These sources include soda fountain trade journal ads, early city directories, industrial directories, and patent records. It is practically impossible to get a complete listing of all manufacturers, but this list should help date and place most ice cream dishers, when the manufacturer is already known.

I have tried to give the address of the company, as accurately as possible, at the time they were manufacturing the dishers. Some of the listings only give the city, however. It is interesting to note that not all of the companies actually made the dishers. This was sometimes contracted out to the local machine shop.

The dates given are only estimates of when the company was in the business of producing dishers. It is very hard to establish exact dates, so in many cases only the decade is given. It is possible that the company was in business either the full decade, or only part of it.

*Bob Bruce*

Erie Specialty Co., Erie, Pa. (ca. 1909)

*Allan Mellis*

V. Clad and Sons, Philadelphia, Pa. (ca. 1905)

*James Denaro*

Automatic Cone Co., Cambridge, Mass. (ca. 1928)

## Manufacturers List

| Company | Date |
| --- | --- |
| Arnold Electric Co.<br>Racine, Wisc. | 1920's–1931 |
| Automatic Cone Co.<br>83–93 Clark St.<br>Cambridge, Mass. | 1903–Present<br>scoops in 1920's |
| Benedict Mfg. Co.<br>East Syracuse, N.Y. | 1920's–1930's |
| Bohlig Mfg Co.<br>St. Paul, Minn. | 1900's–1910's |
| Bunker-Clancy Mfg. Co.<br>1110 Woodland Ave.<br>Kansas City, Mo. | 1920's |
| C. and G. Co.<br>N.Y. | 1900's |
| Cake Cone Co.<br>715 Victor<br>St. Louis, Mo. | 1920's |
| Caron Brothers, Inc.<br>Montreal, Canada | 1920's |
| Cecil Mfg. Co.<br>206–212 Canal St.<br>New York, N.Y. | late 1920's–1930's |
| V. Clad and Sons<br>117–123 So. 11th St.<br>Philadelphia, Pa. | 1870's–1930's |
| Erie Specialty Co.<br>510–518 W. 12th St.<br>Erie, Pa. | 1900's–early 1920's |
| Dan Dee Dipper Co.<br>Knoxville, Tenn. | 1920's |
| Debus Mfg. Co.<br>Hastings, Neb. | 1920's |

## Manufacturers List—*Continued*

| Company | Date |
|---|---|
| Dover Mfg. Co.<br>Dover, N.H. | 1920's |
| F.S. Co.<br>Troy, N.Y. | 1910's |
| Feller Cone Scoop Co.<br>132 Market Ave., South<br>Canton, Ohio | 1940's |
| Fisher Motor Co. LTD<br>Orillia, Ontario, Canada | 1920's |
| Fletcher Mfg. Co. LTD<br>Toronto, Canada | 1920's |
| Franklin Products<br>1220 W. 35th St.<br>Chicago, Ill. | 1930's |
| H. S. Geer Mfg. Co.<br>Troy, N.Y. | 1900's–1910's |
| Gem Spoon Co.<br>4–6 Oakwood Ave.<br>Troy, N.Y. | 1900's–1920's |
| General Ice Cream Corp.<br>Schenectady, N.Y. | 1920's |
| Gilchrist Co.<br>236 Bank St.<br>Newark, N.J. | 1908–1931 |
| Guaranteed Disher Co.<br>N.Y. ? | 1920's |
| Hamilton Beach Mfg. Co.<br>Racine, Wisc. | 1930's–Present |
| Jiffy Sales Co.<br>37 S. Wabash Ave.<br>Chicago, Ill. | 1920's |

## Manufacturers List—*Continued*

| Company | Date |
|---|---|
| Keiner-Williams Stamping Co.<br>8746–82 123rd St.<br>Long Island, N.Y. | 1900's–1930's |
| Kingery Mfg. Co.<br>31 E. Pearl St.<br>Cincinnati, Ohio | 1890's–1920's |
| Lloyd Disher Co.<br>Decatur, Ill. | 1940's |
| McDowell and Co.<br>2020 Knox/816 Western<br>Pittsburgh, Pa. | 1900's |
| McLaren Consolidated Cone Co.<br>Bacon and McDonough Sts.<br>Dayton, Ohio | 1928 |
| Manos Novelty Co.<br>Toronto, Ohio | 1920's |
| Maryland Baking Co.<br>Baltimore, Md. | 1930's |
| Matthews | 1900's |
| Mayer Mfg. Co.<br>1612 S. Wabash<br>Chicago, Ill. | 1920's |
| Thomas Mills and Bro.<br>1301 N. 8th St.<br>Philadelphia, Pa. | 1870's–1940's |
| Modern Specialty Co.<br>St. Paul, Minn. | 1920's |
| Mosteller Mfg. Co.<br>127 Indiana St.<br>Chicago, Ill. | 1900's–1910's |
| Myers Products Corp.<br>240 E. Ferris St.<br>Galesburg, Ill. | 1930's |

## Manufacturers List—*Continued*

| Company | Date |
|---|---|
| N. and Co. | 1890's ?–1900's |
| New Gem Mfg. Co.<br>52 Badger Ave.<br>Newark, N.J. | 1932–1940 |
| Perfection Disher Co.<br>(Dover Sales Co.)<br>222 Sumner<br>Boston, Mass. | late 1920's |
| Perfection Equipment Co.<br>(Sky-Hi Distribution Co.)<br>3619 Broadway<br>Kansas City, Mo. | 1930's |
| Philadelphia Ice Cream Cone<br>Machinery Co.<br>68 N. 4th St.<br>Philadelphia, Pa. | late 1920's–1930's |
| Pi-Alamoder, Inc.<br>St. Louis, Mo. | 1920's |
| Presto Ice Cream Equipment Co.<br>Schenectady, N.Y. | 1920's |
| Sanitary Mould Co.<br>Brooklyn, N.Y. | 1920's |
| J. Schloemer<br>N.Y. | 1920's |
| Schupfer and Eaton Co., Inc.<br>88 Benefit St.<br>Pawtucket, R.I. | 1930's |
| Shore Machine Corp.<br>455 W. 43rd St.<br>New York, N.Y. | 1950's |
| Standard<br>Germany | 1950's |

# Manufacturers List—*Continued*

| Company | Date |
|---|---|
| United Products Co., Inc.<br>37 Winnisimmet St.<br>Chelsea, Mass. | late 1920's–early 1930's |
| Veeder Mfg. Co.<br>Hartford, Ct. | 1900's |
| William F. Wendell<br>Girard, Pa. | 1920's |
| Wiley Small Mfg. Co.<br>509–11 N. LaSalle St.<br>Chicago, Ill. | 1910's |
| Zeroll Co.<br>2410 Robinwood Ave.<br>Toledo, Ohio | 1935–Present |

# Chapter 5

## Patent Records

The records of the U.S. Patent Office provide invaluable source material, in the study of the evolution of the ice cream disher. The different sections of the patent record give us basic and useful information concerning both the invention and the inventor.

The patent record is divided into two parts, the drawing and the specifications. The drawing comprises the visual part of the record. This is a sketch of the invention, as the inventor sees it. Usually, different views are

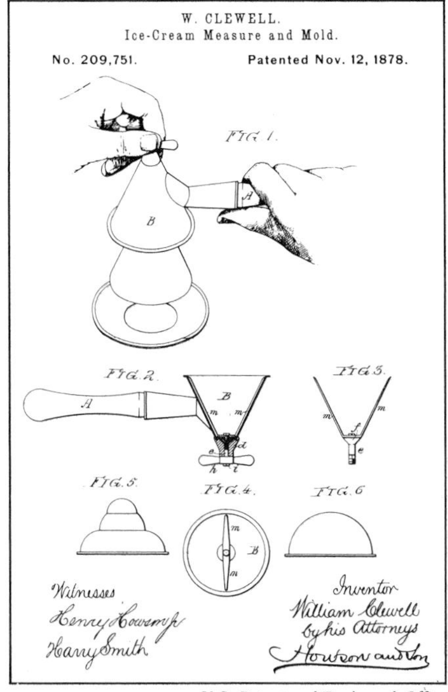


*U.S. Patent and Trademark Office*

Patent drawing

shown, to include all the working parts. In most cases, the drawing looks exactly like the final product, however, not always. Before production, certain improvements and changes might be made, provided they didn't alter the original claims of the patent. One of the most obvious of these changes can be seen in the Gem Spoon Co. disher, pat. no. 538693. The patent drawing also gives the name of the inventor, patent no., and patent date.

The other section of the patent record comprises the specifications. This section explains the use of the disher and the novel features that distinguish this from other dishers. It is most helpful, particularly in the case of some of the more unusual ones, such as Frank Hayden's ice cream soda dipper, pat. no. 659146. Great detail is used to describe the function of every part. This section also gives us the town of residence of the inventor, and the date that he filed his application. In some cases, the inventor assigned his patent to a particular company or individual. This information would be listed here, also.

Probably more interesting than the official patent records, are the patent application files. These files comprise *all* of the correspondence between the inventor or his attorney, and the Patent Office Examiners, up until the date the patent was actually issued. By studying them, we can get a feeling for the complexities of Patent Office procedures. If the patent application was initially rejected, for one reason or another, and many of them were, the

UNITED STATES PATENT OFFICE.

WILLIAM CLEWELL, OF READING, PENNSYLVANIA.

IMPROVEMENT IN ICE-CREAM MEASURE AND MOLD.

Specification forming part of Letters Patent No. **209,751**, dated November 12, 1878; application filed April 29, 1878.

*To all whom it may concern:*

Be it known that I, WILLIAM CLEWELL, of Reading, Pennsylvania, have invented a new and useful Improvement in Ice-Cream Measure and Mold, of which the following is a specification:

The object of my invention is to provide retailers of ice-cream with an implement for measuring the same and for depositing it on a plate or saucer in a molded and attractive condition.

In the accompanying drawing, Figure 1 is a perspective view illustrating the implement and the mode of using the same; Fig. 2, a sectional view; Fig. 3, a detached view of part of Fig. 2; Fig. 4, a view of the open end of the measure; and Figs. 5 and 6, views showing modified forms of the measure.

To a suitable handle, A, is secured the measure B, which consists of a tapering vessel, made in the present instance of thin metal, the small end of the vessel being secured to a metal base, *d*, through which passes a spindle, *e*, having a conical head, *f*, adapted to a countersunk recess in the said base, to which the spindle is confined by its handle *h* and a nut, *i*. To the head of the spindle are attached two arms or scrapers, *m m*, which bear against the measure in the interior of the same.

In using the implement, it is held in one hand, with the mouth of the measure uppermost, as in Fig. 2, and by a spoon held in the other hand the vessel is filled with ice-cream to its upper edge, the cream being properly smoothed off to this edge. The implement is then inverted and held above a plate or saucer, as shown in Fig. 1, while the handle *h* is turned, thereby causing the arms to detach the frozen cream from the sides of the measure, the mass of cream then falling onto the plate, ready for presentation to the consumer, in a molded and attractive condition.

It is not essential that the measure should be of the conical form represented in Figs. 1 and 2. It may, for instance, be made in the form shown in Figs. 5 and 6, or in any other form which will permit the free escape of the mass of frozen cream, the scraping-arms being in all cases made to conform with the shape of the measure. Neither is it necessary that the vessel should be made of metal, as glass, china, or other like material might in some cases be deemed desirable.

It will be evident that more than two scraping-arms may be used, and that one only would serve the desired purpose; but I prefer two arms.

I claim as my invention—

1. The combination of the measuring-vessel B, having a suitable handle, with a scraping arm or arms adapted to the said vessel, and admitting of being turned therein, all substantially as set forth.

2. The combination of the measuring-vessel A, the spindle *e*, passing through and arranged to turn in the said vessel, and carrying a scraping arm or arms, *m*, with a handle, *h*, secured to the spindle, all substantially as described.

In testimony whereof I have signed my name to this specification in the presence of two subscribing witnesses.

WILLIAM CLEWELL.

Witnesses:
MATTHIAS MENGEL,
J. W. EDES.

*U.S. Patent and Trademark Office*

Patent specifications

*In the Matter of the Application of*
2902

William Clewell

*For Letters Patent*

For Ice Cream Measure and Mould

Howsons' Patent Agency,
Philadelphia, Apl. 27th 1878.

To the Hon. Commissioner of Patents:

Sir

We herewith enclose specification, and drawing ~~and assignment~~ relating to the above application. The first government fee has been this day forwarded by check, and the model accompanies the papers

Very respectfully your's,
Howson and Son
Attorneys for Wm. Clewell

National Archives

Part of William Clewell's patent application.

reason is given in great detail. Most often, the reason was a similarity to other patents. Generally, a patent application, with no complications, took from 6 months to a year to be issued a number. In the cases where a patent took 4 or 5 years to be granted, the files are usually thick with conflicting claim correspondence. Raymond Gilchrist and Edwin Walker's files are unusually thick. Some of their claims conflicted with each others, as letters between their attorney's showed.

The following list gives the patent number and the year the patent was issued, as well as the inventor's name and residence. A company name in ( ) indicates to whom the inventor assigned his patent rights. Under, *Type of scoop,* the one or two words listed are a *brief* description of the main characteristics. An * next to the patent date, denotes a scoop that is known to have been produced. A (P) indicates the patents connected with the "Pittsburgh Mystery".

The wealth of information these records provide, help us in the study of these early dishers. Without the use of them, much of the information in this book would not be available.

## Ice Cream Dishers—Patent List

| Patent number | Pat. date | Inventor | Residence | Type of scoop |
|---|---|---|---|---|
| 209751 | 1878* | William Clewell | Reading, Pa. | cone/key |
| 384776 | 1888* | Thomas A. Naylor | Baltimore, Md. | cone/key |
| 432905 | 1890 | Martin L. Schoch | New Berlin, Pa. | cup |
| 514038 | 1894 | Martin L. Schoch | New Berlin, Pa. | |
| 525382 | 1894* | Edson Clemant Baughman | Topeka, Kansas | cone |
| 538693 | 1895* | Bernice J. Noyes | Boston, Mass. | round |
| 554550 | 1896 | Hans M. O. Thode | Mattoon, Ill. | cylinder |
| 561727 | 1896 | Alfred L. Riggs | Knoxville, Pa. | cone (P) |
| 568274 | 1896 | Clarence L. Phillis, Harry E. McCoy | Pittsburgh, Pa. | cone (P) |
| 571118 | 1896 | Fred D. Clark | McDonald, Pa. | cone (P) |
| 571170 | 1896 | Henry J. Pfeiffer | Pittsburgh, Pa. | cone (P) |
| 572987 | 1896 | Charles W. Harmon, James E. Harmon, Charles E. Boyd | Allegheny, Pa. | round (P) |
| 573681 | 1896 | Henry G. Morris | Hoboken, Pa. | round (P) |
| 574185 | 1896 | John & Susanna Zimmer | Pittsburgh, Pa. | cone (P) |
| 576395 | 1897 | Alfred L. Cralle | Pittsburgh, Pa. | cone (P) |
| 578195 | 1897 | Charles M. Beatty | Tarentum, Pa. | cone (P) |
| 584221 | 1897 | H. R. Hageman | | round |
| 586181 | 1897 | Thomas F. Handly | Allegheny, Pa. | cone (P) |
| 586807 | 1897 | James and William H. Crae | Allegheny, Pa. | cone |
| 591635 | 1897 | Thomas F. Rankin | Allegheny, Pa. | cone |
| 595954 | 1897 | Arthur W. Lockwood | Everett, Pa. | cone |
| 599157 | 1898 | Herman August Weber | Pittsburgh, Pa. | cone (P) |
| 618205 | 1899 | Philip Howell | Frank, Pa. | cone |
| 626468 | 1899 | Frederick E. Schmits | Oakland, Ca. | cone |
| 659146 | 1900* | Frank D. Hayden | Richmond, Va. | cylinder |
| 671788 | 1901* | Maximillan Bach | Pittsburgh, Pa. | cone |
| 689368 | 1901 | Arminda B. Rush | Pittsburgh, Pa. | cone |
| 693360 | 1902 | William G. Bahl | Pittsburgh, Pa. | cone |
| 697677 | 1902 | George W. Sherer | Rockford, Ill. | cone |

** Known to have been produced*

*(P) Pittsburgh Mystery*

## Ice Cream Dishers—Patent List—*Continued*

| Patent number | Pat. date | Inventor | Residence | Type of scoop |
|---|---|---|---|---|
| 708987 | 1902 | Edson C. Baughman | Topeka, Kansas | cone |
| 713897 | 1902 | William Maxwell | Pittsburgh, Pa. | cup |
| 714440 | 1902 | William J. Bolland | Pittsburgh, Pa. | cone |
| 741015 | 1903 | James F. Craven (McDowell Mfg. Co.) | Pittsburgh, Pa. | round |
| 772674 | 1904 | Isaac A. Rommer | Newark, N.J. | cup |
| 781899 | 1905 | Rasmus Nielsen (Gilchrist Co.) | Troy, N.Y. | round |
| 785742 | 1905 | Louis Philip Lipps | Cleveland, Ohio | dispenser |
| 803906 | 1905* | Henry A. Keiner, Edward C. Williams | Brooklyn, N.Y. | cone |
| 809663 | 1906 | Arthur E. Bennett (Bennett Mfg. Co.) | Buffalo, N.Y. | cone/key |
| 819373 | 1906 | Albert P. Olmstead | Watervliet, N.Y. | cone |
| 820061 | 1906 | Dosier H. Mosteller | Chicago, Ill. | spoon |
| 820473 | 1906 | Rea Buchanan | Peoria, Ill. | round |
| 825147 | 1906 | Dosier H. Mosteller (Mosteller Mfg. Co.) | Chicago, Ill. | round |
| 833620 | 1906* | Rasmus Nielsen | Troy, N.Y. | cone |
| 841097 | 1907 | Thomas McG. Aiken, James E. Harmon | Allegheny, Pa. | round |
| 845421 | 1907 | Nick W. Kline | Longbeach, Ca. | cone |
| 864550 | 1907* | Dosier H. Mosteller (Mosteller Mfg. Co.) | Chicago, Ill. | round/flips over |
| 866079 | 1907 | Thaddeus S. Smith | Indianapolis, Ind. | cylinder |
| 869879 | 1907 | William R. Cameron | New York, N.Y. | cylinder |
| 892633 | 1908* | Edwin Walker | Erie, Pa. | cone |
| 900348 | 1908* | Martin Bohlig (Bohlig Mfg. Co.) | St. Paul, Minn. | round/divides |
| 900573 | 1908* | Charles E. McCarren | Cinn., Ohio | round |
| 901437 | 1908 | Lory J. Graffort, Peter L. Hoffman | New Carlisle, Ind. | cone |
| 903563 | 1908 | Lory J. Graffort, Peter L. Hoffman | New Carlisle, Ind. | cone |
| 909550 | 1909 | Tobias Cohn | New York, N.Y. | sandwich |
| 925275 | 1909 | Frank Benjamin | Troy, N.Y. | cup |
| 938628 | 1909 | Joseph A. Aubry | Hammond, Ind. | slicer |
| 950525 | 1910 | Albert Wilcox | Wheeling, W. Va. | cone |
| 951571 | 1910* | Dosier H. Mosteller (Mosteller Mfg. Co.) | Chicago, Ill. | cone |

* *Known to have been produced*

## Ice Cream Dishers—Patent List—*Continued*

| Patent number | Pat. date | Inventor | Residence | Type of scoop |
|---|---|---|---|---|
| 953901 | 1910* | Albert John Daniel | Boone, Iowa | cone filler |
| 954498 | 1910 | Herman Bieder | Ashtabula, Ohio | bricks |
| 961429 | 1910 | Samuel J. Clark | Cornwall-on-the-Hudson, N.Y. | slicer |
| 964225 | 1910 | Ernest A. Erickson | Wilson, Pa. | cone |
| 968945 | 1910 | William B. Hogan | Albany, N.Y. | round |
| 977382 | 1910 | James Geier | Troy, N.Y. | round |
| 978938 | 1910 | Alphonse Roos | L.A., Ca. | mold |
| 987470 | 1911 | Savo B. Ljutica | | cone |
| 990479 | 1911 | Joseph Edwards | Duncan, Okla. | coneholder |
| 993508 | 1911 | Robert A. D. Colmery | Mt. Gilead, Ohio | cup |
| 999018 | 1911 | John W. Duncan | | coneholder |
| 1012944 | 1911* | Edwin Walker, Clarence L. Walker | Erie, Pa. | round/sundae creme |
| 1016711 | 1912 | David Henry Roller | Muncie, Ind. | round |
| 1042080 | 1912 | Martin L. Burkhart | Minn., Minn. | cone |
| 1045015 | 1912* | James Geier | Troy, N.Y. | coneholder |
| 1045166 | 1912 | James W. Murray | Fort McPherson, Ga. | cone |
| 1049585 | 1913 | Jacob J. Honecker | Cleveland, Ohio | round |
| 1052370 | 1913* | Rasmus Nielsen | Troy, N.Y. | round |
| 1057065 | 1913 | William Krist | Milwaukee, Wis. | cone |
| 1062940 | 1913 | Ben T. Wilson, Wilton F. Ratcliff | Nacogdoches Texas | coneholder |
| 1069226 | 1913 | Theodore J. Brandt | Gresham, Ore. | cone |
| 1078209 | 1913 | Rasmus Nielsen | Troy, N.Y. | coneholder |
| 1109576 | 1914* | Raymond B. Gilchrist (Gilchrist Co.) | Newark, N.J. | round |
| 1109577 | 1914 | Raymond B. Gilchrist (Gilchrist Co.) | Newark, N.J. | cone |
| 1109578 | 1914 | Raymond B. Gilchrist | Newark, N.J. | round |
| 1109579 | 1914 | Raymond B. Gilchrist | Newark, N.J. | round |
| 1112802 | 1914 | Charles N. & Casper J. Jager | Baltimore, Md. | cone |
| 1120888 | 1914 | Edson C. Baughman | Topeka, Kansas | cone |
| 1121489 | 1914 | Tuckerman C. Fuqua | Richmond, Va. | cone |

** Known to have been produced*

## Ice Cream Dishers—Patent List—*Continued*

| Patent number | Pat. date | Inventor | Residence | Type of scoop |
|---|---|---|---|---|
| 1132657 | 1915* | Raymond B. Gilchrist (Gilchrist Co.) | Newark, N.J. | round |
| 1132870 | 1915* | Rasmus Nielsen (Gilchrist Co.) | Troy, N.Y. | round |
| 1132871 | 1915 | Rasmus Nielsen | Troy, N.Y. | round |
| 1138533 | 1915 | Theodore J. Brandt (National Specialty Co.) | Gresham, Ore. | cone |
| 1138703 | 1915* | Edwin Walker | Erie, Pa. | cone/key |
| 1138704 | 1915* | Edwin Walker | Erie, Pa. | cone |
| 1138705 | 1915* | Edwin Walker | Erie, Pa. | round |
| 1138706 | 1915* | Edwin Walker | Erie, Pa. | round |
| 1142354 | 1915 | Dosier H. Mosteller | Chicago, Ill. | round |
| 1153172 | 1915 | William A. Robinson | Old Fort, N.C. | |
| 1162116 | 1915* | Edwin Walker | Erie, Pa. | cone |
| 1168919 | 1916 | Samuel Ellsworth Surface | Stickney, S.D. | cone |
| 1174564 | 1916 | John E. Golden | Dunmore, Pa. | double cone |
| 1188757 | 1916 | George E. Holmes, Frank W. Grant | Dover, N.H. | slicer |
| 1194685 | 1916* | Edwin Walker | Erie, Pa. | round |
| 1197531 | 1916 | Rasmus Nielsen | Troy, N.Y. | round |
| 1199590 | 1916 | Samuel F. Martin | Waynesboro, Pa. | cylinder |
| 1199880 | 1916 | William Eichelberger, Walter W. Brewer | Pierce, W. Va. | cone filler |
| 1200224 | 1916 | Rasmus Nielsen | Troy, N.Y. | cone |
| 1200225 | 1916 | Rasmus Nielsen | Troy, N.Y. | round |
| 1204167 | 1916 | Wayne Like | | cone holder |
| 1205396 | 1916 | William Ross | Troy, N.Y. | round |
| 1224007 | 1917 | August E. Moos | Nokomis, Ill. | round |
| 1232309 | 1917 | Frank Hillix | Weston, Mo. | cone |
| 1236279 | 1917 | Rinhold F. Fenchel | Beaver Falls, Pa. | cone |
| 1238429 | 1917* | Rasmus Nielsen (Gilchrist Co.) | Troy, N.Y. | cone |
| 1246032 | 1917 | Joseph Bluhm (Dana Mfg. Corp.) | Troy, N.Y. | round |
| 1253057 | 1918 | Arthur McDowell Larrowe, Azel Lewis Kline | Canisteo, N.Y. | cone |

** Known to have been produced*

## Ice Cream Dishers—Patent List—*Continued*

| Patent number | Pat. date | Inventor | Residence | Type of scoop |
|---|---|---|---|---|
| 1255785 | 1918 | Napoleon Pepin | Woonsocket, R.I. | cone |
| 1255906 | 1918 | Frank P. Miller, Jr. | Hoboken, N.J. | round |
| 1265392 | 1918 | Max Schwarz | Richmond, Va. | coneholder |
| 1268046 | 1918 | Oliver Newman | Madrid, Iowa | sandwich |
| 1271327 | 1918 | Theofil Klugiewicz | Erie, Pa. | cone filler |
| 1278686 | 1918* | Herman Landman | Kansas City, Mo. | mold |
| 1279553 | 1918 | Frank C. Kistler | Greensburg, Pa. | coneholder |
| 1282731 | 1918 | James T. Bickle | Mt. View, Mo. | disher/dispenser |
| 1282993 | 1918 | Arlie H. Vincent | Burlington, Kansas | coneholder |
| 1296745 | 1919 | Joseph Bluhm (Dana Mfg. Corp.) | Troy, N.Y. | cone |
| 1320885 | 1919 | Harry V. Melick | Columbus, Ohio | double round |
| 1323582 | 1919 | William B. Dow | Waltham, Mass. | cone filler |
| 1325082 | 1919 | Benjamin F. Englar | Baltimore, Md. | cone |
| 1352755 | 1920 | Samuel Levy | Knoxville, Tenn. | sandwich |
| 1352756 | 1920* | Samuel Levy | Knoxville, Tenn. | sandwich |
| 1360324 | 1920 | Hermann J. Schubert | Hackensack, N.J. | cone filler |
| 1387613 | 1921 | Russell H. Proper | New York, N.Y. | sandwich |
| 1430979 | 1922 | John M. Gibbs | Parsons, Kansas | cone |
| 1450886 | 1923 | William Glock Heimerdinger | Louisville, Ky. | cone filler |
| 1459638 | 1923 | Michael P. Rodopulos | Chicago, Ill. | banana split |
| 1460551 | 1923 | William G. Lyman | Peoria, Ill. | cone |
| 1472533 | 1923 | William R. Ripley | Turlock, Ca. | round |
| 1480398 | 1924 | Frederick C. Kirchoff | San Francisco, Ca. | round |
| 1481125 | 1924 | Stephen Cuper, Anthony Daniels, Frank Klens | Scranton, Pa. | sandwich |
| 1481890 | 1924 | Guy M. Causey | Salem, Ore. | sandwich |
| 1482094 | 1924 | William Roddie Ripley | Modesto, Ca. | round |
| 1483938 | 1924* | George E. Holmes, Frank W. Grant | Dover, N.H. | slicer |
| 1484716 | 1924 | Frederick C. Kirchoff | San Francisco, Ca. | round |
| 1485273 | 1924 | Charles Kleintop | Allentown, Pa. | cone filler |

* *Known to have been produced*

## Ice Cream Dishers—Patent List—*Continued*

| Patent number | Pat. date | Inventor | Residence | Type of scoop |
|---|---|---|---|---|
| 1485622 | 1924 | Charles J. Manuel | Tarrytown, N.Y. | round |
| 1485677 | 1924* | George E. Holmes, Frank W. Grant | Dover, N.H. | slicer |
| 1507698 | 1924 | William H. Craven | Philipsburg, Pa. | dispenser |
| 1508915 | 1924 | Earl E. Bidwell | Omaha, Neb. | slicer |
| 1526753 | 1925* | Maurice L. Levene | Chicago, Ill. | sandwich |
| 1528406 | 1925 | Isadore Davidson | Newark, N.J. | coneholder |
| 1529319 | 1925* | John A. Manos | Toronto, Ohio | heart |
| 1529782 | 1925* | Barnett Gerstein | College Point, N.Y. | sandwich |
| 1531179 | 1925* | William L. Daly | Schenectady, N.Y. | cylinder |
| 1532275 | 1925 | David L. Strumph | | cylinder |
| 1540089 | 1925 | Oscar H. Schmelter | Erie, Pa. | cone |
| 1561558 | 1925* | John A. Manos | Toronto, Ohio | heart |
| 1562432 | 1925 | Arthur William Bersch | Milwaukee, Wis. | round |
| 1574788 | 1926 | William H. Brueseke | St. Louis, Mo. | electric |
| 1581493 | 1926* | Johannes Schloemer | New York, N.Y. | sandwich |
| 1583072 | 1926* | Herman Landman | Kansas City, Mo. | sandwich |
| 1584757 | 1926 | William B. Dow | Waltham, Mass. | egg shape |
| 1588413 | 1926 | Henry A. Hardy | Topeka, Kansas | round |
| 1587538 | 1926 | Patrick McLaughlin | Dover, N.H. | slicer |
| 1588599 | 1926 | Fred N. Martin | Spokane, Wash. | round |
| 1595393 | 1926* | Harlan P. Gardner, Alvin O. Olafson (Par-Pie Co.) | St. Paul, Minn. | pie ala mode |
| 1595635 | 1926* | Frederick W. Vollans | Orillia, Ontario, Canada | cylinder |
| 1595661 | 1926 | Burton L. Huntley (Kreampak Carton Co.) | Minn., Minn. | dispenser |
| 1607115 | 1926 | Morris L. Cecil | New York, N.Y. | round |
| 1609655 | 1926 | Fred N. Martin | Spokane, Wash. | round |
| 1615641 | 1927 | Steven B. Long, John C. Pimm | | |

* *Known to have been produced*

## Ice Cream Dishers—Patent List—*Continued*

| Patent number | Pat. date | Inventor | Residence | Type of scoop |
|---|---|---|---|---|
| | | (Long Sales Co.) | Syracuse, N.Y. | sandwich |
| 1615939 | 1927* | Harrison D. Flegel (Arnold Electric Co.) | Racine, Wisc. | round |
| 1620110 | 1927* | Herman Landman | Kansas City, Mo. | sandwich |
| 1622348 | 1927 | John C. Ritter | Portland, Ore. | cone |
| 1627132 | 1927* | William F. Wendel | Girard, Pa. | sandwich |
| 1634594 | 1927 | John H. Pieper | | dispenser |
| 1639122 | 1927 | Louis J. Whitman | Cinn., Ohio | mold |
| 1639809 | 1927 | George T. Parr (Parr Pie Co.—St. Paul) (Pi-Alamoder, Inc.—St. Louis) | St. Paul, Minn. | pie ala mode |
| 1642726 | 1927* | Harlan P. Gardner | St. Paul, Minn. | pie ala mode |
| 1645208 | 1927 | Jink Thompson | Huntington, W. Va. | slicer |
| 1657470 | 1928* | George E. Holmes, Frank W. Grant | Dover, N.H. | slicer |
| 1661734 | 1928 | Peter D. Pearce | Grand Rapids, Mich. | dispenser |
| 1667734 | 1928 | Charles O. Mook | Kansas City, Mo. | slicer attach. |
| 1669703 | 1928 | Harrison D. Flegel (Arnold Electric Co.) | Racine, Wisc. | round |
| 1675776 | 1928* | Sidney B. Whiteside | New York, N.Y. | round |
| 1677984 | 1928 | George T. Parr | St. Paul, Minn. | pie ala mode |
| 1687813 | 1928 | Earl W. Werner | Muskegon Hts., Mich. | cylinder |
| 1688079 | 1928 | Otto Hinz, Russell Merrell | Los Angeles, Ca. | round |
| 1688595 | 1928 | George T. Parr (Pi-Alamoder, Inc.) | St. Paul, Minn. | pie ala mode |
| 1698716 | 1929 | John W. Cox (Gilchrist Co.) | Erie, Pa. | foot pump |
| 1703023 | 1929 | George C. White | Irvington, N.J. | round |
| 1705533 | 1929 | William E. Patzer | Hastings, Neb. | dispenser |
| 1710397 | 1929 | Valentin Bach | | pie ala mode |
| 1712042 | 1929* | Charles H. Jockmus | Ansonia, Conn. | round |
| 1718555 | 1929 | Christ J. Halset, John W. Hose | Chicago, Ill. | round |
| 1721045 | 1929 | Edward J. Martineau | Seattle, Wash. | cylinder |
| 1728505 | 1929 | Charles G. Palmer | Newark, N.J. | round |

** Known to have been produced*

## Ice Cream Dishers—Patent List—*Continued*

| Patent number | Pat. date | Inventor | Residence | Type of scoop |
|---|---|---|---|---|
| 1732328 | 1929 | John W. Cox (Gilchrist Co.) | Erie, Pa. | round |
| 1732502 | 1929 | John W. Cox | Erie, Pa. | electric |
| 1747737 | 1930 | George D. Ruetz | Racine, Wisc. | round |
| 1748204 | 1930 | Charles W. Campbell | St. Paul, Minn. | cone holder |
| 1752560 | 1930 | Thomas Jameson (Gilchrist Co.) | Newark, N.J. | round |
| 1756609 | 1930 | Elliott M. Story | Worcester, Mass. | cylinder |
| 1757799 | 1930 | Frederick H. Harm | Le Sueur Center, Minn. | cylinder |
| 1760358 | 1930 | Carl G. Hertzer | Tiffin, Ohio | triangular |
| 1761986 | 1930 | Joseph H. Grummer | Cleveland, Ohio | pie ala mode |
| 1763389 | 1930 | Penrose E. Chapman | St. Louis, Mo. | |
| 1765973 | 1930 | Harrison D. Flegel (Arnold Electric Co.) | Racine, Wisc. | round |
| 1769218 | 1930 | Gus G. Garvis | Des Moines, Iowa | pie ala mode |
| 1772489 | 1930 | Mack D. Jeffries | Boston, Mass. | cone holder |
| 1773013 | 1930* | Raymond Schupfer | Pawtucket, R.I. | round |
| | | Lawrence B. Eaton | Saylesville, R.I. | |
| 1774154 | 1930? | Willard A. Phillips (T. N. Benedict Mfg. Co.) | East Syracuse, N.Y. | round |
| 1776258 | 1930 | Arthur S. Hood | Kenmore, N.Y. | cylinder |
| 1789065 | 1931* | Joseph Brezin (Phila. I. C. Cone Mach. Co.) | Philadelphia, Pa. | round |
| 1789588 | 1931* | Thomas Jameson (Gilchrist Co.) | Newark, N.J. | round |
| 1798490 | 1931 | George Y. Parr | St. Paul, Minn. | pie ala mode |
| 1805387 | 1931 | James L. Balton (Md. Baking Co.?) | Baltimore, Md. | sandwich |
| 1826009 | 1931* | Edward J. Martineau | Seattle, Wash. | cylinder |
| 1826651 | 1931 | Jolliette E. Chisholm | Portland, Ore. | round |
| 1826818 | 1931 | Charles G. Palmer | Irvington, N.J. | round |
| 1829442 | 1931* | Harrison D. Flegel (Hamilton Beach) | Racine, Wisc. | round |
| 1842709 | 1932 | Edson C. Baughman | Kansas City, Mo. | round |
| 1843873 | 1932* | Wellsley D. Gray | Lorain, Ohio | cone |

* *Known to have been produced*

## Ice Cream Dishers—Patent List—*Continued*

| Patent number | Pat. date | Inventor | Residence | Type of scoop |
|---|---|---|---|---|
| 1854265 | 1932 | Harold Lawson | Little Rock, Ark. | cylinder |
| 1847328 | 1932 | Louis Berzon (Phila. I. C. Cone Mach. Co.) | Philadelphia, Pa. | round |
| 1857685 | 1932 | Joseph B. Friedman | Los Angeles, Ca. | round |
| 1862527 | 1932* | John W. Cox (Gilchrist Co.) | Newark, N.J. | round |
| 1868656 | 1932* | Joseph Brezin (Phila. I. C. Cone Mach. Co.) | Philadelphia, Pa. | sandwich |
| 1877935 | 1932* | Ernest S. Millo | Bronx., N.Y. | disk |
| 1888739 | 1932 | Leo I. Sanders | Estherville, Iowa | round |
| 1896083 | 1933* | Ora E. Harris | Kearney, Neb. | cylinder |
| 1903791 | 1933? | Louis Myers | Chicago, Ill. | round |
| 1923257 | 1933 | William M. Dean | Oyster Bay, N.Y. | round |
| Re.19084 | 1934 | Ora E. Harris | Kearney, Neb. | sandwich |
| 1956224 | 1934? | Louis Myers | Chicago, Ill. | round |
| 1961655 | 1934* | Robert J. Albrecht (Hamilton Beach) | Racine, Wisc. | trunnion |
| 1966089 | 1934 | Frank R. Chester (Chester Bros. Ltd.) | Vancouver, B.C., Canada | round |
| 1974051 | 1934? | Sherman L. Kelly | Toledo, Ohio | electric |
| 1978942 | 1934* | Ora E. Harris | Kearney, Neb. | cylinder |
| 1978943 | 1934? | Ora E. Harris | Kearney, Neb. | cylinder |
| 2013265 | 1935 | Frank R. Chester (Chester Bros. Ltd.) | Vancouver, B.C., Canada | round |
| 2019566 | 1935? | Harold P. Gray (T. N. Benedict Mfg. Co.) | Leominster, Mass. | spade |
| 2034117 | 1936 | Robert L. Pflieger | Dayton, Ohio | double sandwich |
| 2041200 | 1936* | Louis Myers (Myers Mfg. Co.) | Chicago, Ill. | round |
| 2063754 | 1936 | Robert J. Price | Uniontown, Pa. | cone |
| 2076416 | 1937 | Edwin G. Rust | Sioux City, Iowa | slicer |
| 2077501 | 1937 | Maximilian E. Weiss | Philadelphia, Pa. | spade/slicer |
| 2085381 | 1937? | Louis Myers (Myers Mfg. Co.) | Galesburg, Ill. | round |

* *Known to have been produced*

## Ice Cream Dishers—Patent List—*Continued*

| Patent number | Pat. date | Inventor | Residence | Type of scoop |
|---|---|---|---|---|
| 2108585 | 1938 | Andrew M. Healy | Streator, Ill. | cone |
| 2109598 | 1938 | Joseph Stasinski, Frederick Edinger, John E. Thebaud | Philadelphia, Pa. | electric |
| 2129753 | 1938 | Joseph D. Wilhoit | Louisville, Ky. | round |
| 2154806 | 1939 | Irene L. Clave, Alfred O. Clave | St. Paul, Minn. | pie ala mode |
| 2155700 | 1939* | Patrick F. Donahue (Scoville Mfg. Co.) | Waterville, Conn. | round |
| 2157813 | 1939 | Leopold Biskup | Philadelphia, Pa. | round |
| 2160023 | 1939* | Sherman L. Kelly | Toledo, Ohio | half round |
| 2160585 | 1939* | Harry C. Gessler | Brooklyn, N.Y. | round |
| 2164429 | 1939 | John C. Ritter | Los Angeles, Ca. | cone |
| 2165941 | 1939* | Robert J. Price | Uniontown, Pa. | cone |
| 2166810 | 1939 | John R. Gammeter | Akron, Ohio | electric |
| 2168737 | 1939 | Alexander S. Mackey | Clearview, Ont., Canada | cylinder |
| 2171606 | 1939 | Rex M. Shultz | Ventura, Ca. | half round |
| 2173253 | 1939 | John W. Gallo | Mineola, N.Y. | cylinder |
| 2176752 | 1939 | James L. Taggart | Mt. Pleasant, Pa. | V spade |
| 2178648 | 1939 | Ray E. Rothenbush | Los Angeles, Ca. | |

* *Known to have been produced*

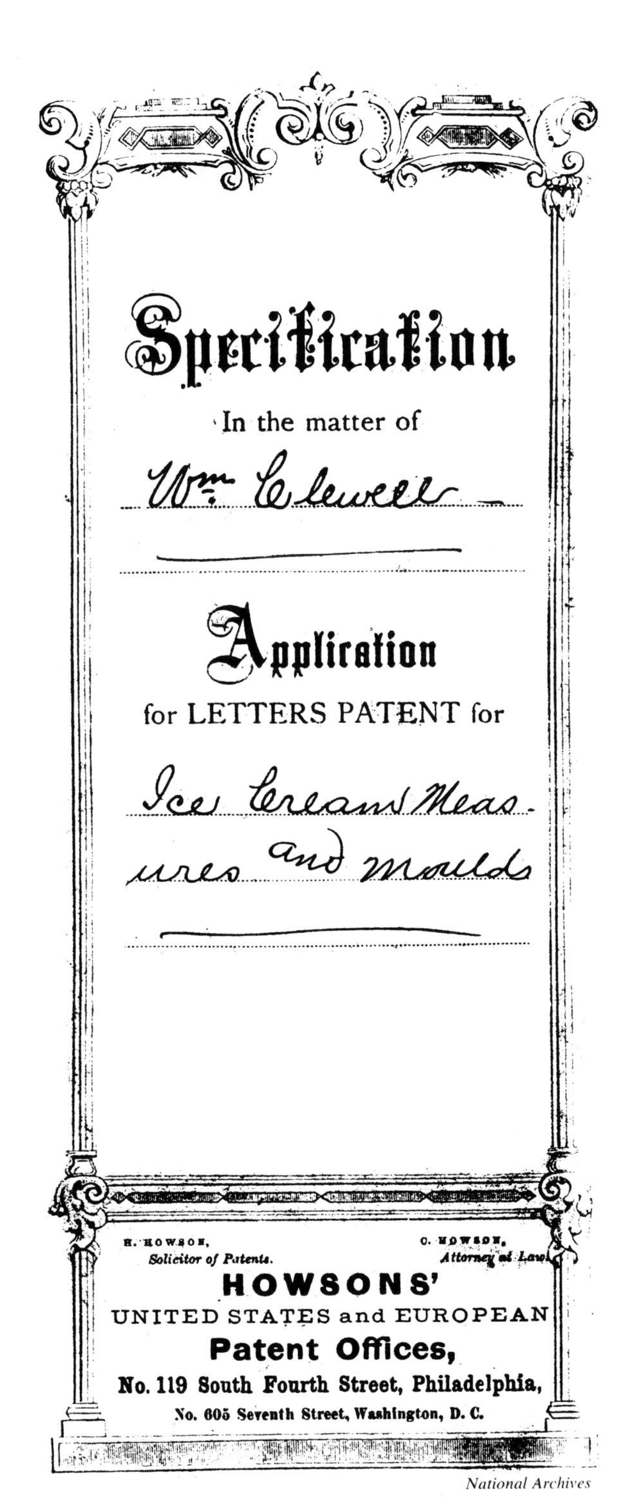


*National Archives*

Cover of Wm. Clewell's patent application.

# Chapter 6

## The Pioneer Era
## 1876–1900

The year was 1876, the Centennial of the founding of the United States and the signing of the Declaration of Independence. Americans were still trying to forget the bitter Civil War. The United States was emerging as a great industrial power, with railroads, steel, and petroleum as the leading industries. Names like Carnegie, Vanderbilt, and Rockefeller were household words. A larger majority of the 46 million people in the country, were centered in the East. The West was still a frontier. This was the year General Custer was defeated at Little Big Horn and Mark Twain wrote his, *Adventures of Tom Sawyer*. America was gearing up for it's largest celebration in history, the Centennial Exhibition at Philadelphia. Alexander Graham Bell's telephone, the Corliss Engine, and Tuft's magnificent soda fountain were just some of the popular attractions at the seven month long event. These were just some of the events occurring at the time of a significant development in the early ice cream industry.

A soda fountain owner in Reading, Pa., William Clewell, invented what was probably the first mechanical ice cream disher. Up until this time, ice cream was served with a spoon. Clewell's device formed ice cream into a conical pyramid and released it onto a plate. Valentine Clad, a Philadelphia tinsmith, located at 123 S. 11th St., was the first to manufacture Clewell's disher. Later, Thomas Mills, a Philadelphia ice cream and confectionary machinery manufacturer, produced the same disher. These were marked "Clad's Disher". The next two decades saw many imitations in it's style because of it's popularity and usefulness.

The early dishers of this period were constructed of tin and steel, with a key operated release mechanism. The handles were usually also made of tin and steel and the bowl shape was mostly conical. The Naylor Co., N. and Co., and a number of other unidentified companies used primarily the same design.

In the 1890's, the Kingery Co., makers of Crystal Flake ice cream powder, introduced a new type of disher. This "rapid" disher, invented by

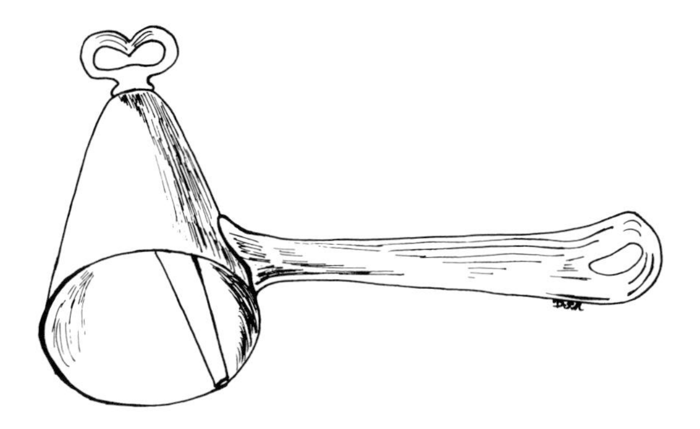

E. C. Baughman, was the first *one-handed* type. It's squeeze handle action was an improvement over the earlier key release type. The german silver plating used on this disher was a sanitary feature lacking in the tin and steel models.

In the late 1890's, the ice cream sundae was rapidly becoming the most popular ice cream creation since Robert Green concocted the ice cream soda, in 1874. This was coupled with the fact that the annual ice cream production skyrocketed from 59,000 gals. to 5 million gals., in the same period. This increased demand for supplies foretold of more changes to come in the industry. The last five years of the 1890's accounted for 19, out of a total of 24, ice cream disher patents for the entire period.

Typical trade card from the 1880's.

A-1. V. Clad Co., Philadephia, Pa.
**Inventor:** William Clewell? (Reading, Pa.)
**Material:** steel
**Handle:** steel, tubular
**Length:** 8½″
**Bowl:** conical
**Guide number:** 1
**Note:** round seal on end of handle marked "Clewell's V. Clad Maker Pat. May 3, 1876"
no patents were issued on that date

A-2. V. Clad Co., Philadelphia, Pa.
**Inventor:** William Clewell? (Reading, Pa.)
**Material:** steel, enamel coated
**Handle:** same, flat
**Length:** 7½″
**Bowl:** conical
**Guide number:** 1
**Note:** marked "Pat. May 3, 1878" on scrape
no patents were issued on that date

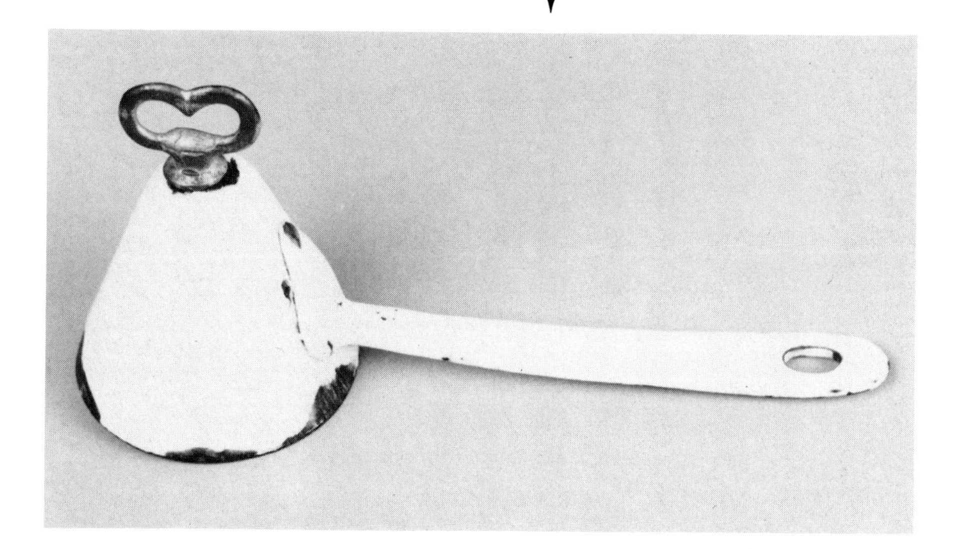

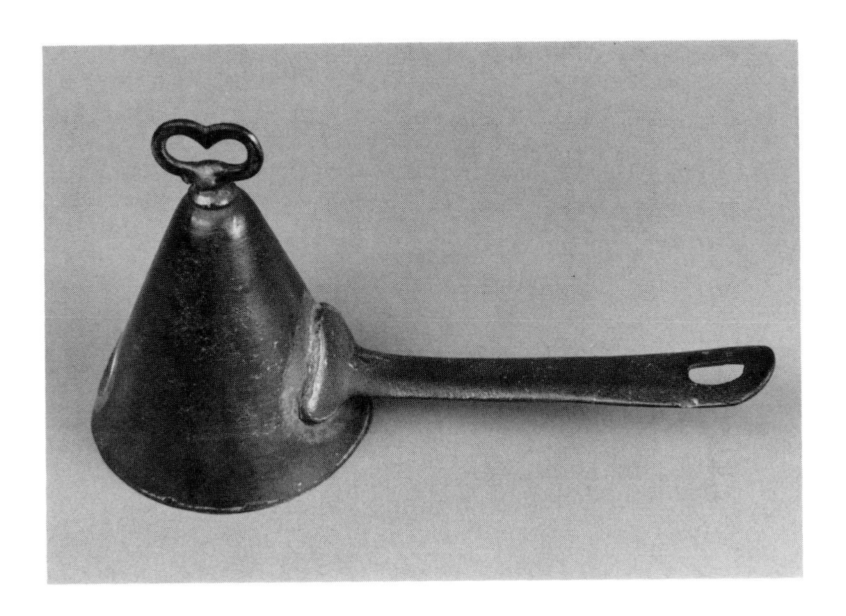

A-3. V. Clad Co., Philadelphia, Pa.
**Patent number:** 209,751
**Patent filed:** 1878
**Patent issued:** 12 Nov. 1878
**Inventor:** William Clewell (Reading, Pa.)
**Material:** steel
**Handle:** steel, flat (also tubular)
**Length:** 8″
**Bowl:** conical
**Guide number:** 1
**Note:** round company seal found on front of cone or end of tubular handle

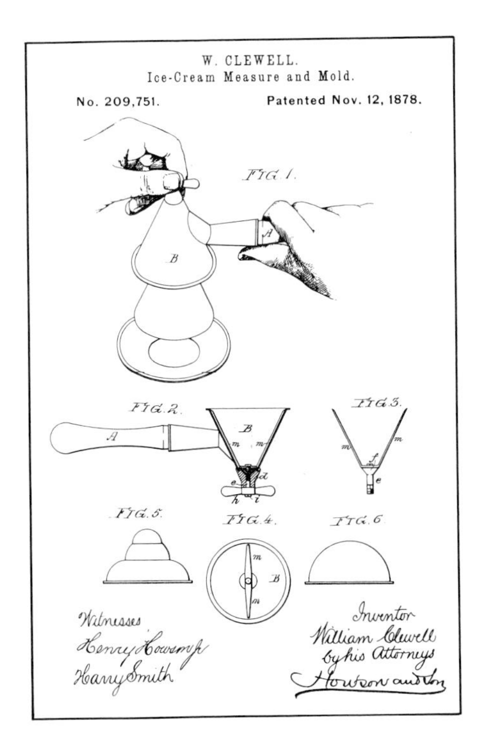

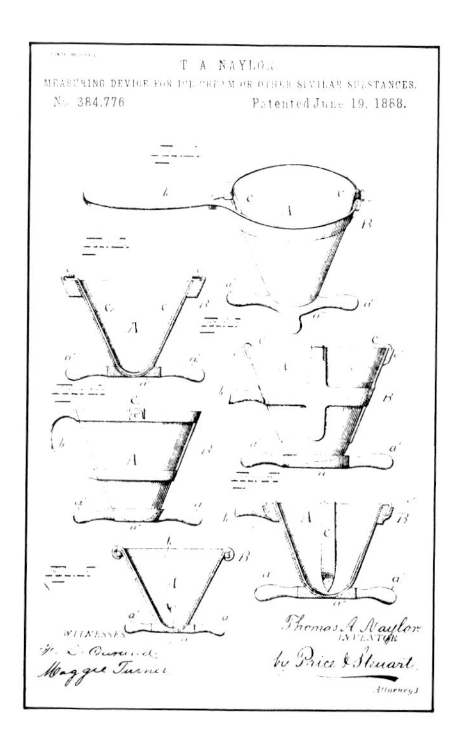


A-4. Naylor

**Patent Number:** 384,776
**Patent filed:** 2 Feb. 1888
**Patent issued:** 19 June 1888
**Inventor:** Thomas A Naylor (Baltimore, Md.)
**Material:** steel
**Handle:** steel, flat
**Length:** 8″
**Bowl:** conical
**Guide number:** 1
**Note:** top of handle marked "Naylor's Pat. 6-19-88" when key is turned, bowl moves, while scraper remains stationary

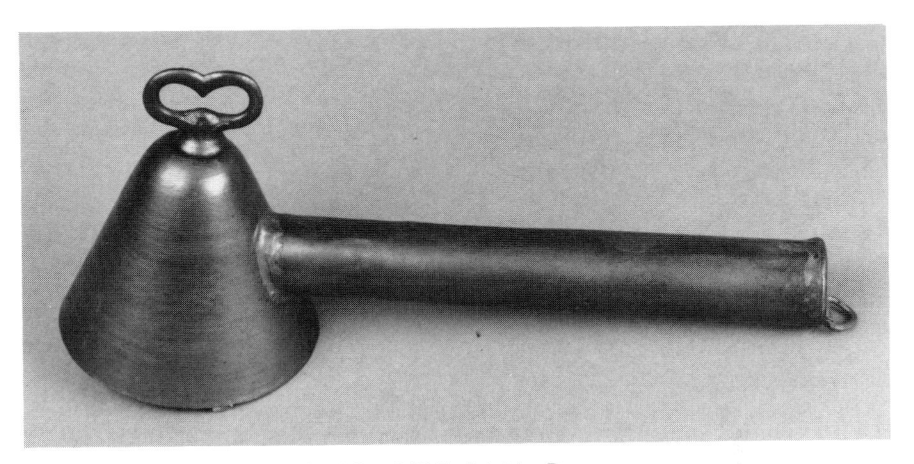

A-5. V. Clad Co.,? Philadelphia, Pa.
**Inventor:** William Clewell? (Reading, Pa.)
**Material:** steel, copper plated
**Handle:** same, tubular, with attached hook
**Length:** 8½″
**Bowl:** conical
**Guide number:** 1
**Note:** no markings
ca. 1890–1900

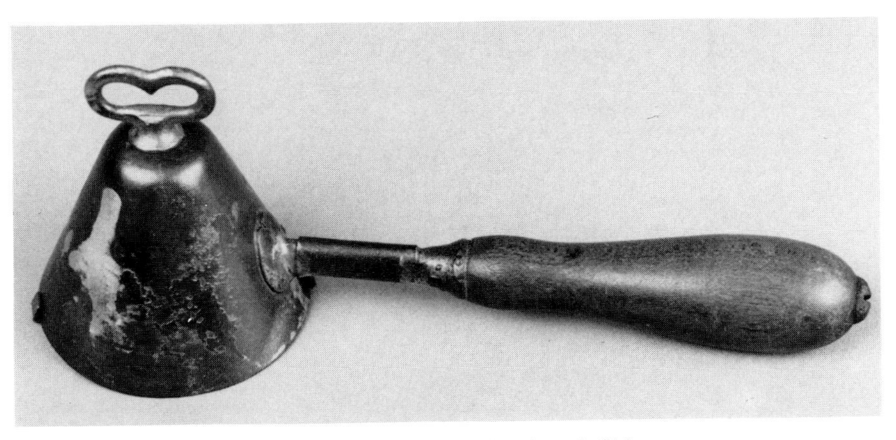

A-6. Kingery Mfg. Co., Cincinnati, Ohio
**Material:** steel
**Handle:** wood
**Length:** 8¼″
**Bowl:** conical
**Guide number:** 1
**Note:** scraper marked
"Pat. Apl'd For
Kingery Mfg. Co."

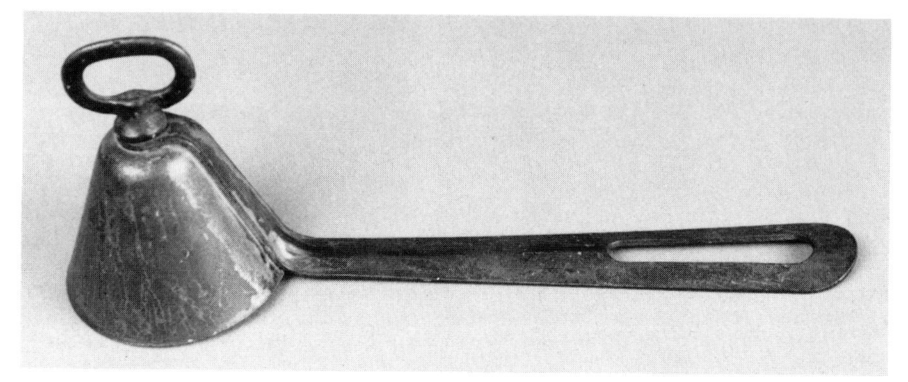

A-7. Unknown maker
**Material:** steel
**Handle:** same, flat
**Length:** 7½″
**Bowl:** conical
**Guide number:** 1
**Note:** no markings
ca. 1890–1900

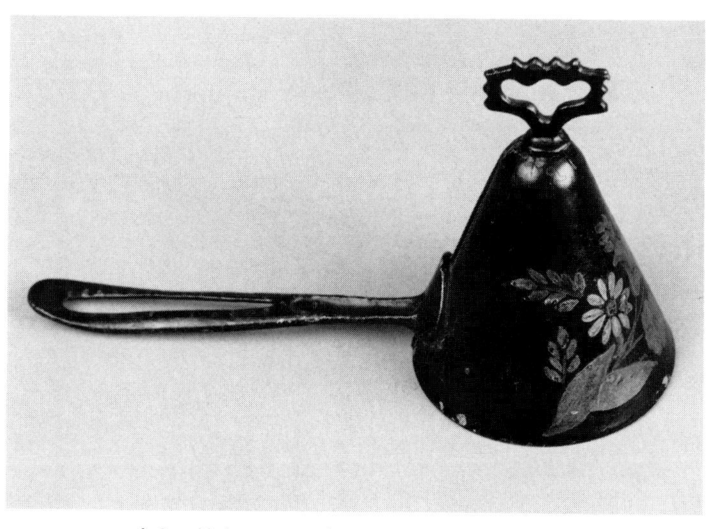

A-8. Unknown maker
**Material:** steel
**Handle:** same
**Length:** 8¼″
**Bowl:** conical
**Guide number:** 1
**Note:** no markings
this example has been painted
ca. 1890–1900

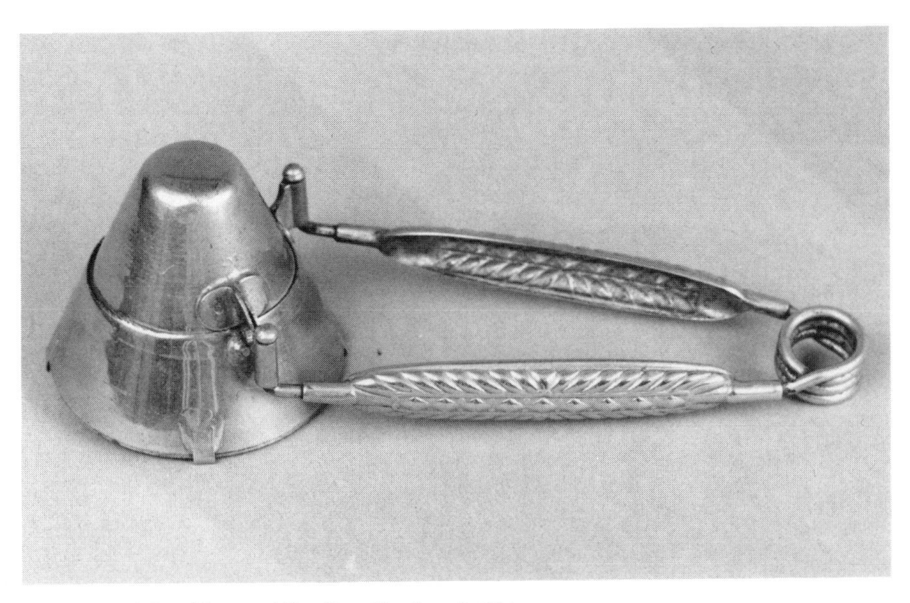

A-9. Kingery Mfg. Co., Cincinnati, Ohio
**Patent number:** 525,382
**Patent filed:** 19 Sept. 1892
**Patent issued:** 4 Sept. 1894
**Inventor:** Edson Clemant Baughman (Topeka, Kansas)
**Material:** nickel plated metal
**Handle:** same, squeeze type
**Length:** 8½″
**Bowl:** conical
**Guide number:** 3
**Note:** first disher made for "one handed" use as bowl rotates when handle is squeezed
fancy handles probably made after 1904, while earlier models most likely had wire handles

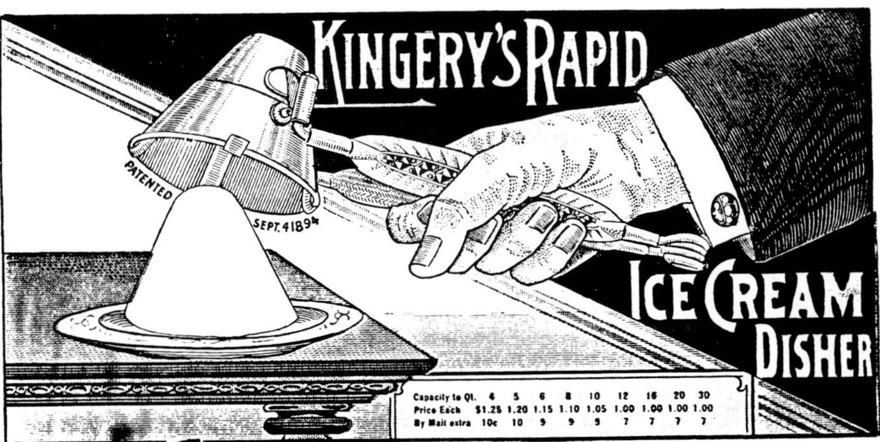


*Allan Mellis*

Gem Spoon Co. catalog

A-10. Gem Spoon Co., Troy, N.Y.
**Patent number:** 538,693
**Patent filed:** 2 Jan. 1895
**Patent issued:** 7 May 1895
**Inventor:** Bernice J. Noyes (Boston, Mass.)
**Material:** brass, nickel plated
**Handle:** wood
**Length:** 10½″
**Bowl:** round
**Guide number:** 2
**Note:** possibly the first round disher produced

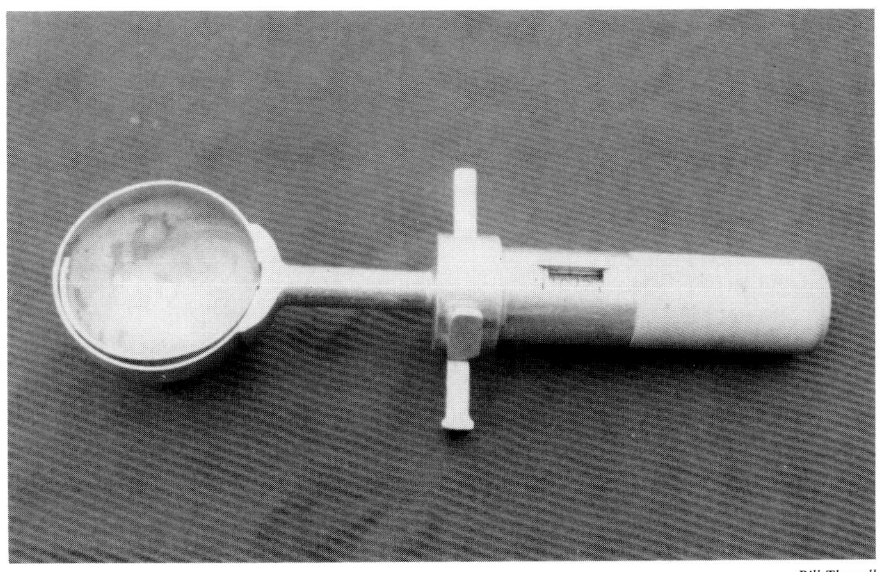

*Bill Thunell*

A-11. Veeder Mfg. Co., Hartford, Conn.
**Patent issued:** 3 Oct. 1899
**Material:** brass, nickel plated
**Handle:** same
**Length:** 8¼″
**Bowl:** round
**Guide number:** 5
**Note:** has an automatic counter in handle
inside handle marked
"Veeder Mfg. Co., Hartford, Conn. Pat. Oct. 3, 1899"

# Chapter 7

## The Innovative Era
## 1900–1910

The first decade of the 20th Century was an important era of innovation and change for the country, as well as the ice cream industry. The country was in the midst of a huge tidal wave of immigration, the likes of which it had never seen before. Over 14 million immigrants arrived in the first twenty years of this century. Inventors, James Denaro and John Manos were among them. With these immigrants came new ideas. The technological advances of the era were also responsible for changes and improvements.

Several important events occurred in the ice cream industry. In 1904, the ice cream cone was "born" at the St. Louis World's Fair, as a result of an enterprising vendor combining ice cream and a rolled up waffle. It was an instant success. That same year, the homogenizer was introduced in the United States, which resulted in a vastly improved texture of ice cream. In 1906, President Theodore Roosevelt signed the long needed Food and Drug Act, which regulated standards for food, including ice cream. In addition to these, the need for proper sanitation was beginning to get attention from the industry. To help unify the industry, the International Association of Ice Cream Manufacturers was formed in 1900.

At least 32 ice cream dishers were patented this decade. In their designs, one can see a reflection of the changes in the industry. First, there was a trend towards greater variety and styles. The round bowl was introduced because of it's utilitarian function. It was easily used for sundaes, sodas and cones. The cone shaped bowl, however, still remained popular. The handles were made of wood, probably for ease of use. The concern for sanitation was reflected in the fact that dishers were increasingly being made of nickel-plated brass, instead of the unsanitary tin and steel. Also, the spring mechanisms being introduced, were much more sophisticated than the key release type. A good example of this is the 1906 Mosteller disher, where the spring action causes the bowl to flip over.

The number of manufacturers that dominated production during this pe-

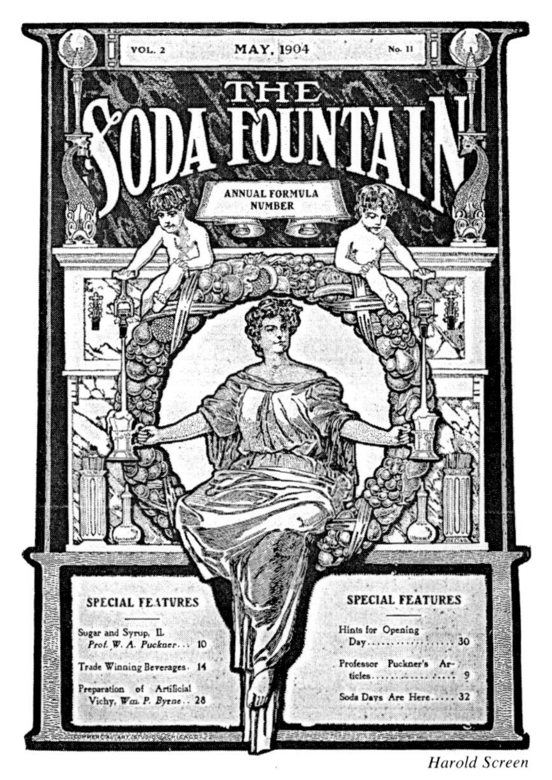


*Harold Screen*

*The Soda Fountain* magazine, official publication of the International Association of Ice Cream Manufacturers.

riod, increased over the previous one. In addition to the V. Clad Co., Thomas Mills Co., and the Kingery Co., some of the newer ones were: the Erie Specialty Co., of Erie, Pa., Mosteller Mfg. Co., of Chicago, Ill., and the Bohlig Mfg. Co., of St. Paul, Minn. Several other new manufacturers, the Gem Spoon Co. and the H.S. Geer Co., were both from the same city, Troy, N.Y. As the end of the decade approached and the ice cream production increased to 30 million gallons a year, a new company made it's entry into the field. The Gilchrist Co., of Newark, N.J., introduced it's line of "better than need be goods", and proceeded to dominate the market for the next two decades, through it's advertising and sales.

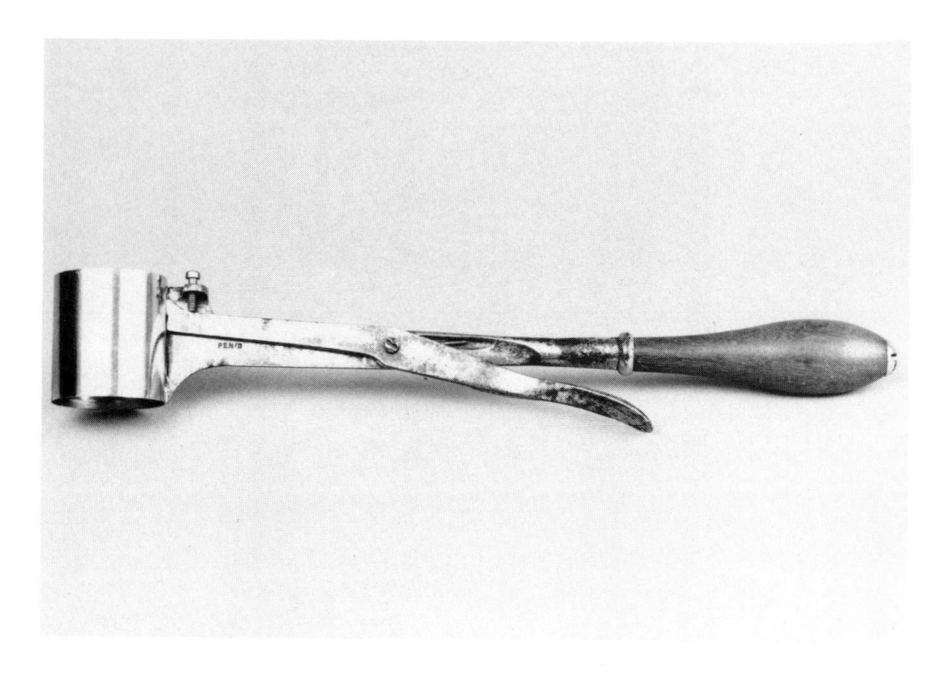


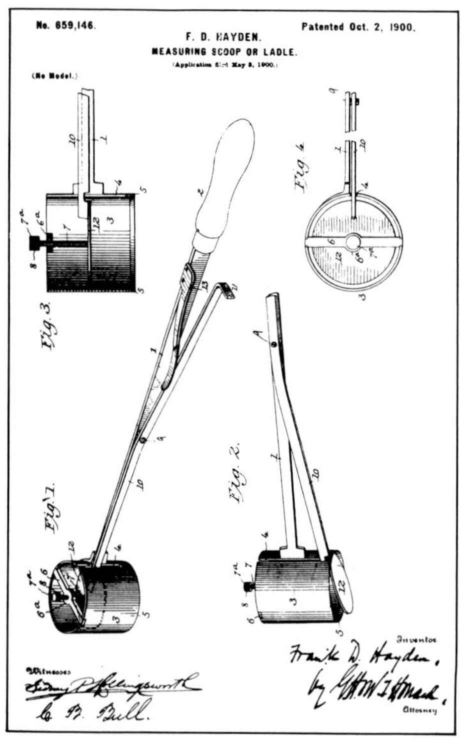


B-1. C. + G. Co., N.Y.
**Patent number:** 659,146
**Patent filed:** 3 May 1900
**Patent issued:** 2 Oct. 1900
**Inventor:** Frank D. Hayden (Richmond, Va.)
**Material:** steel
**Handle:** wood
**Length:** 13″
**Bowl:** cylindrical
**Guide number:** 5
**Note:** used to make ice cream sodas
shank marked "C. + G. Co. N.Y. Patent Pen'd"

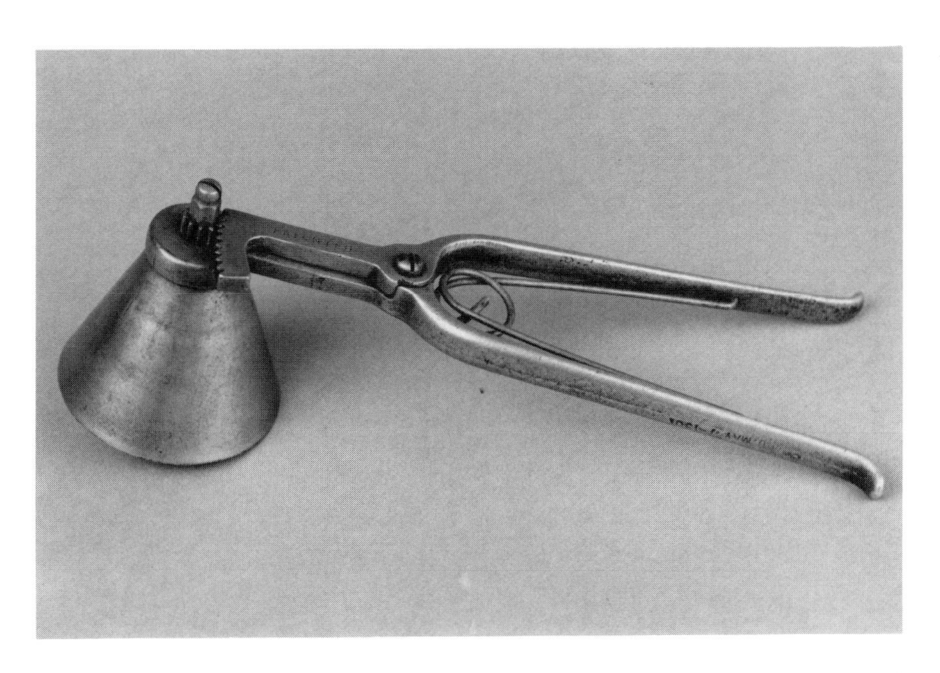

B-2. Unknown maker
**Patent number:** 671,788
**Patent filed:** 16 Jan. 1900
**Patent issued:** 9 Apr. 1901
**Inventor:** Maximilian Bach (Pittsburgh, Pa.)
**Material:** steel
**Handle:** steel
**Length:** 10″
**Bowl:** conical
**Guide number:** 4
**Note:** handle marked "Patented U.S.A. April 9 1901 E. of G. May 7 1901"

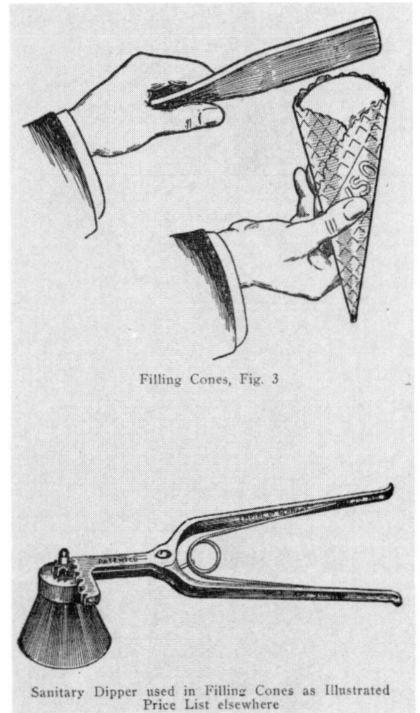


Sayso Cone manual

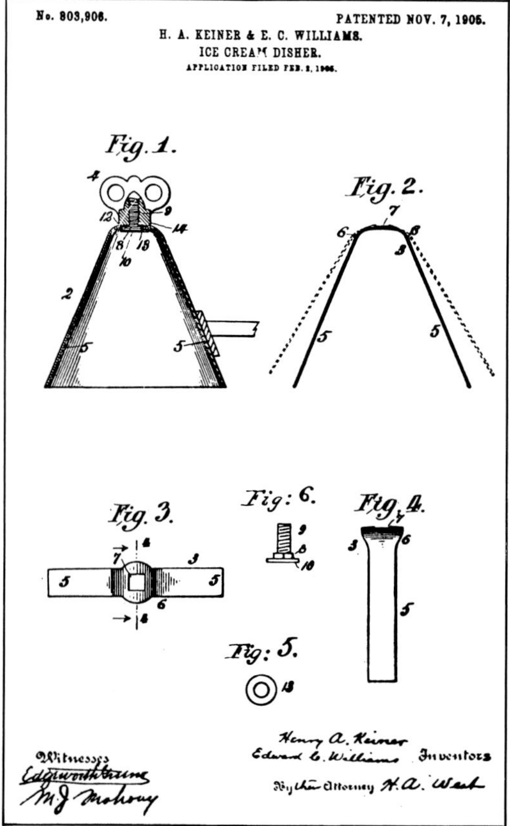


B-3. Keiner-Williams Stamping Co., Richmond Hill, L.I., N.Y.
**Patent number:** 803,906
**Patent filed:** 2 Feb. 1905
**Patent issued:** 7 Nov. 1905
**Inventors:** Henry A. Keiner
Edward C. Williams
(Brooklyn, N.Y.)
**Material:** steel
**Handle:** steel wire loop
**Length:** 7½"
**Bowl:** conical
**Guide number:** 1
**Note:** "KW" on key
scraper marked
"Pat. Nov. 7, 1905"

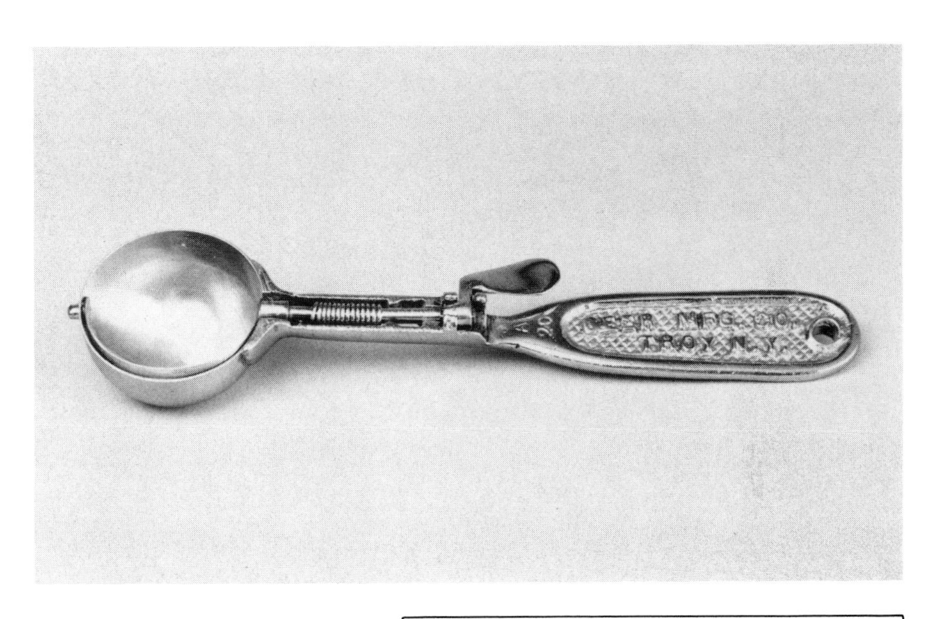


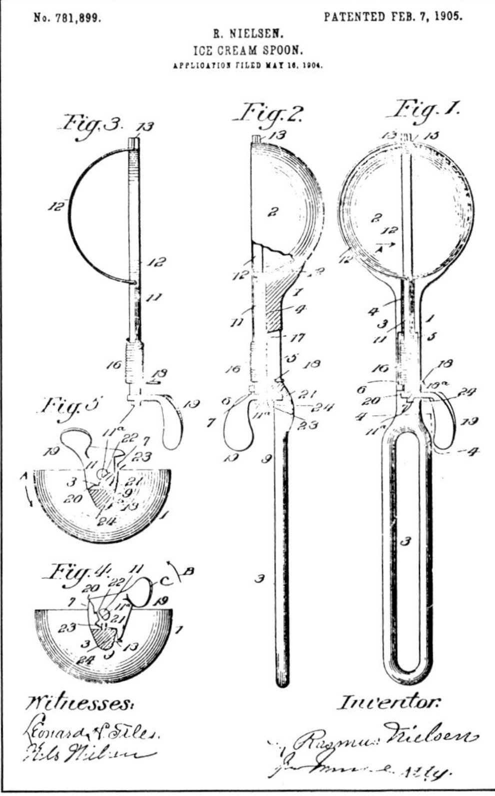
No. 781,899. PATENTED FEB. 7, 1905.

R. NIELSEN.

ICE CREAM SPOON.

APPLICATION FILED MAY 16, 1904.



B-4. Geer Mfg. Co., Troy, N.Y.
**Patent number:** 781,899
**Patent filed:** 16 May 1904
**Patent issued:** 7 Feb. 1905
**Inventor:** Rasmus Nielsen (Troy, N.Y.)
**Material:** brass, nickel plated
**Handle:** same, flat
**Length:** 9¼″
**Bowl:** round
**Guide number:** 3
**Note:** front handle marked "Geer Mfg. Co., Troy, N.Y."
back handle marked "Clipper Disher, Pat. Feb. 7, 1905"
has a double scraper
earlier model marked "Giles and Nielsen The Clipper Spoon"

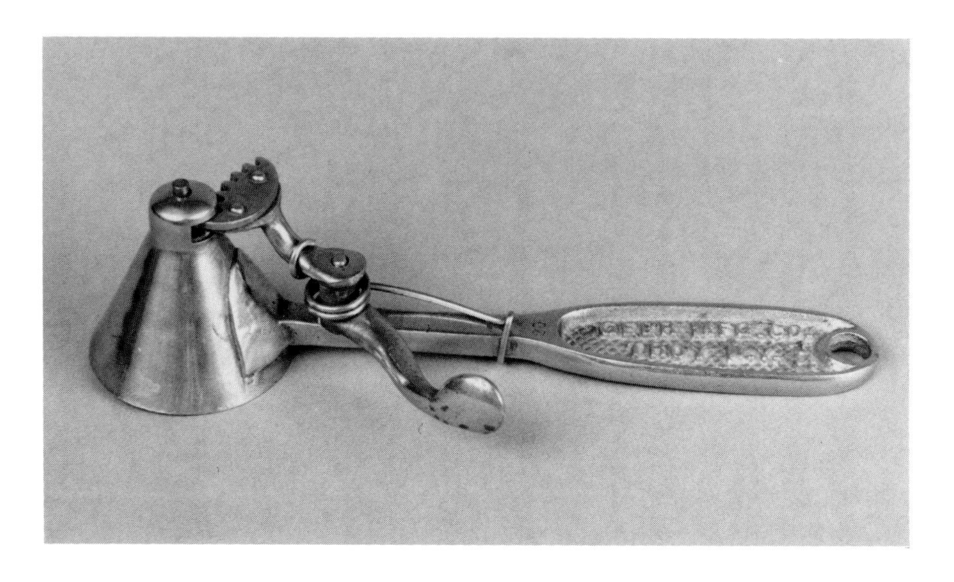

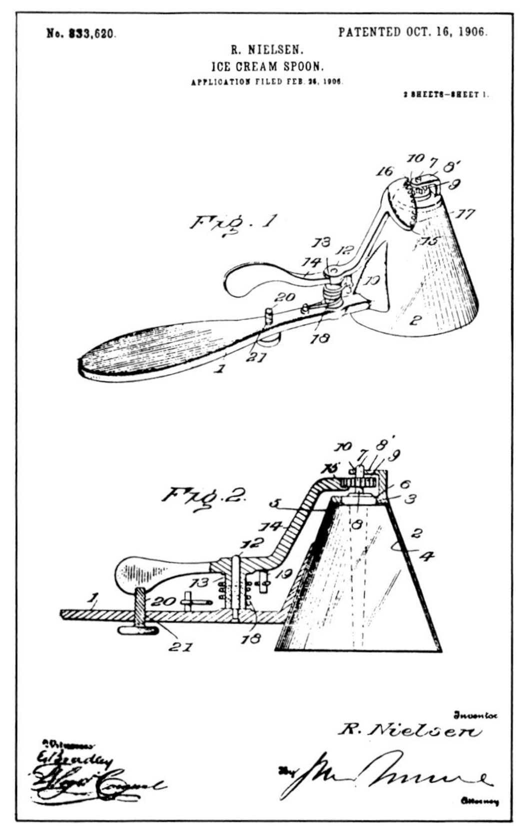


B-5. Geer Mfg. Co., Troy, N.Y.
**Patent number:** 833620
**Patent filed:** 26 Feb. 1906
**Patent issued:** 16 Oct. 1906
**Inventor:** Rasmus Nielsen (Troy, N.Y.)
**Material:** brass, nickel plated
**Handle:** same, flat
**Length:** 9″
**Bowl:** conical
**Guide number:** 3
**Note:** back handle marked "Geer Mfg. Co. Troy, N.Y."
front handle marked "Cone Clipper Pat. Oct. 16, 1906"

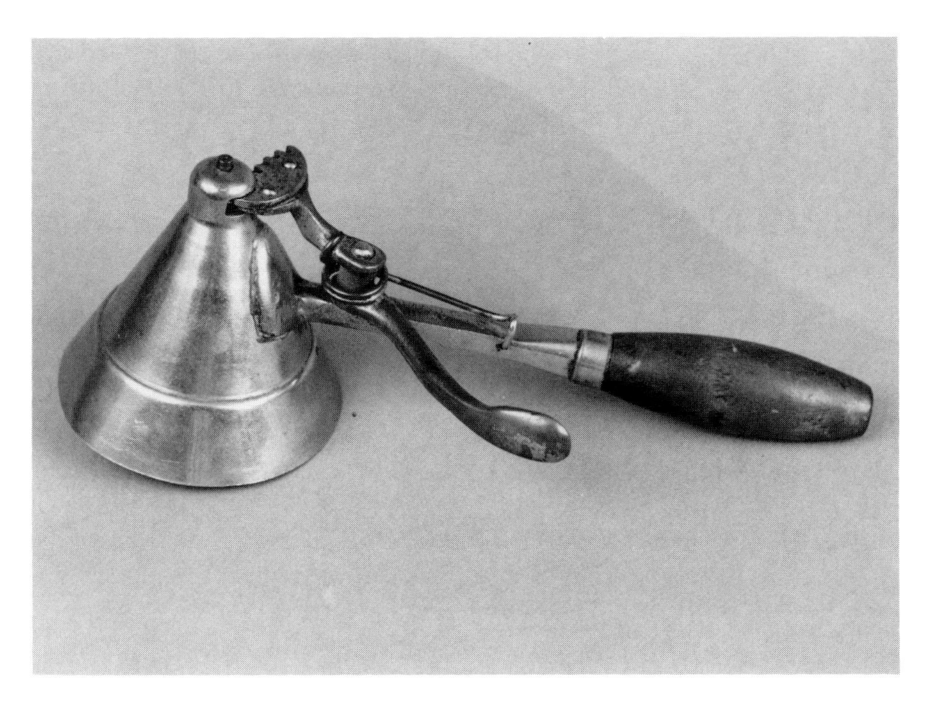

B-6. H. S. Geer Co., Troy, N.Y.
**Patent number:** 833,620
**Patent filed:** 26 Feb. 1906
**Patent issued:** 16 Oct. 1906
**Inventor:** Rasmus Nielsen (Troy, N.Y.)
**Material:** brass, nickel plated
**Handle:** wood
**Length:** 9½″
**Bowl:** conical
**Guide number:** 3
**Note:** front shank marked
"Pat. Oct. 16, 06"
back shank marked
"H. S. Geer Co., Troy, N.Y."

## Clipper Cone Disher

Very strong, works easily and cannot clog. Requires no tools of any kind, and cannot get out of order. Just lift the spring from the handle, then a quick twist and the disher is ready for cleansing. State size: 6, 8, 10, 12, 16, 20 to a quart. Price, any size, each, **$2.00**

*Ed Marks*

Creamery Package Mfg. Co. catalog—1917

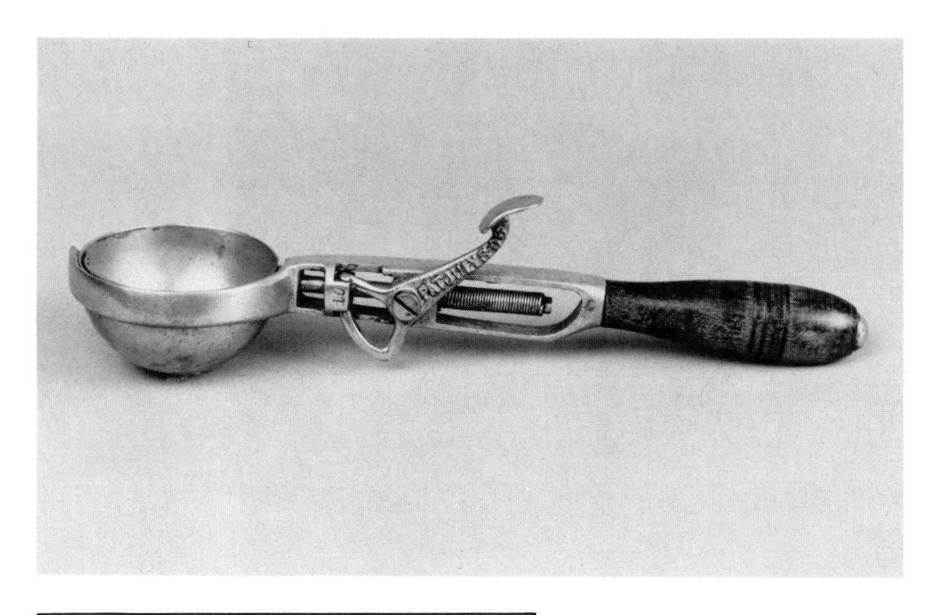

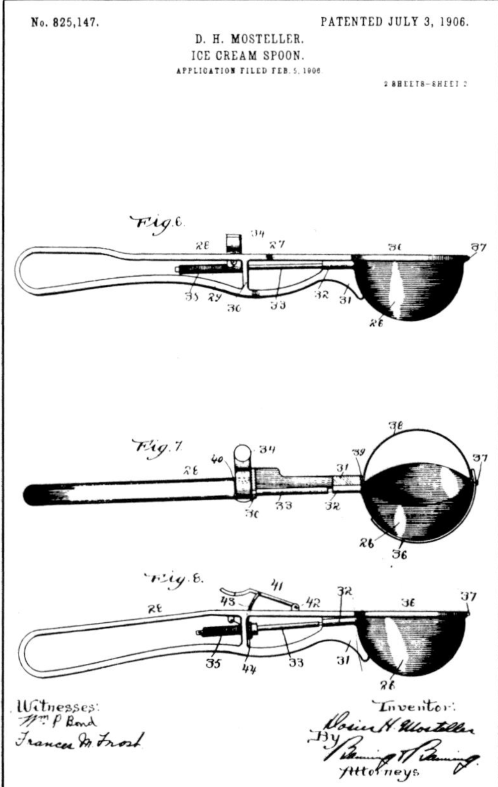


B-7. Mosteller Mfg., Chicago, Ill.
**Patent number:** 825,147
**Patent filed:** 5 Feb. 1906
**Patent issued:** 3 July 1906
**Inventor:** Dosier H. Mosteller (Chicago, Ill.)
**Material:** aluminum and nickel plated brass
**Handle:** wood
**Length:** 10½″
**Bowl:** round
**Guide number:** 5
**Note:** thumb lever marked "Pat. July 3, 06" mechanism is extremely unusual because bowl flips upside down when thumb lever is depressed

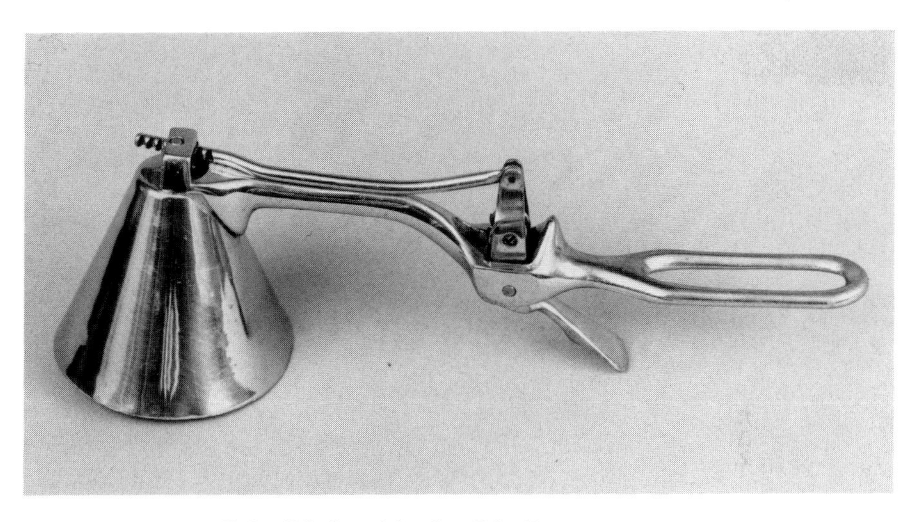

B-8. Erie Specialty Co., Erie, Pa.
**Patent number:** 892,633
**Patent filed:** 1 Dec. 1905
**Patent issued:** 7 July 1908
**Inventor:** Edwin Walker (Erie, Pa.)
**Material:** brass and copper, nickel plated
**Handle:** brass, loop
**Length:** 11¼″
**Bowl:** conical
**Guide number:** 4
**Note:** thumb lever marked
"Erie Spec. Co., Erie, Pa."

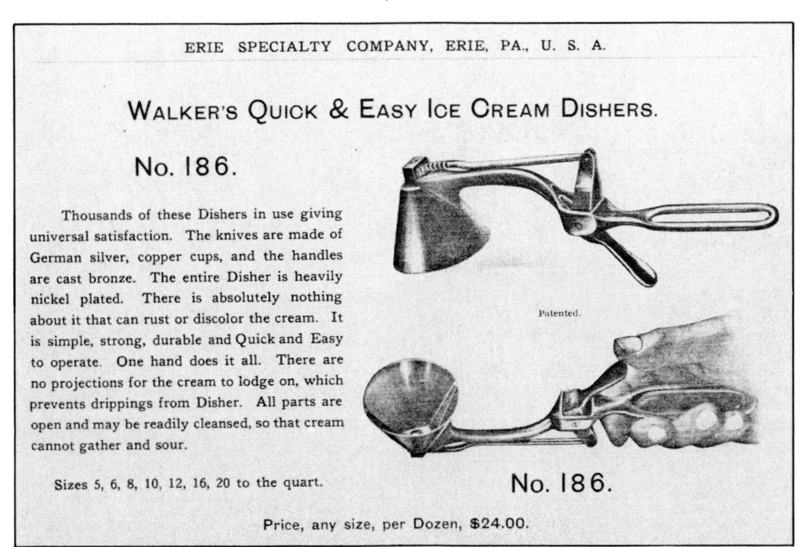

ERIE SPECIALTY COMPANY, ERIE, PA., U. S. A.

WALKER'S QUICK & EASY ICE CREAM DISHERS.

No. 186.

Thousands of these Dishers in use giving universal satisfaction. The knives are made of German silver, copper cups, and the handles are cast bronze. The entire Disher is heavily nickel plated. There is absolutely nothing about it that can rust or discolor the cream. It is simple, strong, durable and Quick and Easy to operate. One hand does it all. There are no projections for the cream to lodge on, which prevents drippings from Disher. All parts are open and may be readily cleansed, so that cream cannot gather and sour.

Patented.

Sizes 5, 6, 8, 10, 12, 16, 20 to the quart.

No. 186.

Price, any size, per Dozen, $24.00.

*Bob Bruce*

Erie Specialty Co. catalog—1909

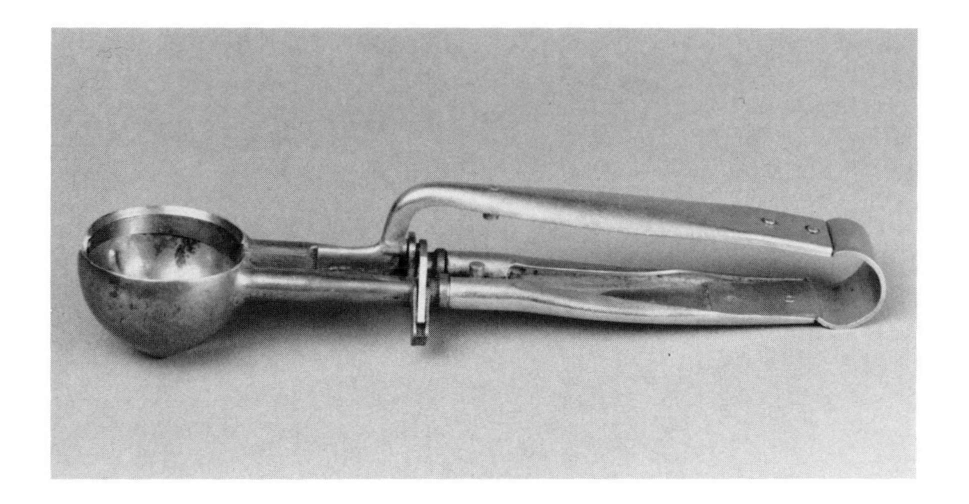

B-9. Bohlig Mfg. Co., St. Paul, Minn.
**Patent number:** 900,348
**Patent filed:** 7 Oct. 1907
**Patent issued:** 6 Oct. 1908
**Inventor:** Martin Bohlig (St. Paul, Minn.)
**Material:** aluminum and white metal
**Handle:** white metal
**Length:** 10″
**Bowl:** round
**Guide number:** 5
**Note:** handle marked
"Bohlig Mfg. Co.
St. Paul, Minn.
Pat. Oct. 6, 1908
Other Pats. Pend."
rare mechanism, when handle is squeezed, bowl divides in half to drop ice cream through bottom

NEW BOHLIG ICE CREAM CONE DISHER $2.00 Each

860.1

The Bohlig Disher, No. 860.1, is a new all-metal Disher for serving ice cream in cones direct from the can to the cone. Pressure on the spring handle of the Disher depresses the scraper on the inside of the bowl and at the same time opens both halves of the bowl out flat. In this way the scraper forces the ice cream from the Disher into the cone, point first; it can then be pushed down solid with the opened halves of the bowl. The Disher is made of steel, highly nickel plated. It has no working parts that can get out of order or gather dirt. It will not corrode or rust and is always sanitary.

No. **860.1** Bohlig Disher, 16 to quart....each **$2.00**
No. **860.2** Bohlig Disher, 12 to quart....each **2.00**
No. **860.3** Bohlig Disher, 20 to quart....each **2.00**

*Harold Screen*

Liquid Carbonic catalog—1916

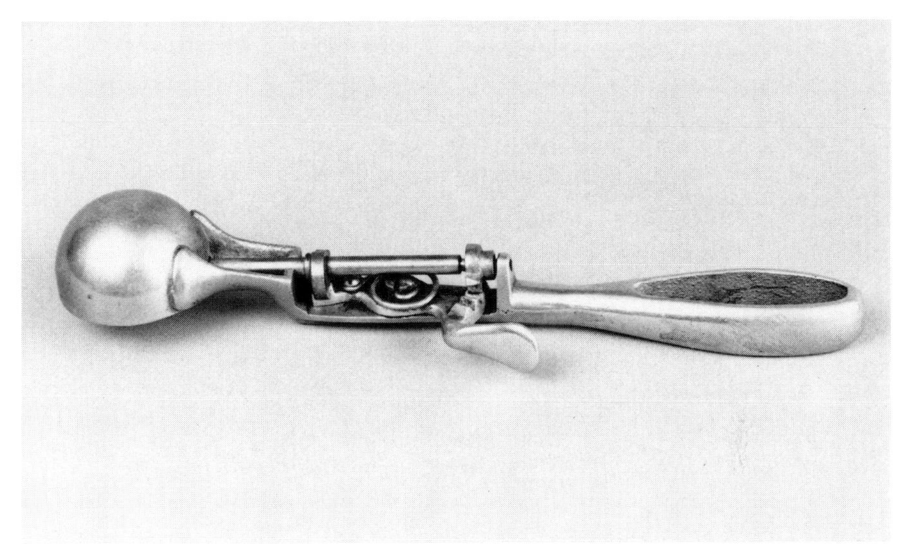

B-10. Kingery Mfg. Co., Cincinnati, Ohio
**Patent number:** 900,573
**Patent filed:** 26 June 1908
**Patent issued:** 6 Oct. 1908
**Inventor:** Charles E. McCarren (Cincinnati, Ohio)
**Material:** bronze, nickel plated
**Handle:** bronze loop or wood
**Length:** 11″
**Bowl:** round
**Guide number:** 2
**Note:** scrapers marked "Kingery Mfg. Co. Cin'ti, O. Victor Pat'd. Oct. 6, 1908"
double scrapers move in opposite directions

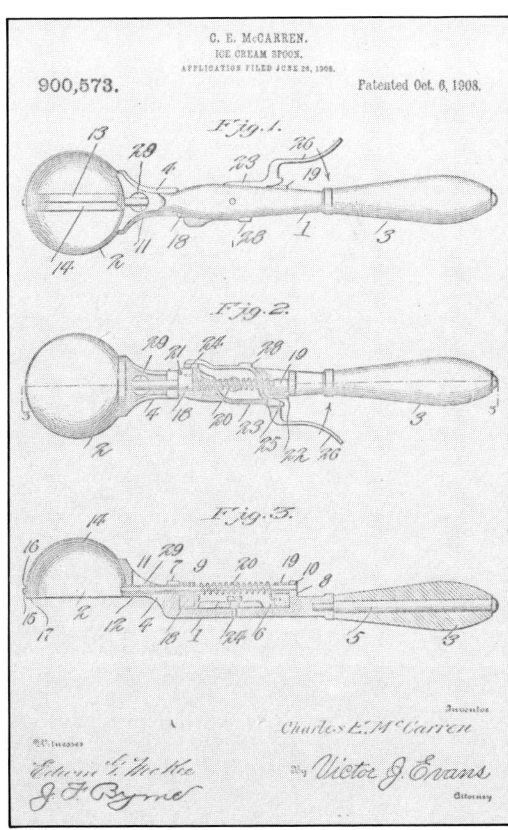

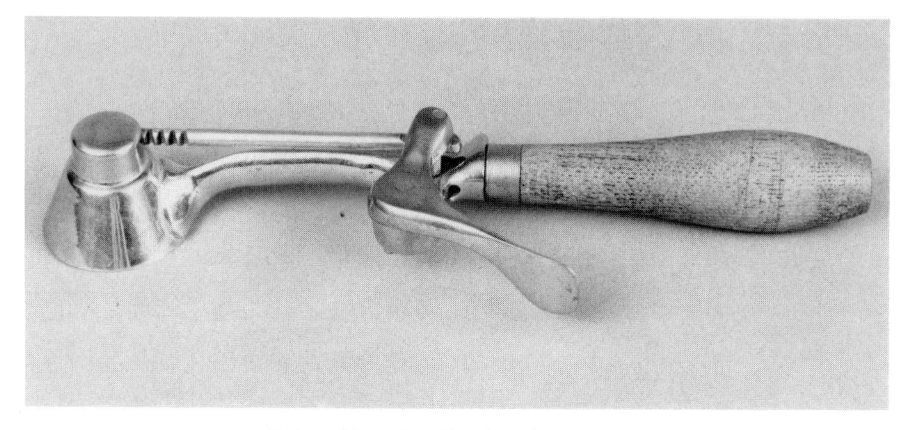

B-11. Mosteller Mg. Co., Chicago, Ill.
**Material:** brass, nickel plated
**Handle:** wood
**Length:** 9¼″
**Bowl:** conical
**Guide number:** 2
**Note:** scraper marked
"Mosteller Pat. Apl'd"
made as small as size 50

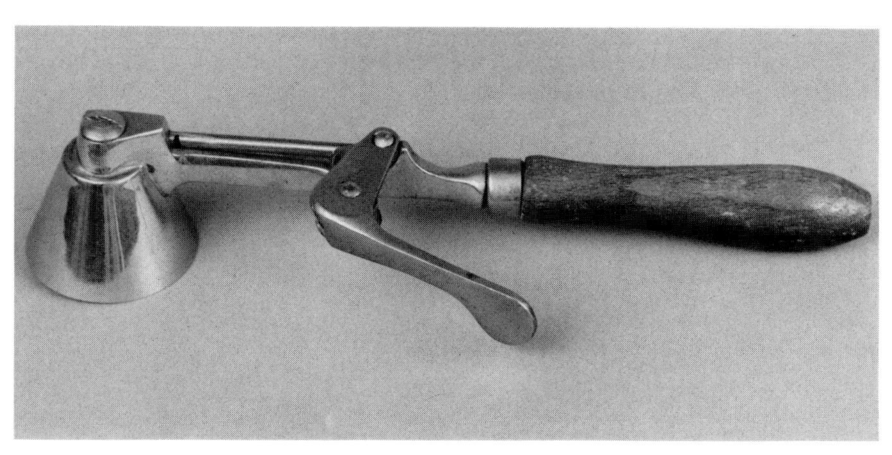

B-12. Erie Specialty Co., Erie, Pa.
**Patent issued:** 1908
**Inventor:** Edwin Walker?
**Material:** brass, nickel plated
**Handle:** wood
**Length:** 10¼″
**Bowl:** conical
**Guide number:** 2
**Note:** scraper marked
"Quick and Easy Specialty Co.
Pat. 1908 Erie, Pa."

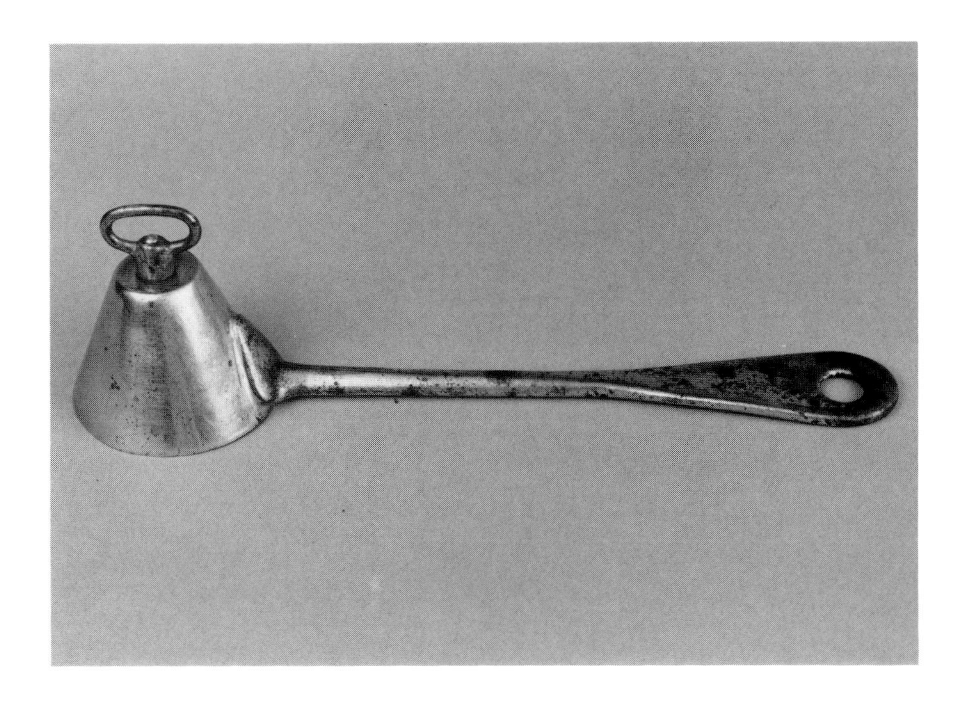

B-13. Erie Specialty Co., Erie, Pa.
**Material:** copper bowl, nickel plated
**Handle:** iron, nickel plated
**Length:** 10¼″
**Bowl:** conical
**Guide number:** 2
**Note:** pictured in 1909 catalog with three different handle lengths

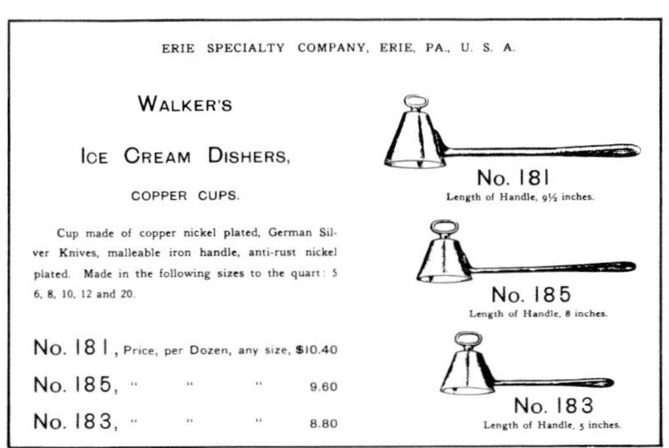

ERIE SPECIALTY COMPANY, ERIE, PA., U. S. A.

WALKER'S

ICE CREAM DISHERS,

COPPER CUPS.

Cup made of copper nickel plated, German Silver Knives, malleable iron handle, anti-rust nickel plated. Made in the following sizes to the quart: 5 6, 8, 10, 12 and 20.

No. 181, Price, per Dozen, any size, $10.40
No. 185, " " " 9.60
No. 183, " " " 8.80

No. 181
Length of Handle, 9½ inches.

No. 185
Length of Handle, 8 inches.

No. 183
Length of Handle, 5 inches.

*Bob Bruce*

Erie Specialty Co. catalog—1909

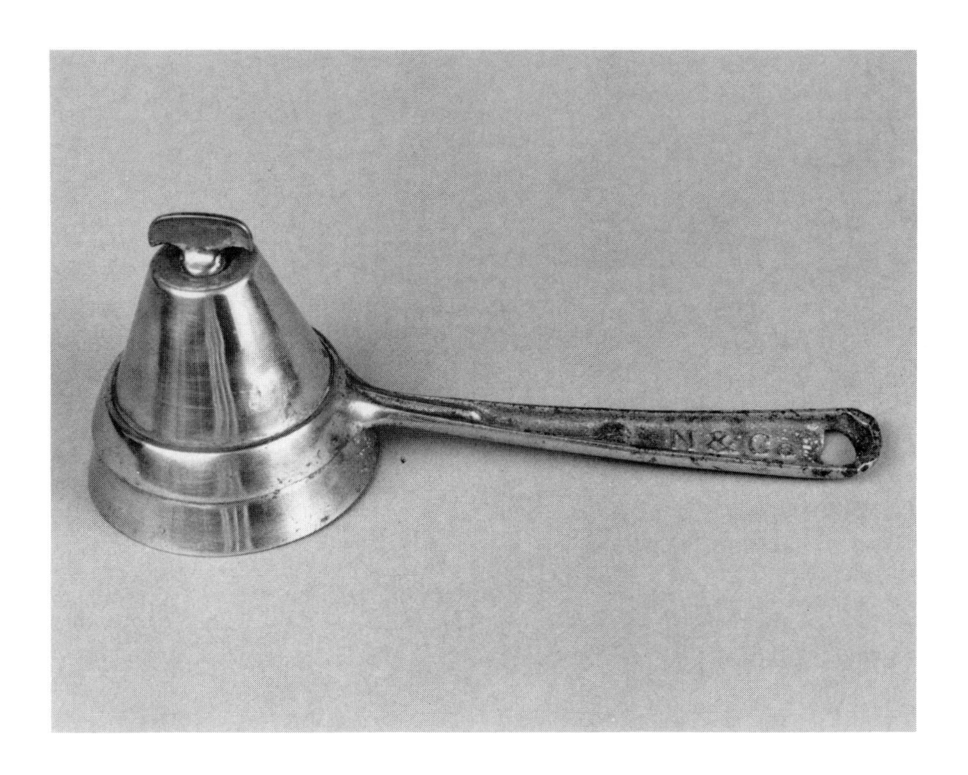


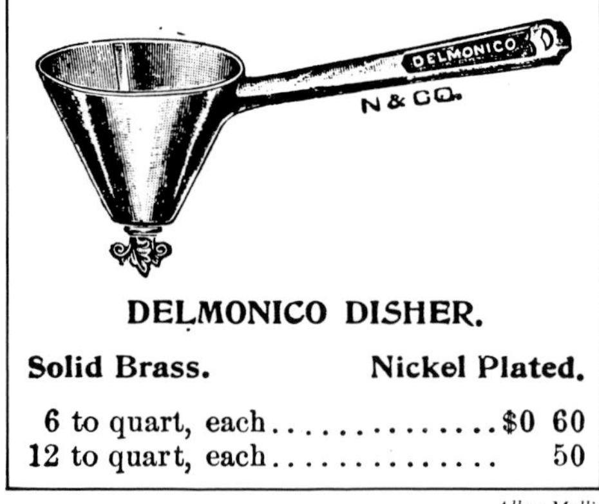


*Allan Mellis*

Horizontal Freezer Company catalog—1908

B-14. N and Co.
**Material:** brass, nickel plated
**Handle:** same
**Length:** 8″
**Bowl:** conical
**Guide number:** 2
**Note:** handle marked "N & Co Delmonico"
ca. 1900–1910

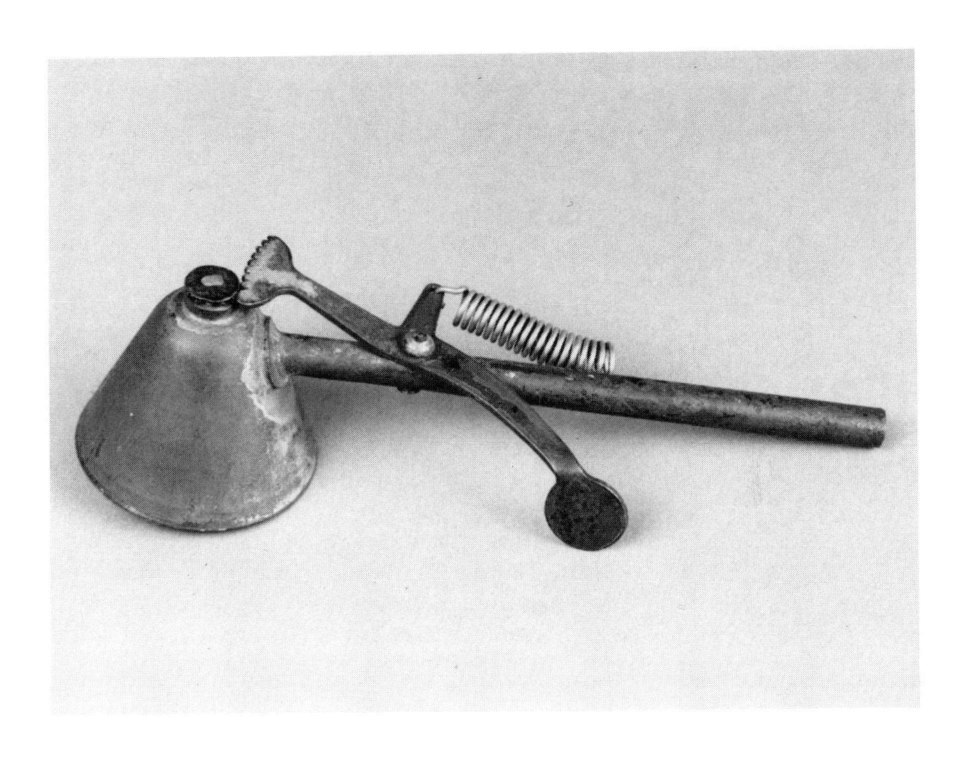

B-15. Unknown maker
**Material:** steel, tin plated
**Handle:** wood
**Length:** about 10″
**Bowl:** cone
**Guide number:** 2
**Note:** no markings
listed in V. Clad's 1905 catalog as the "Duquesne Disher"
this example is missing the wood handle
ca. 1900–1910

Duquesne Disher

Tinned.

16, 12, 10, 8 to Quart.

Each . . . . . . . . . . . . . $0 50

*Allan Mellis*

1905 V. Clad catalog

*Bill Burg*

B-16. Unknown maker
**Material:** steel
**Handle:** same, loop
**Length:** 7½″
**Bowl:** cone
**Guide number:** 1
**Note:** no markings
ca. 1900–1910

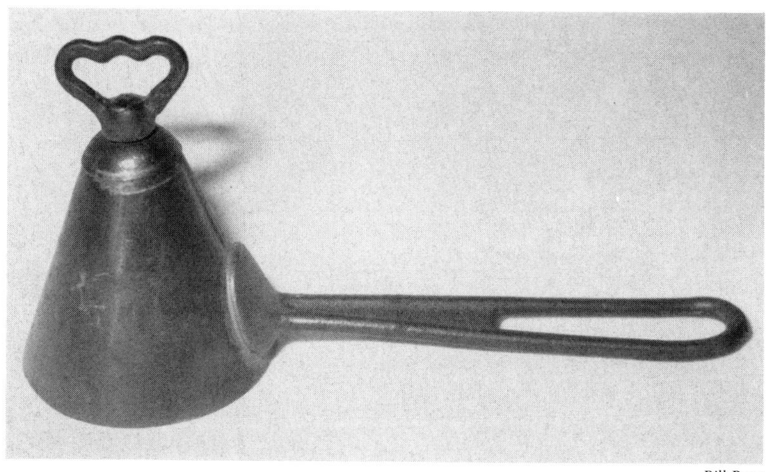

*Bill Burg*

B-17. Unknown maker
**Material:** steel
**Handle:** same, loop
**Length:** 8″
**Bowl:** cone
**Guide number:** 1
**Note:** handle marked
"Royal"
ca. 1900–1910

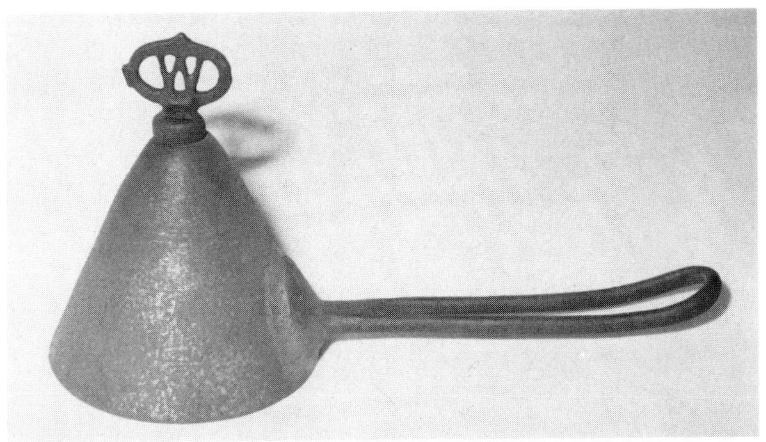


*Bill Burg*

B-18. John W. Wallace Co.
**Material:** steel
**Handle:** same, loop
**Length:** 8″
**Bowl:** cone
**Guide number:** 1
**Note:** scraper marked
"Pat. Apl'd. John W. Wallace Co."
ca. 1900–1910
"W" on key

*Bill Burg*

B-19. V. Clad Co., Philadelphia, Pa.
**Material:** steel, tin plated
**Handle:** steel wire loop
**Length:** 8″
**Bowl:** cone
**Guide number:** 1
**Note:** no markings
ca. 1900–1910

# Chapter 8

# The Mass Production Era
## 1910–1920

Continuing improvements in the ice cream industry increased production and helped to modernize the ice cream plant. It's not surprising that ice cream consumption also increased dramatically during this period. By 1920, the average American enjoyed 6.4 quarts of ice cream per year, as compared to 1.3 quarts, in 1909. The first World War helped to influence the change in status of ice cream, from a confection, to an essential food. Since sugar was rationed during the war, the ice cream industry had to convince the government that ice cream was a necessary food, thereby qualifying for the sugar. Needless to say, it did.

This mass production era was characterized by large numbers of dishers, manufactured by relatively few companies. There were primarily three men and three manufacturing centers responsible for most of the ice cream disher production, during this period. The men were: Raymond Gilchrist, Edwin Walker, and Rasmus Nielsen. The centers were: Newark, N.J., Erie, Pa., and Troy, N.Y., all within several hundred miles of each other. Raymond Gilchrist and his Gilchrist Co., held at least 5 different patents and produced probably more ice cream dishers than any other company. Edwin Walker and the Erie Specialty Co., manufactured the most variety of dishers during this decade, at least 12. Rasmus Nielsen, of Troy, N.Y., held at least 10 different disher patents, himself. Some were made by the H. S. Geer Co., of Troy, and some were assigned to the Gilchrist Co. There is evidence that these three men knew each other. Troy, N.Y. was the home of three major ice cream disher manufacturers; the H. S. Geer Co., the F. S. Co., and the Gem Spoon Co.

The shortage of materials, during W.W.I, undoubtedly slowed down production, during the last half of the decade. Nevertheless, this didn't seem to slow down the output of ideas. The number of patents issued almost doubled the number issued the previous decade. At least 72 were issued between 1910–1920. Of these Gilchrist, Walker, and Nielsen were responsible for at least 20.

There are some common characteristics of dishers made in this era. First, the shape of the bowl was either round or conical. The working mechanisms usually consisted of some type of spring. The body was made of nickel-plated brass. Finally, the handle was usually made of wood. Two representative examples of typical dishers, are the Gilchrist #31 and #33. These characteristics are only generalized, as there were always exceptions.

The Gilchrist Co. and the Erie Specialty Co., were two of the largest manufacturers, each having 85 and 32 employees, respectively. There were joined by the three Troy manufacturers, the Geer Co., Gem Spoon Co., and the F.S. Co. Other active companies included the Mosteller Mfg. Co. and the Wiley-Small Co., both of Chicago. The Keiner-Williams Co. was still producing it's early style tin and steel dishers, as was the V. Clad Co. and the Thomas Mills Co. The Kingery Co. was also still in business, at this date.

*Dairy and Food Industries Supply Assoication*

Some of the exhibits at the ice cream industry's first trade show, held in Boston, in 1917.

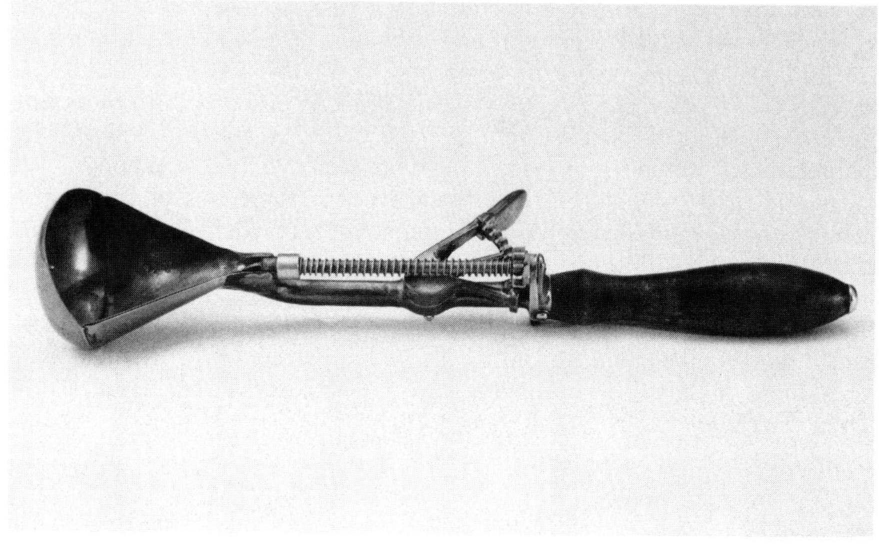

*Bill Thunell*

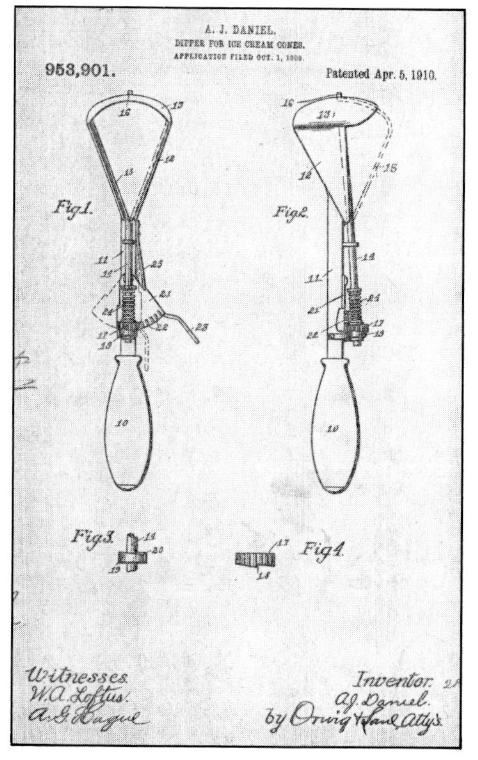


C-1. Unknown maker
**Patent number:** 953901
**Patent filed:** 1 Oct 1909
**Patent issued:** 5 Apr 1910
**Inventor:** Albert J. Daniel (Boone, Iowa)
**Material:** brass, nickel plated
**Handle:** wood
**Length:** 12″
**Bowl:** cone, inverted
**Guide number:** 5
**Note:** shank marked "Patented"
used for filling ice cream cones

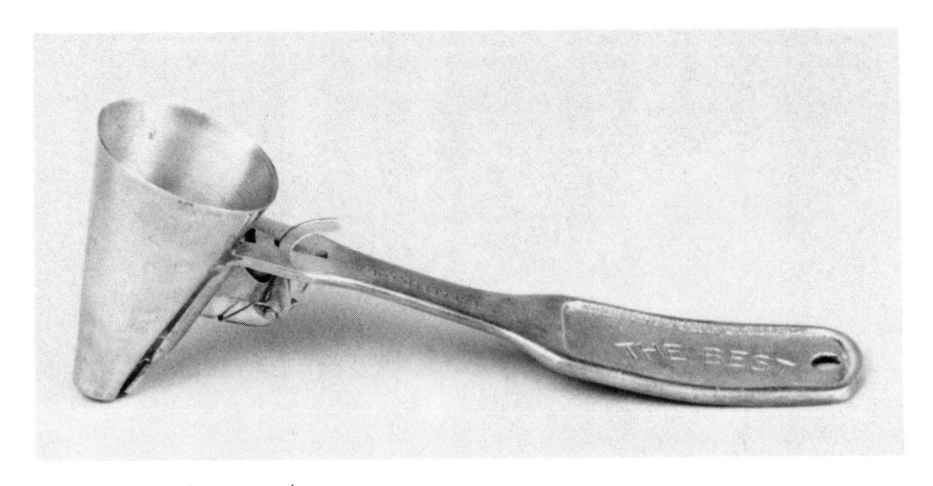


C-2. Unknown maker
**Material:** brass
**Handle:** same
**Length:** 6½″
**Bowl:** conical
**Guide number:** 5
**Note:** handle marked
"The Best Pat. Appld. For"
probably a coneholder to hold 1¢ size cones, while filling them
ca. 1910

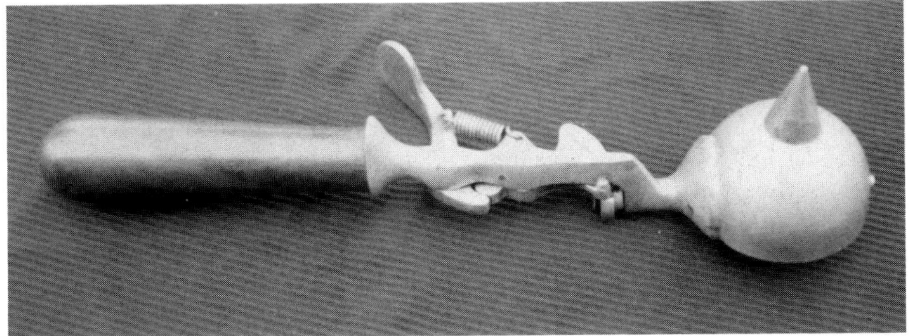

*Bill Thunell*

C-3. Unknown maker
**Material:** brass, nickel plated
**Handle:** wood
**Length:** 11″
**Bowl:** round
**Guide number:** 3
**Note:** gear piece marked
"Pat. Pend."
bowl has point on outside, possibly for making "sundae creams"

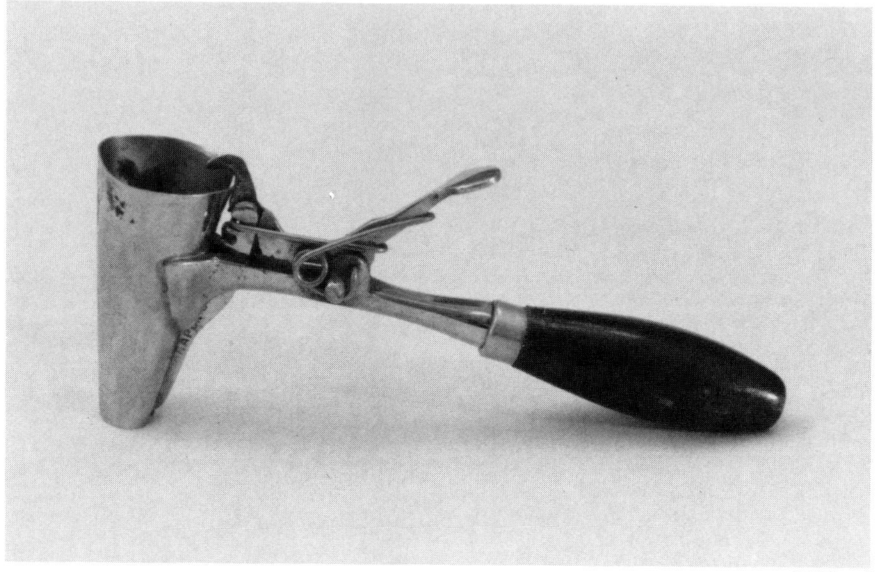

*Bill Thunell*

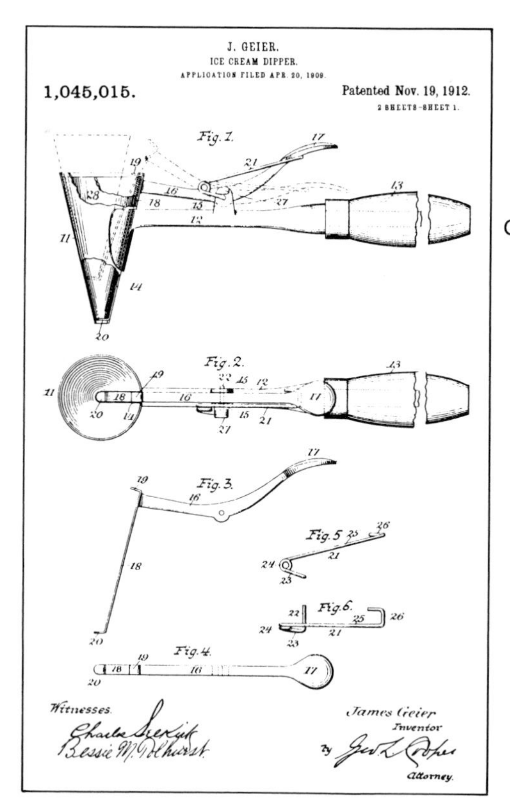


C-4. H. S. Geer Co., Troy, N.Y.
**Patent number:** 1045015
**Patent filed:** 20 Apr 1909
**Patent issued:** 19 Nov 1912
**Inventor:** James Geier (Troy, N.Y.)
**Material:** brass, nickel plated
**Handle:** wood
**Length:** 8″
**Bowl:** conical
**Guide number:** 5
**Note:** lifting lever marked "H. S. Geer Co. Troy, N.Y." coneholder, used to hold ice cream cones while filling them

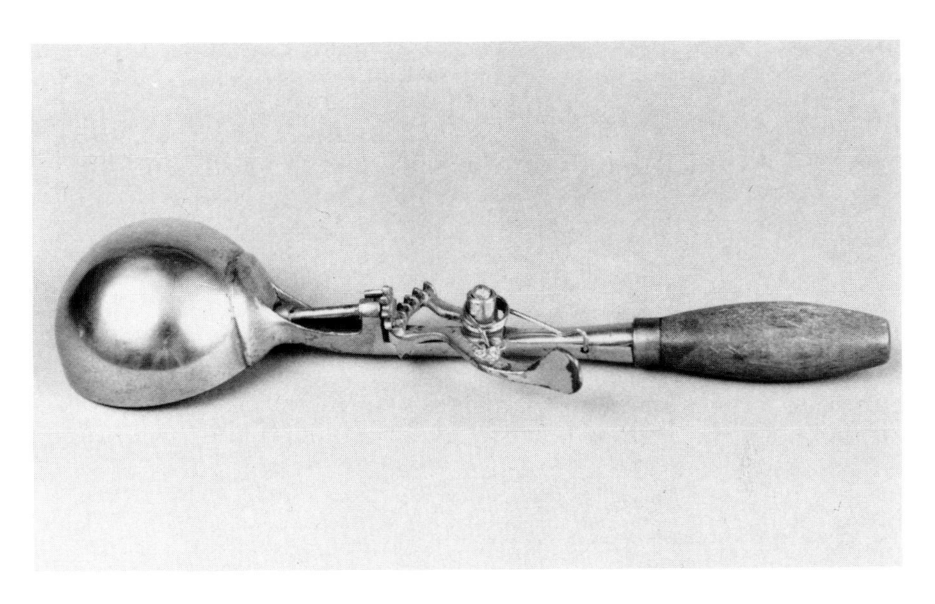

C-5. H. S. Geer Co., Troy, N.Y.
**Patent number:** 1052370
**Patent filed:** 2 Mar. 1911
**Patent issued:** 4 Feb. 1913
**Inventor:** Rasmus Nielsen
**Material:** brass, nickel plated
**Handle:** wood
**Length:** 11½″
**Bowl:** round
**Guide number:** 2
**Note:** shank marked
"H. S. Geer Co.
Troy, N.Y."
thumb lever marked
"Pat. Apd. For"
later model had "Trojan Disher" on shank, and a shorter scraper rod

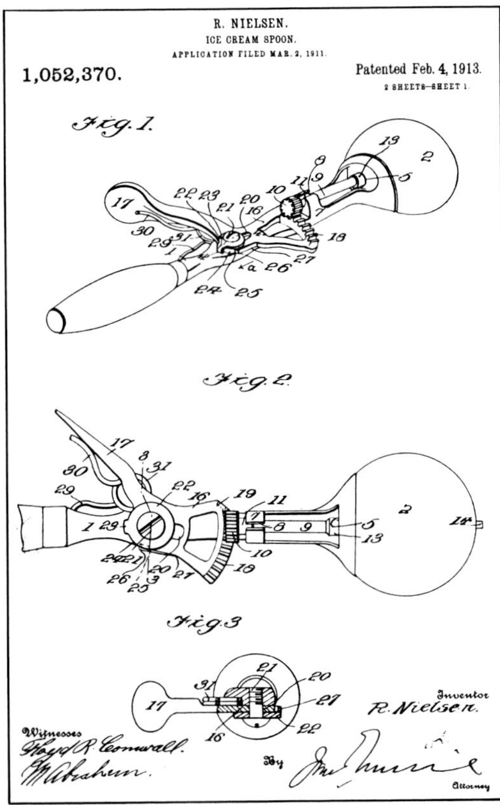

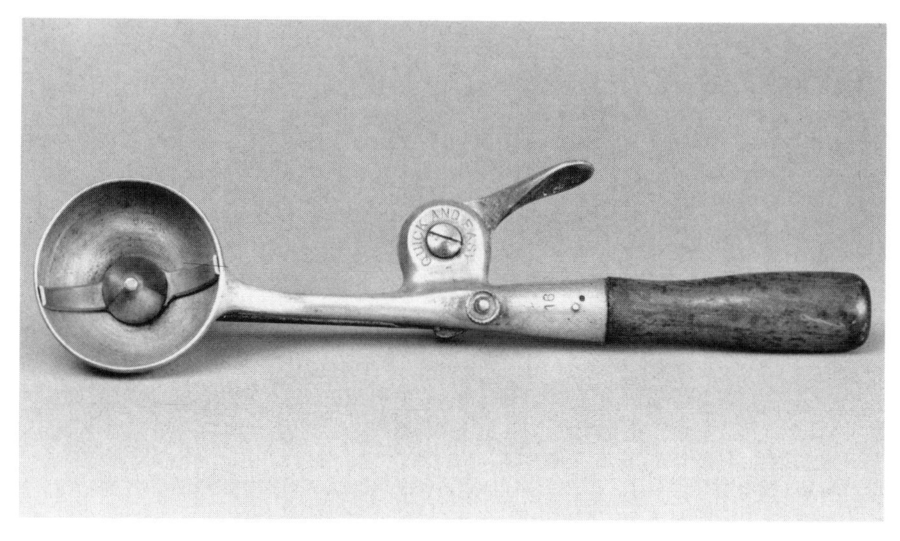


C-6. Erie Specialty Co., Erie, Pa.
**Patent number:** 1,012,944
**Patent filed:** 7 Feb. 1910
**Patent issued:** 26 Dec. 1911
**Inventors:** Edwin Walker
Clarence L. Walker
(Erie, Pa.)
**Material:** aluminum
**Handle:** wood
**Length:** 10½″
**Bowl:** round
**Guide number:** 3
**Note:** beneath thumb mechanism marked
"Quick and Easy"
unusual feature is a conical projection inside bowl
used for making "sundae creams"

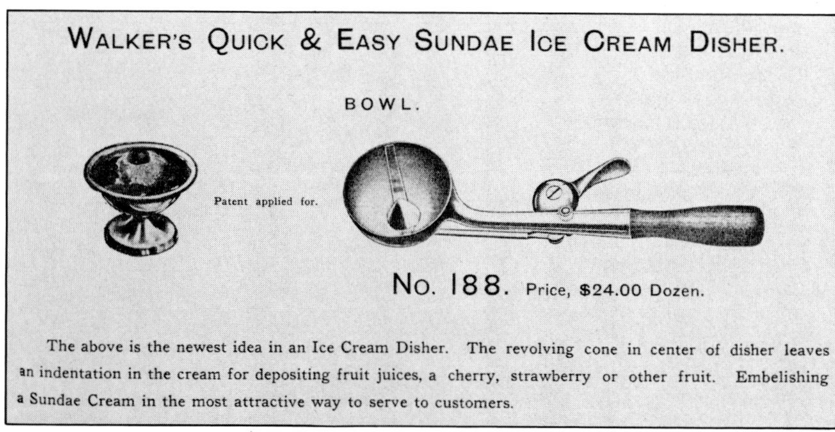


*Bob Bruce*

Erie Specialty Co. catalog—1909

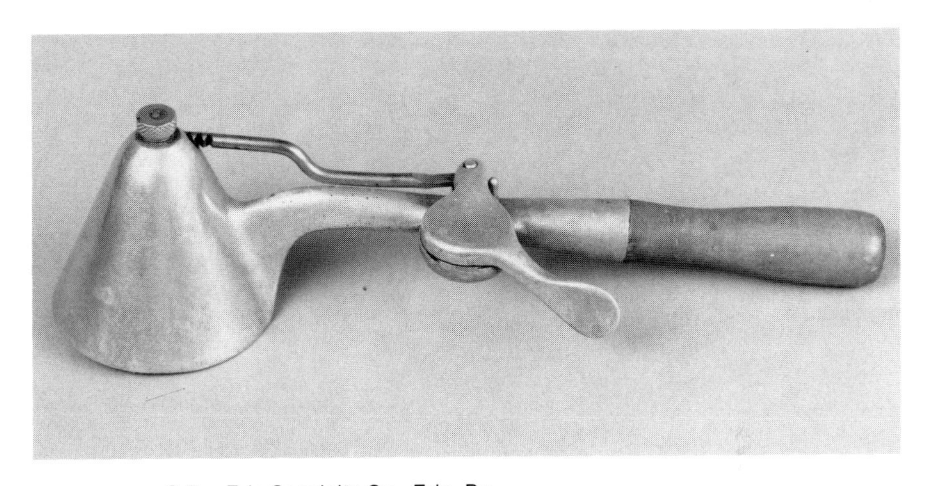

C-7. Erie Specialty Co., Erie, Pa.
**Patent number:** 1162116
**Patent filed:** 19 July 1910
**Patent issued:** 30 Nov. 1915
**Inventor:** Edwin Walker (Erie, Pa.)
**Material:** aluminum
**Handle:** wood
**Length:** 11″
**Bowl:** conical
**Guide number:** 3
**Note:** beneath thumb mechanism marked
"Quick and Easy"
scraper marked
"Erie Specialty Co. Erie, Pa."
unusual feature is a conical projection inside bowl
used for making "sundae creams"

WALKER'S QUICK & EASY ICE CREAM DISHER.

No. 187, Cone Shape

Price, $24.00 Dozen.

The center cone can be had in any size disher for serving in plate, sundae cup or college Ices. (See page 9.)

Sizes:—8, 10, 12, 14, 16, 20 to quart.

*Bob Bruce*

Erie Specialty Co. catalog—1909

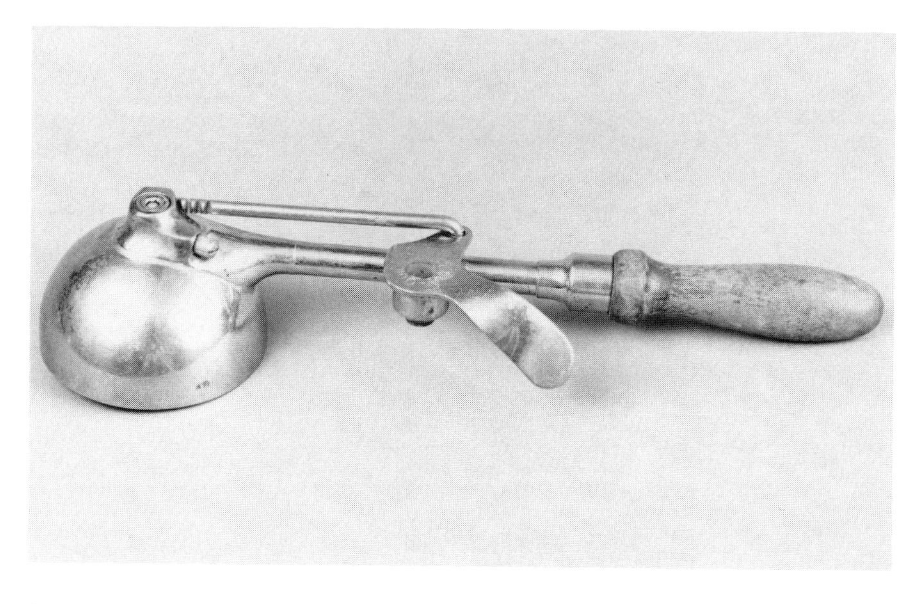

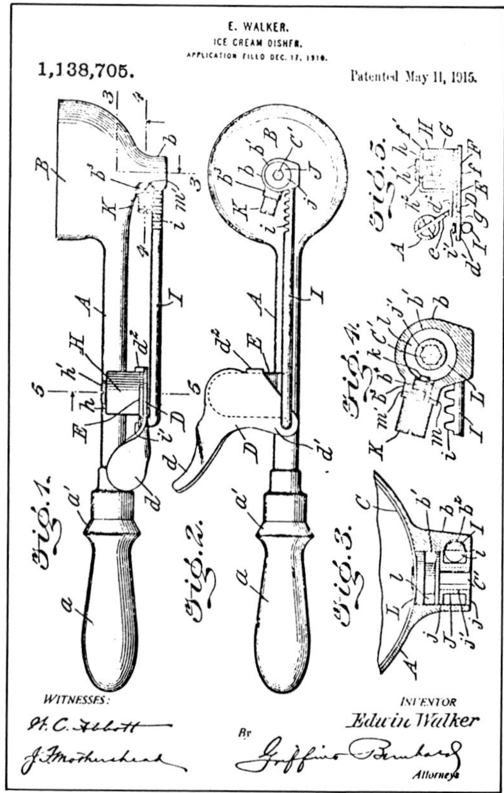


C-8. Erie Specialty Co., Erie, Pa.
**Patent number:** 1,138,705
**Patent filed:** 17 Dec. 1910
**Patent issued:** 11 May 1915
**Inventor:** Edwin Walker
(Erie, Pa.)
**Material:** brass, nickel plated
**Handle:** wood
**Length:** 11″
**Bowl:** round
**Guide number:** 2
**Note:** thumb lever marked
"Quick and Easy"
scraper marked
"Erie Specialty Co.
Erie, Pa."

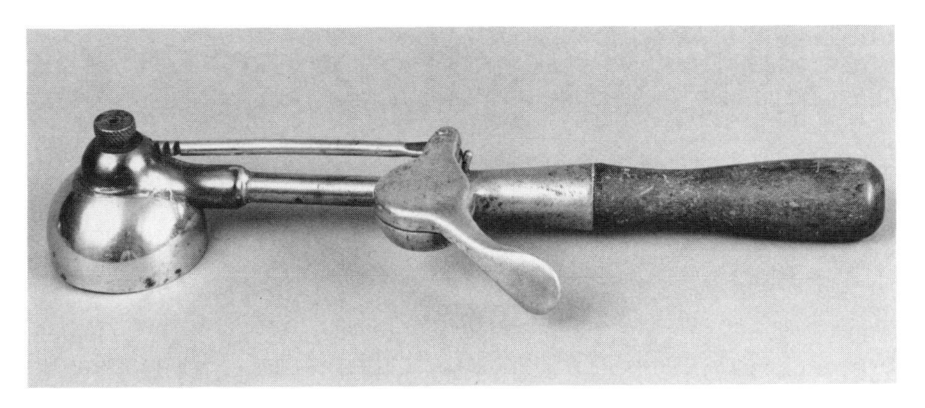

C-9. Erie Specialty Co., Erie, Pa.
**Patent number:** 1,138,704
**Patent filed:** 4 Oct. 1909, renewed 12 Oct. 1912
**Patent issued:** 11 May 1915
**Inventor:** Edwin Walker (Erie, Pa.)
**Material:** brass. copper, aluminum
**Handle:** wood
**Length:** 10½″
**Bowl:** round
**Guide number:** 2
**Note:** beneath thumb mechanism marked "Quick and Easy"

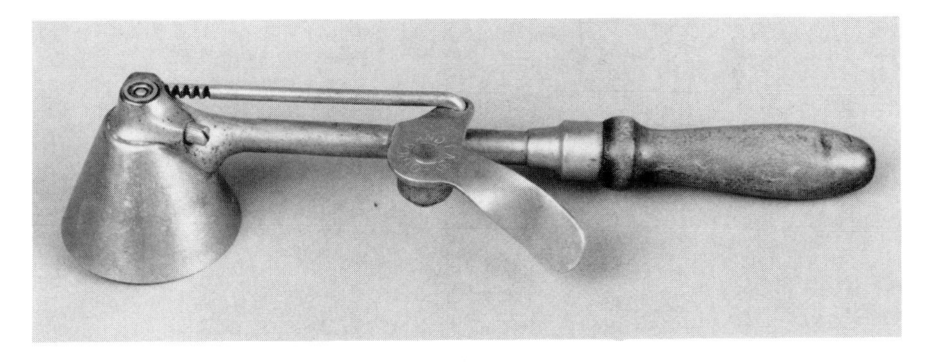

C-10. Erie Specialty Co., Erie, Pa.
**Patent number:** 1138705
**Patent filed:** 17 Dec. 1910
**Patent issued:** 11 May 1915
**Inventor:** Edwin Walker (Erie, Pa.)
**Material:** brass, nickel plated
**Handle:** wood
**Length:** 10½″
**Bowl:** conical
**Guide number:** 2
**Note:** thumb lever marked "Quick and Easy"

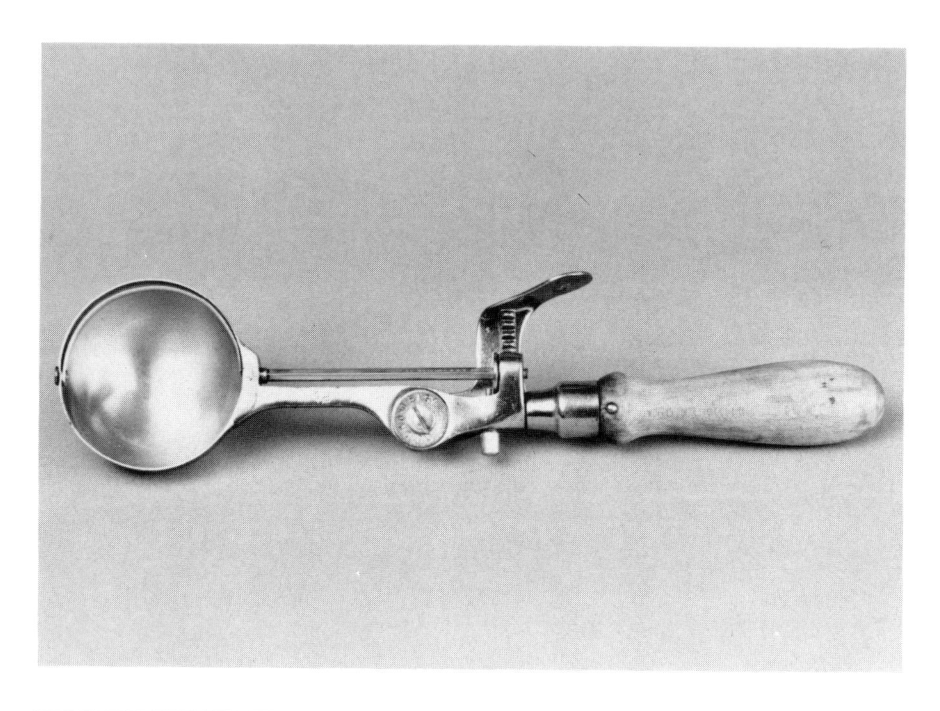

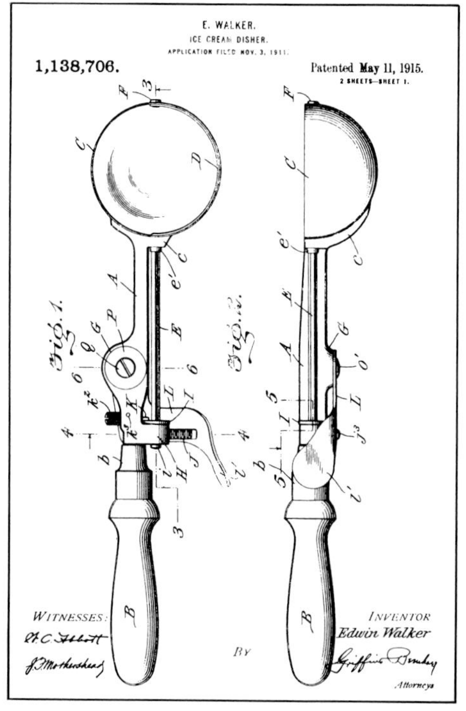


C-11. Erie Specialty Co., Erie, Pa.
**Patent number:** 1,138,706
**Patent filed:** 3 Nov. 1911
**Patent issued:** 11 May 1915
**Inventor:** Edwin Walker (Erie, Pa.)
**Material:** brass, nickel plated
**Handle:** wood
**Length:** 11″
**Bowl:** round
**Guide number:** 2
**Note:** thumb plate marked "Erie Specialty Co. Erie, Pa.
bottom shank marked "Quick and Easy"

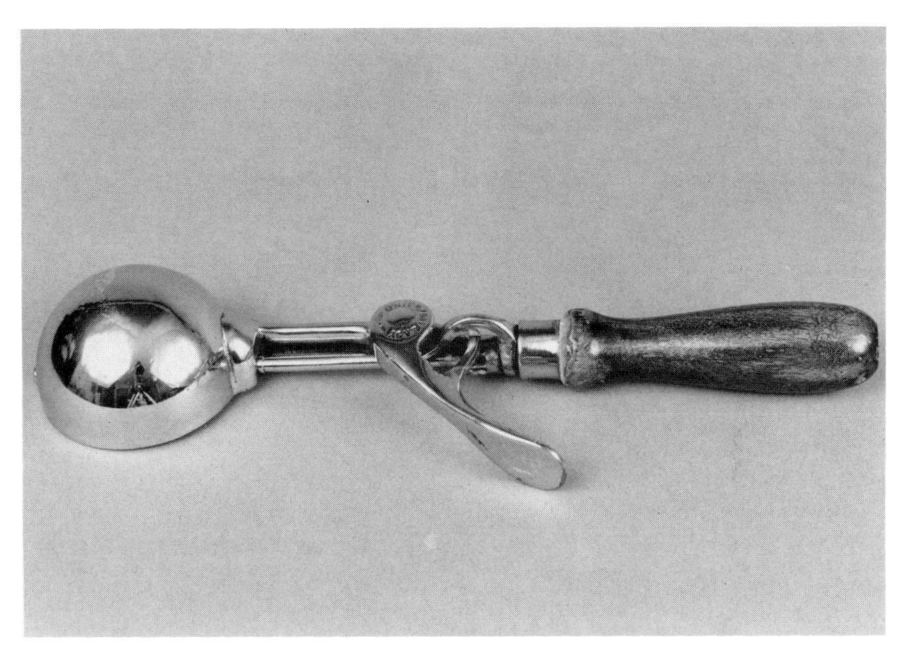

C-12. Erie Specialty Co., Erie, Pa.
**Patent number:** 1194685
**Patent filed:** 15 Nov. 1915
**Patent issued:** 15 Aug. 1916
**Inventor:** Edwin Walker
(Erie, Pa.)
**Material:** brass, nickel plated
**Handle:** wood
**Length:** 10¼″
**Bowl:** round
**Guide number:** 3
**Note:** top of thumb lever marked
"Quick and Easy"
scraper marked
"Erie Specialty Co.
Erie, Pa."

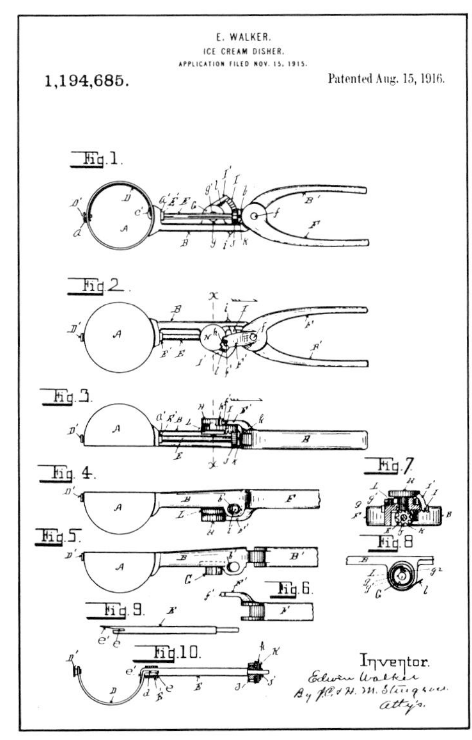

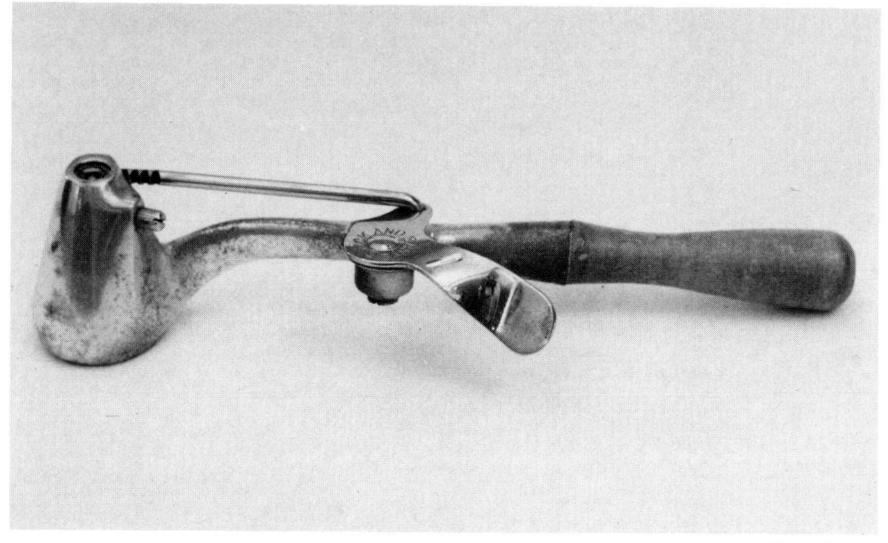

*Morton Burness*

C-13. Erie Specialty Co., Erie, Pa.
**Inventor:** Edwin Walker?
**Material:** aluminum
**Handle:** wood
**Length:** 10½″
**Bowl:** conical
**Guide number:** 4
**Note:** thumb piece marked
"Quick and Easy"
used with a paddle to fill ice cream cones

## WALKER'S QUICK & EASY ICE CREAM CONE DISHER

No. 486

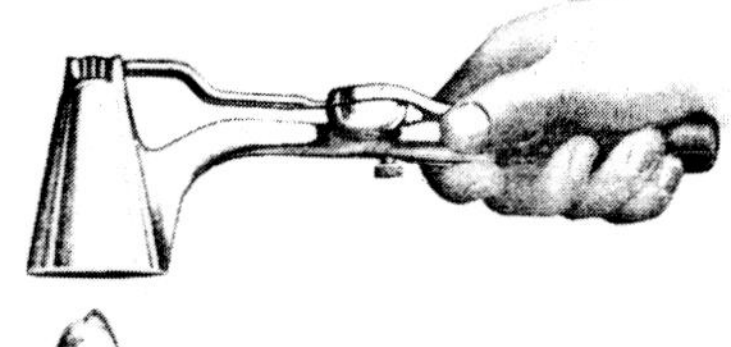

No. 487
Tray.

No. 486
With Tray No. 487
FOR FILLING CONES.

Disher and Tray made of special cast Aluminum that does not corrode. To operate deposit the cream on Tray, place a Cone over the cream, reverse the Tray and cone then remove the Tray and cone is filled 10c size. For 5c size use 286 or 386, 20 to quart.

No. 486 Size 16 to the Quart, Dozen, $24.00
No. 487 - - - - Dozen, 4.00

*Bob Bruce*

Erie Specialty Co. catalog—1909

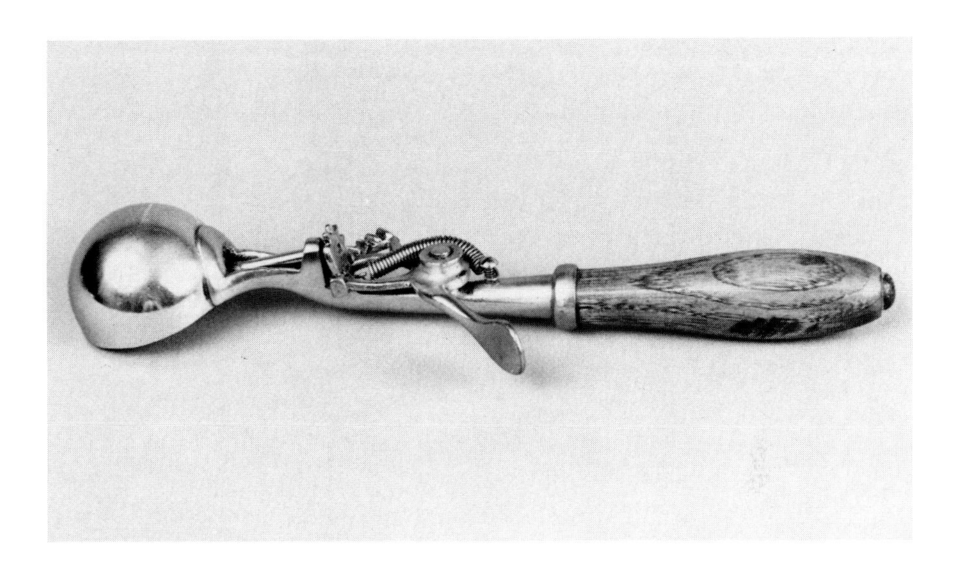

C-14. Gem Spoon Co., Troy, N.Y.
**Patent number:** 1205396
**Patent filed:** 1 June 1915
**Patent issued:** 21 Nov 1916
**Inventor:** William Ross (Troy, N.Y.)
**Material:** brass, nickel plated
**Handle:** wood
**Length:** 10¼″
**Bowl:** round
**Guide number:** 1
**Note:** scraper marked "Gem Spoon Co. Troy, N.Y. Trojan"

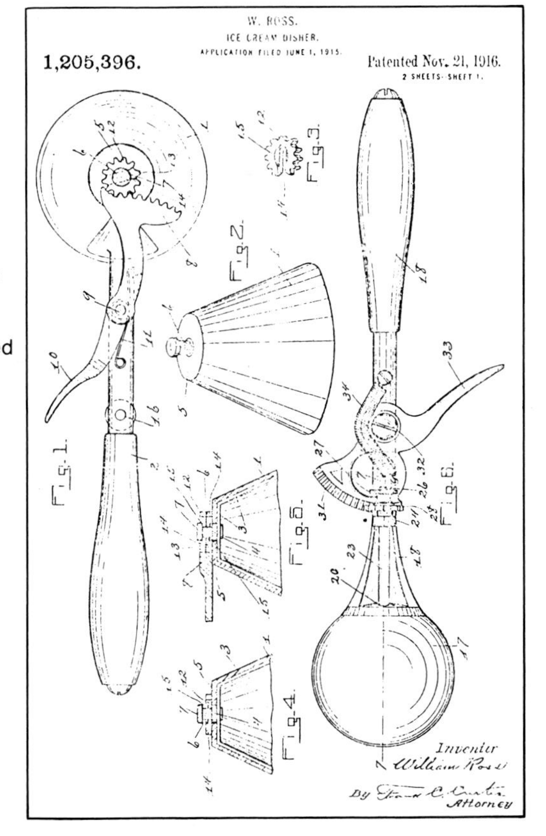

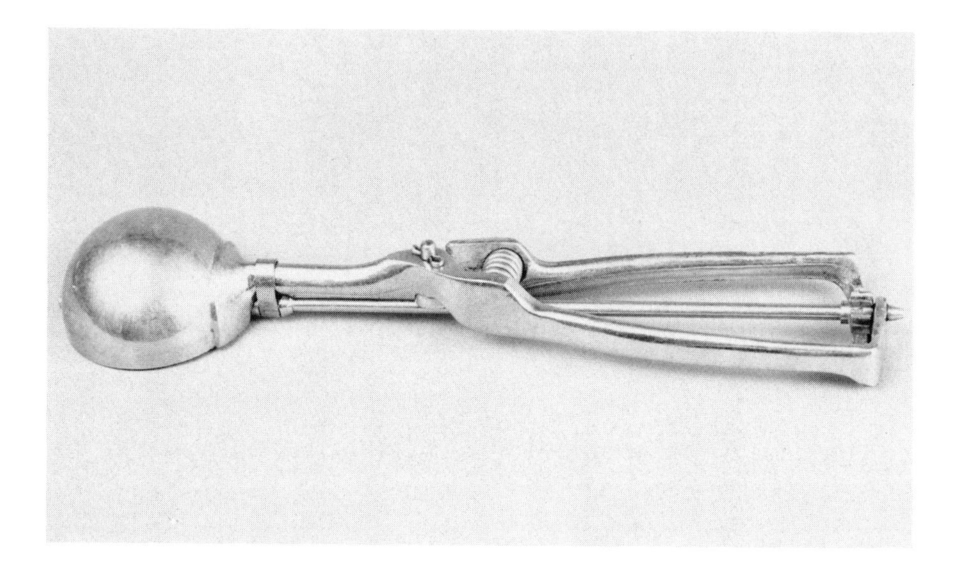

GILCHRIST'S

## Automatic Ice Cream Disher, No. 30

**A perfect device for filling Ice Cream Cones**

This remarkable device will automatically discharge the Ice Cream from the bowl without effort. There is absolutely no limit to its speed.

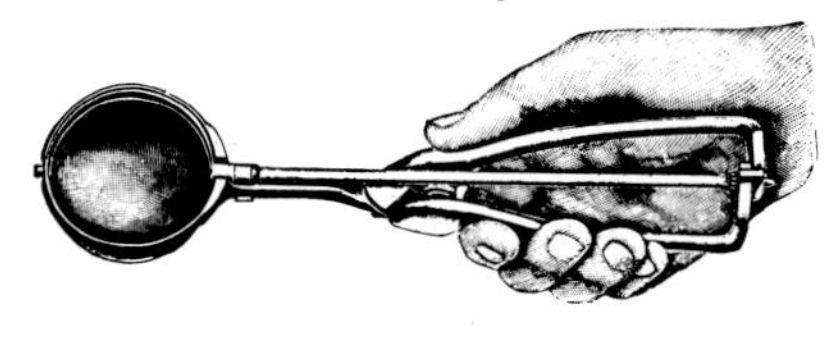

FIGURE 1

There are no thumb or finger pieces to be pressed or turned, as simply a slight closing of the hand does the work.
All parts can be instantly separated and put together without tools of any kind.

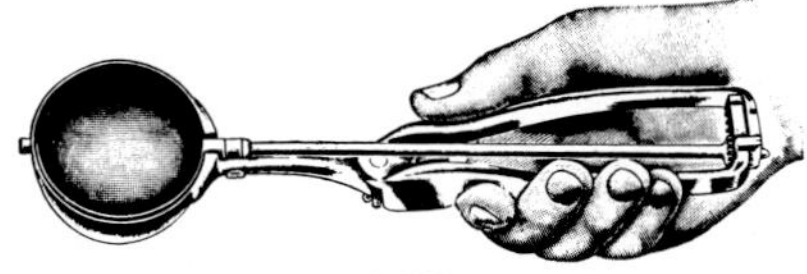

FIGURE 2

Figure 1 shows Gilchrist's No. 30 Automatic Disher in normal or starting position. **Note** how it fits the hand, thus providing a firm hold. **Note the Scraper** is shown at the upper side of the bowl.

Figure 2 shows the Disher in the position it assumes after the ice cream has been discharged from the bowl. This has been accomplished **simply by slightly closing the hand. That's all.**

**Note the Scraper** has been rotated and is now shown at the lower side of the bowl.

*Allan Mellis*

Gilchrist Co. catalog no. 20

C-15. Gilchrist Co., Newark, N.J.
**Patent number:** 1,109,576
**Patent filed:** 26 Sept. 1907
**Patent issued:** 1 Sept. 1914
**Inventor:** Raymond B. Gilchrist (Newark, N.J.)
**Material:** brass, nickel plated
**Handle:** same, squeeze type
**Length:** 10½″
**Bowl:** round
**Guide number:** 2
**Note:** marked either on handle or scraper rod "Gilchrist's No. 30"

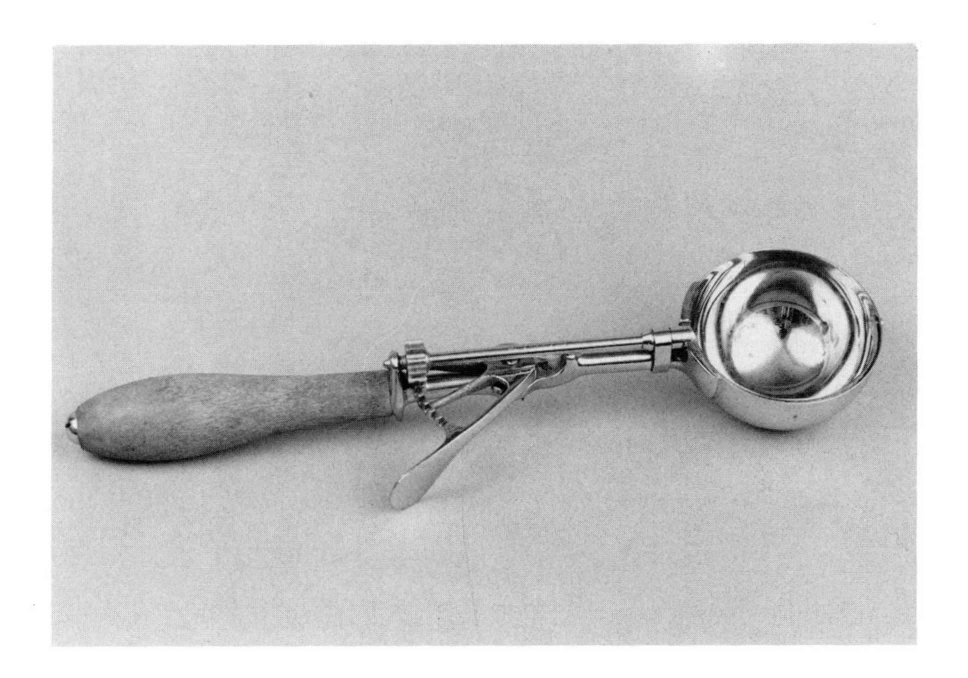

C-16. Gilchrist Co., Newark, N.J.
**Patent number:** 1,132,657
**Patent filed:** 3 Feb. 1908
**Patent issued:** 23 Mar. 1915
**Inventor:** Raymond B. Gilchrist (Newark, N.J.)
**Material:** brass, nickel plated
**Handle:** wood
**Length:** 11″
**Bowl:** round
**Guide number:** 1
**Note:** thumb lever or scraper rod marked "Gilchrist 31" probably the most popular and common ice cream disher ever produced

"Better Than Need Be" Goods

**Gilchrist's No. 31**
**Automatic Ice Cream Disher**

Operating on **well established lines,** constructed in a **most mechanical manner,** having no exposed spring, no works near the bowl, and adapted to **be instantly** cleaned or repaired, is giving the greatest satisfaction.

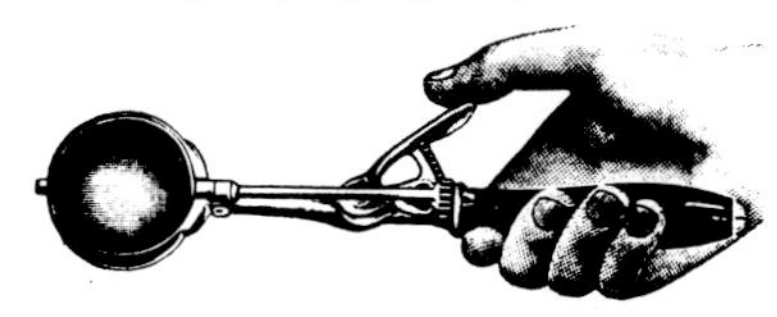

Made of bronze metal, handsomely polished and nickel plated. The **bowl** and **scraper** are made of **German silver.** There are no aluminum parts whatsoever o turn black and to disintegrate and crumble through the effect of the acids in the cream.
Made in six sizes, namely: 6, 8, 10, 12, 16 and 20 to the quart. Price, any size, $1.50.

**GILCHRIST'S SODA FOUNTAIN SPECIALTIES ARE ON SALE BY ALL DEALERS**

*We manufacture other Ice Cream Dishers, also Cork Pullers, Lemon Squeezers, Lime Squeezers, Transfer Ladles, Ice Cream Spoons, Soda Glass Holders, Ice Shredders, Ice Planes, Corking and Capping Machines, Ice Picks and Ice Tools, Ice Scoops, etc.*

**THE GILCHRIST CO.**
MAKERS OF "BETTER THAN NEED BE" GOODS
**NEWARK, N. J.**
CATALOGUE ON REQUEST

*Ed Marks*

*Soda Fountain* magazine—Aug., 1908

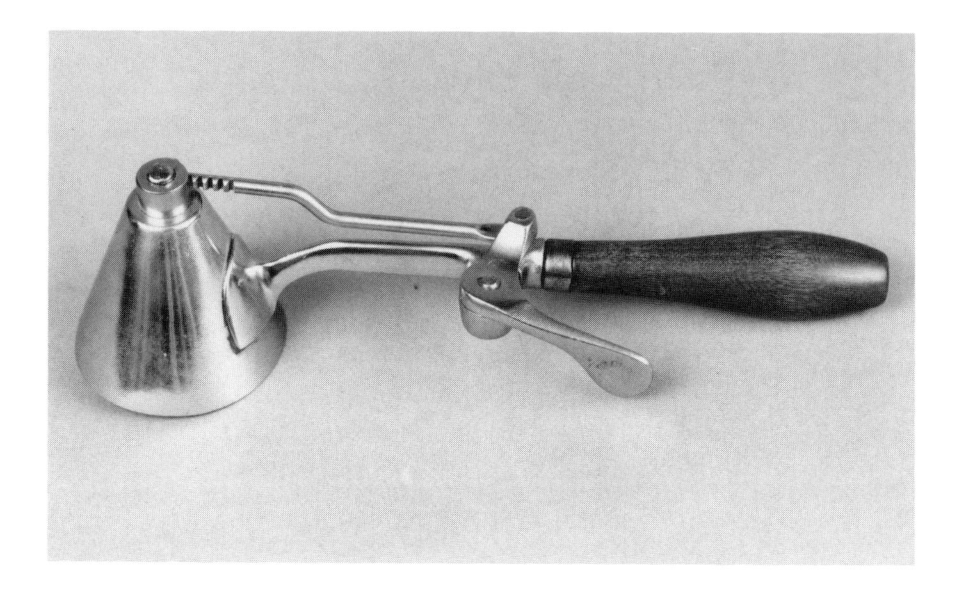

C-17. Gilchrist Co., Newark, N.J.
**Patent number:** 1109577
**Patent filed:** 16 Apr 1910
**Patent issued:** 1 Sept 1914
**Inventor:** Raymond Gilchrist (Newark, N.J.)
**Material:** brass, nickel plated
**Handle:** wood
**Length:** 10½″
**Bowl:** conical
**Guide number:** 2
**Note:** thumb lever marked "Gilchrist 33"

GILCHRIST'S

## No. 33 Pyramid Shape Ice Cream Disher

Dishers having the scraper rotate from the center of the bowl do not compare with those in which the scraper operates from the sides of the bowl, throwing the cream right out, as Gilchrist's No. 31 and No. 30, but for any who still like the cream in pyramid form for plate service only the No. 33 should be used.

It is made of **bronze metal,** handsomely nickel plated. The bowl and scraper are made of nickel silver.

It can be taken apart for cleaning or repairing in **One-Tenth of a Second.** You simply **"Press the button"** (shown by the ☞). It is as easily put together.

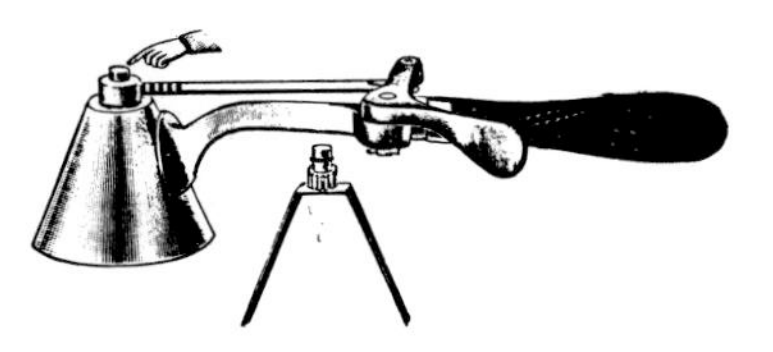

No exposed spring is used; the spring, which is made of phosphor bronze metal, is entirely concealed; the operating gear is also concealed, **in fact there is not a single projection, hollow or crevice to gather and hold the cream.**

**Always specify size wanted.**

Made in six sizes, namely: 6, 8, 10, 12, 16, and 20 to the quart.

**No. 33 Disher, price per dozen................$24.00**

*Allan Mellis*

Gilchrist Co. catalog no. 20

C-18. Gilchrist Co., Newark, N.J.
**Material:** steel, re-tinned
**Handle:** same, loop
**Length:** 7½″
**Bowl:** cone
**Guide number:** 1
**Note:** "G" on key
made until 1931

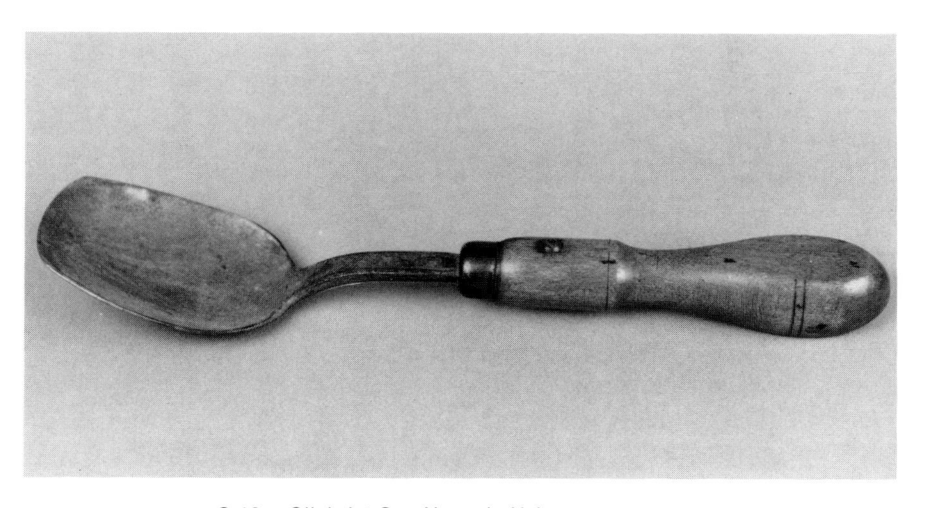

C-19. Gilchrist Co., Newark, N.J.
**Material:** white metal, re-tinned
**Handle:** wood
**Length:** 12″ (also in 10″ and 14″)
**Guide number:** 1
**Note:** used to pack ice cream into cartons

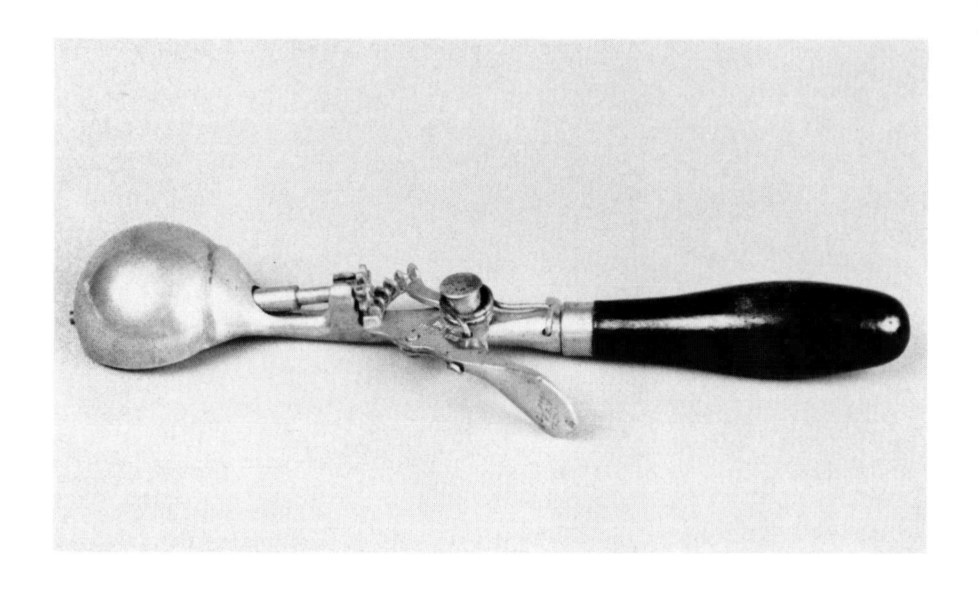

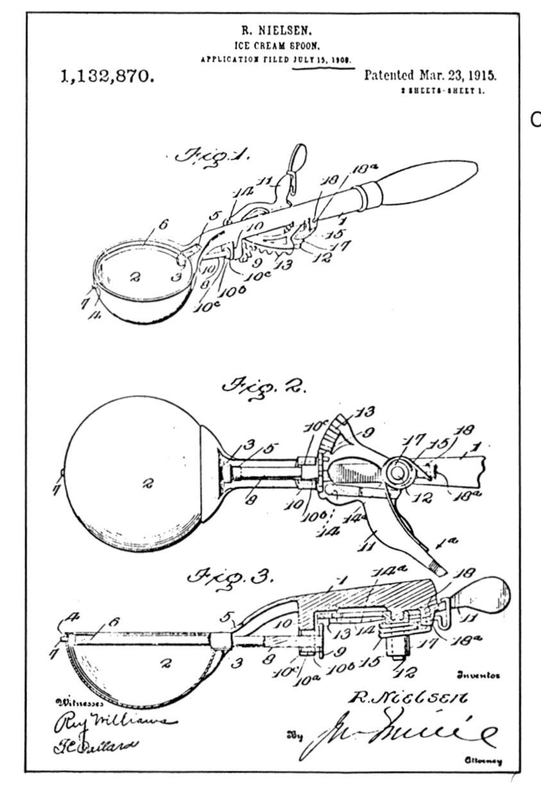


C-20. F.S. Co., Troy, N.Y.
**Patent number:** 1132870
**Patent filed:** 15 July 1908
**Patent issued:** 23 Mar. 1915
**Inventor:** Rasmus Nielsen (Troy, N.Y.)
**Material:** brass, nickel plated
**Handle:** wood
**Length:** 10½″
**Bowl:** round
**Guide number:** 1
**Note:** thumb lever marked "Clipper F.S. Co. Troy, N.Y." "Pat'd. Mar. 23, 1915"

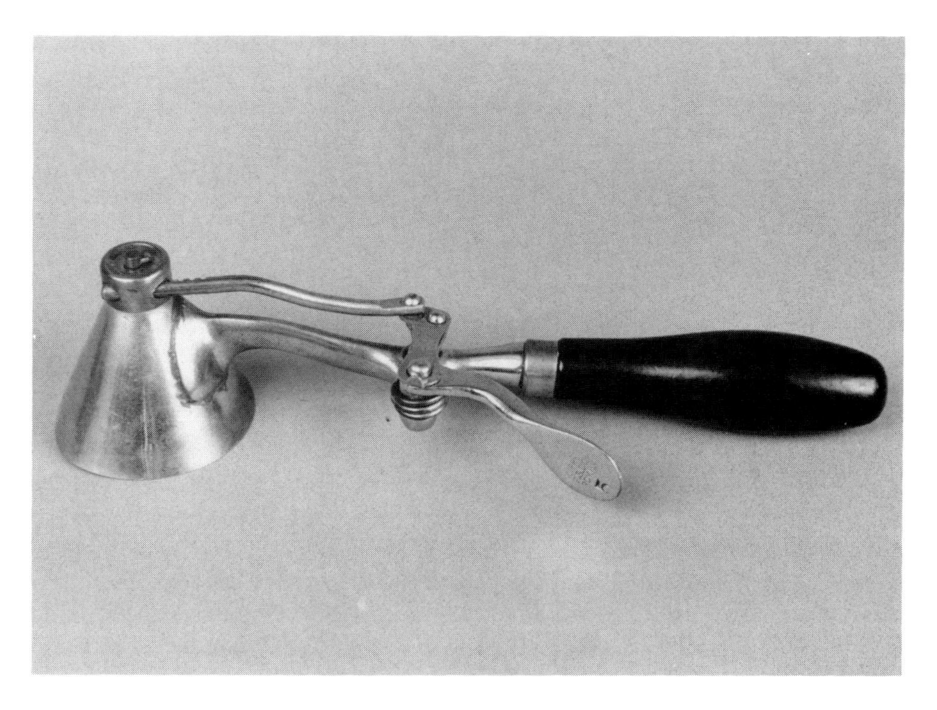

C-21. F.S. Co., Troy, N.Y.
**Patent issued:** 1 Sept. 1914
**Inventor:** Rasmus Nielsen? (Troy, N.Y.)
**Material:** brass, nickel plated
**Handle:** wood
**Length:** 10″
**Bowl:** conical
**Guide number:** 2
**Note:** thumb lever marked
"Clipper F.S. Co. Troy, N.Y."
"Pat'd. Sept. 1, 1914"

# Chapter 9

## The Novelty Era
## 1920–1930

The "Roaring 20's" was one of the most important and interesting eras in the development of the ice cream disher. It was, without a doubt, the most prolific period for the unusual, or novelty type disher. Indeed, the ice cream industry as a whole, saw the introduction of many types of novelties.

There were a number of influences on the ice cream industry at this time, Prohibition being one of them. Without a legal source of liquor, the population was consuming ice cream with a passion. In 1929, the peak year for production, Americans consumed a record breaking, nine quarts per person. Other factors were the first commercial production of dry ice, in 1925, and the 15 million automobiles on the road. These coupled to facilitate the delivery of ice cream to almost any part of the country.

A number of ice cream novelties made their debut in this era. The first was the Eskimo Pie, in 1921, a chocolate covered ice cream bar. It was a phenomenal success for its inventor, Christian Nelson. This was followed closely by the Good Humor and the Popsicle. The ice cream sandwich and the closely related IcyPi, were great favorites, as well as the banana split and the pie-ala-mode. The first three novelties were pre-packaged, but the others had to be created at the soda fountain or ice cream vendor's stand.

To facilitate the dispenser's job, new types of dippers were designed. Perhaps the most popular new style of dipper was the one for making ice cream sandwiches. Like the cone, the ice cream sandwich could be carried and eaten from the hand. This was great for picnics, ballgames and fairs. The easiest method for making these, was for the vendor to dip the ice cream from a bulk container, using an ice cream sandwich dipper. Then, ejecting the slab between two wafers, he completed the ice cream sandwich. A similar and earlier device sometimes used, was the ice cream sandwich wafer holder. It was more like a mold, and kept the dispenser from actually having to handle the food. A common characteristic of all the ice cream sandwich dippers, was that they were either square or rectangular. Most were flat, but at least two were curved, to fit the sides of the container, and eliminate waste.

Beginning with the DanDee dipper, in 1920, at least 15 different ones were produced. The Automatic Cone Co. used it's dipper to make the IcyPi, a modified ice cream sandwich, with three sides closed, to prevent dripping. This sandwich type of dipper could also be used for pie-ala-mode.

It is interesting to note that a number of companies, whose names appear on the dippers, didn't actually produce them. These were cone companies, who were primarily in the business to make the wafers, and sold their dippers only to increase their wafer sales. The Automatic Cone Co. had it's IcyPi scoop manufactured by the Philadelphia Ice Cream Cone Machinery Co., as probably did the Md. Baking Co. and the McLaren Cone Co. The Cake Cone Co. most likely also had their scoop manufactured by an outside firm.

Another popular soda fountain treat was the banana split. Since round scoops of ice cream didn't exactly fit between two banana halves, a special disher was designed to do the job. It had an oval bowl. As far as I know, only three companies made this type of disher, the Gilchrist Co, United Products Co., and Hamilton Beach Co. The Gilchrist disher is the one most often seen by collectors. Even though it is not as rare as some of the other dishers, the banana split disher is one of the most popular.

Pie-ala-mode was another favorite dessert. Ice cream could be put on a piece of pie using a round scoop, a sandwich scoop, or a special pie-ala-mode scoop. The latter was invented by Harlen P. Gardner, of St. Louis, Mo. He designed two different styles. The first one was made by Pi-Alamoder, Inc., the second by the Modern Specialty Co. Both were triangular, to fit the shape of a piece of pie. These are very seldom seen by collectors.

Two other unique scoops worth mentioning here, are the Dover Co. "slicer" disher and F. Vollans' cylinder dispenser. The slicing scoop was a response to the soda fountain operator's concern over decreasing waste and increasing profits. This disher dispensed exactly the same size quantity of ice cream every time, without the extra "overhang". The Vollans dispenser was used to fill an edible type of pastry called a "Cold Dog". It too measured the same quantity of ice cream each time. Both of these appealed to the cost conscious soda fountain operator.

The ultimate novelty scoop was invented by John Manos, in 1925. His heart shaped disher is probably the most beautiful one ever made. With more advertising and promotion it may have become a great success.

In all, at least 69 patents, for various types of ice cream dishers, were granted this decade. A demand was created for different types of dishers, and was filled by ingenious inventors. Another interesting note, is that at least 30 companies were in business producing these dishers, a record for any era.

Ed Marks

1926 *Soda Fountain* ad for L. L. Rowe Co. ice cream disher washer.

In 1929, the collapse of the stock market wiped out many dreams and businesses. This and other events, shocked the country, and for a number of years damaged the ice cream industry. The "heyday" of the ice cream disher was over by 1930, as the demand for the novelty type disher drastically decreased. Food to survive was more important that ice cream. Fortunately, though, a number of these unique dishers are still around, to be enjoyed and treasured by collectors.

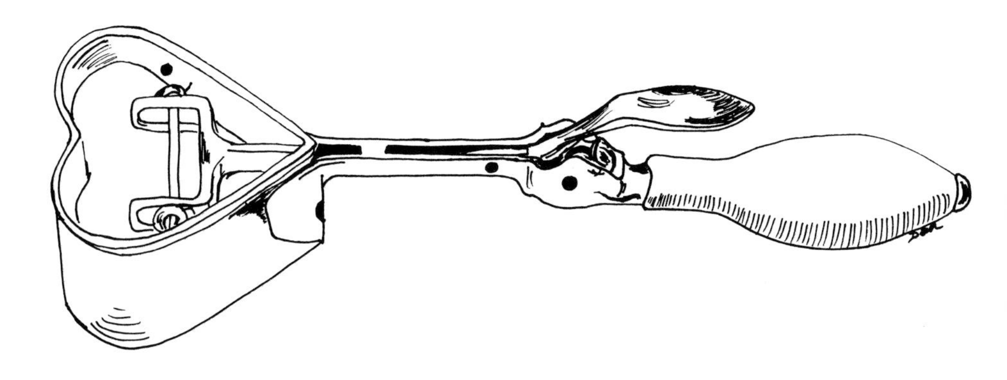

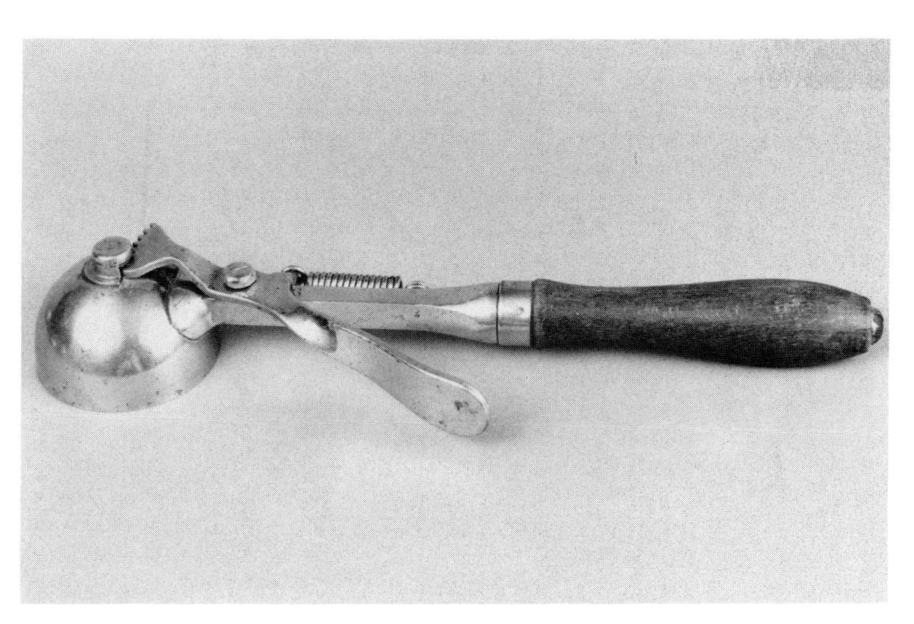

D-1. Benedict Mfg. Co.,
East Syracuse, N.Y.
**Material:** brass, nickel plated
**Handle:** wood
**Length:** 10½″
**Bowl:** round
**Guide number:** 1
**Note:** shank marked
"No. 3 Indestructo"
pre-1928
has a coil spring

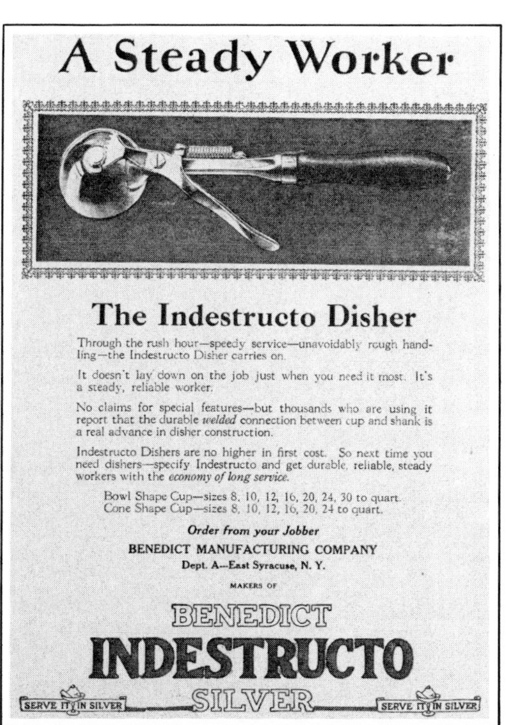


*Ed Marks*

*Soda Fountain* magazine—May, 1926

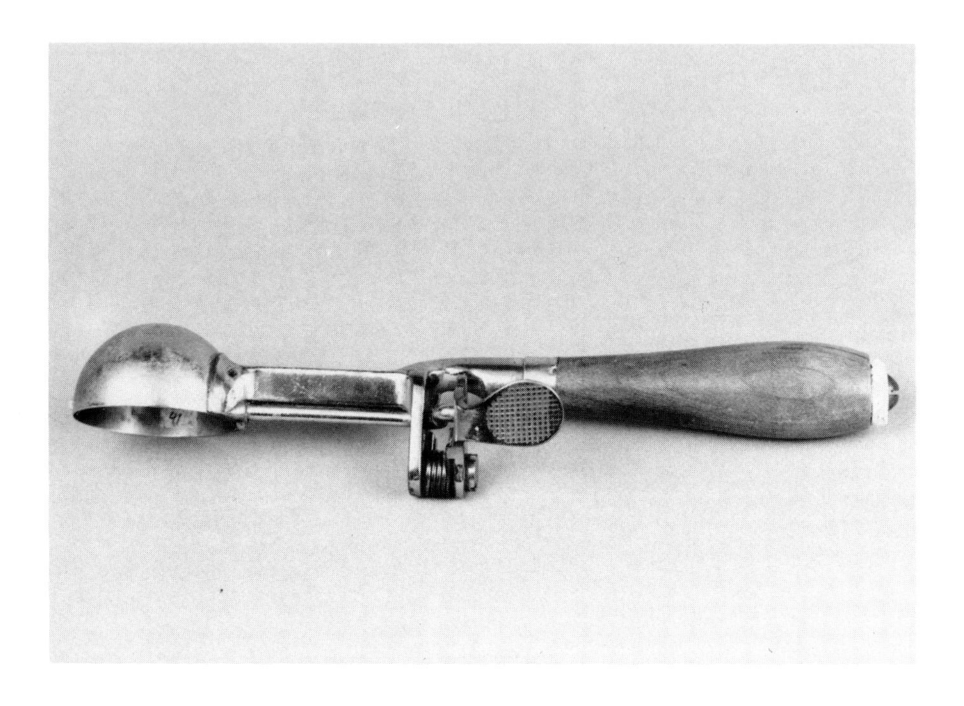

*Allan Mellis*

*Soda Fountain* magazine—June, 1928

D-2. Benedict Mfg. Co.,
East Syracuse, N.Y.
**Patent number:** 1675776
**Patent filed:** 21 July 1926
**Patent issued:** 3 July 1928
**Inventor:** Sidney B. Whiteside
(New York, N.Y.)
**Material:** brass, nickel plated
**Handle:** wood
**Length:** 10″
**Bowl:** round
**Guide number:** 1
**Note:** shank marked
"Indestructo No. 4"
under thumb piece marked
"Patents Applied"
earlier model had a collar
on the scraper rod

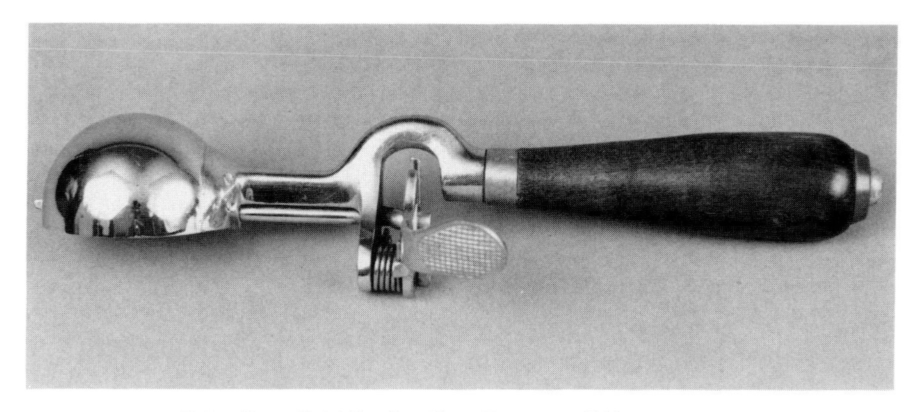

D-3. Benedict Mfg. Co., East Syracuse, N.Y.
**Patent number:** 1675776
**Patent filed:** 21 July 1926
**Patent issued:** 3 July 1928
**Inventor:** Sidney B. Whiteside (New York, N.Y.)
**Material:** brass, nickel plated
**Handle:** wood
**Length:** 9½″
**Bowl:** round
**Guide number:** 1
**Note:** under thumb piece marked
"Indestructo No. 4, Patented July 3, 1928"
also had bakelite handles
colored tips on handle denoted size

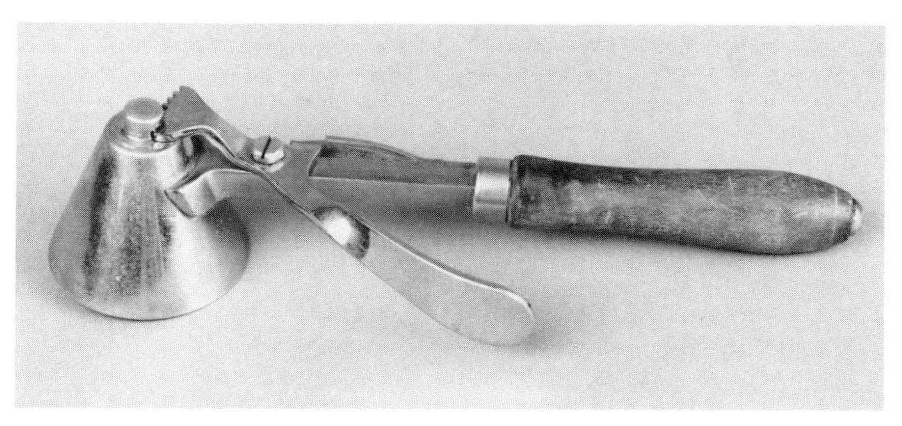

D-4. Benedict Mfg. Co., East Syracuse, N.Y.
**Material:** brass, nickel plated
**Handle:** wood
**Length:** 10¼″
**Bowl:** cone
**Guide number:** 2
**Note:** shank marked
"No. 5 Indestructo"
has leaf spring

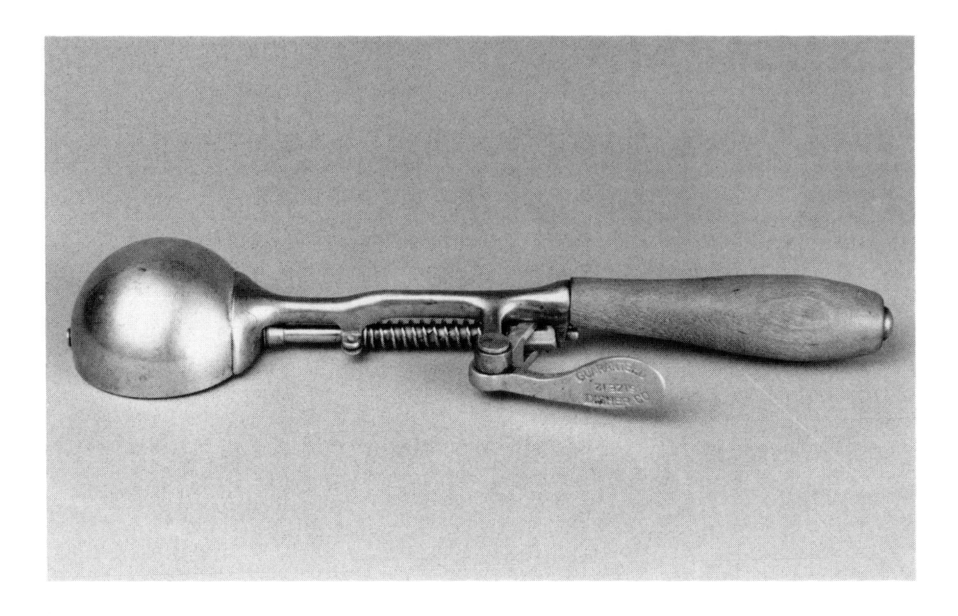

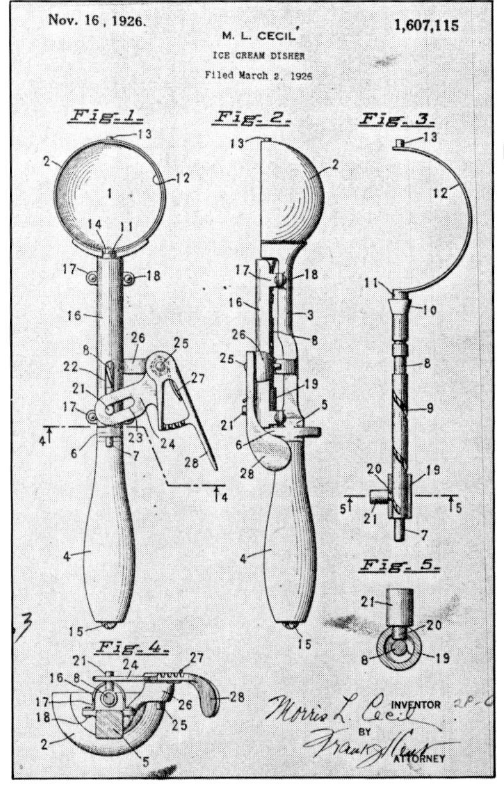


D-5. Guaranteed Disher Co.
**Patent number:** 1607115
**Patent filed:** 2 Mar. 1926
**Patent issued:** 16 Nov. 1926
**Inventor:** Morris L. Cecil (New York, N.Y.)
**Material:** brass, nickel plated
**Handle:** wood
**Length:** 11″
**Bowl:** round
**Guide number:** 2
**Note:** thumb lever marked "Guaranteed Disher Co. Patented Nov. 16, 1926"

D-6. Arnold Electric Co., Racine, Wisc.
**Patent number:** 1615939
**Patent filed:** 17 June 1925
**Patent issued:** 1 Feb 1927
**Inventor:** Harrison D. Flegel
(Racine, Wisc.)
**Material:** brass, nickel plated
**Handle:** wood
**Length:** 9″
**Bowl:** round
**Guide number:** 1
**Note:** thumb piece marked
"No. 50 ARNOLD Racine, Wis. Pat. Feb. 1, 1927"
colored tips on handle denoted size

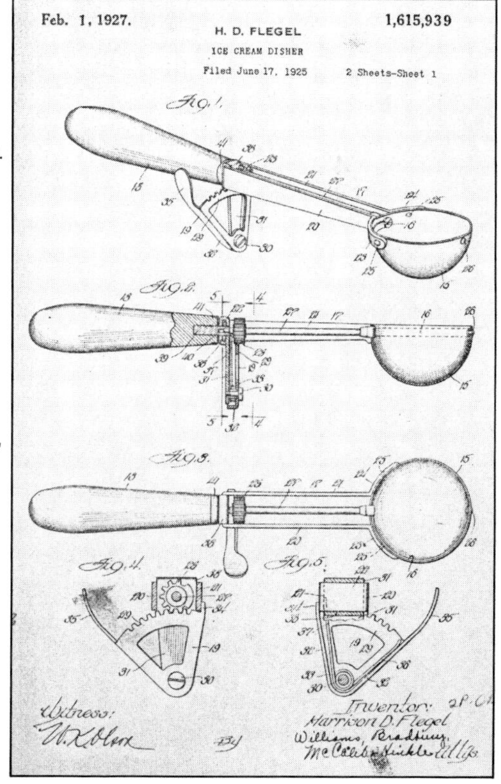

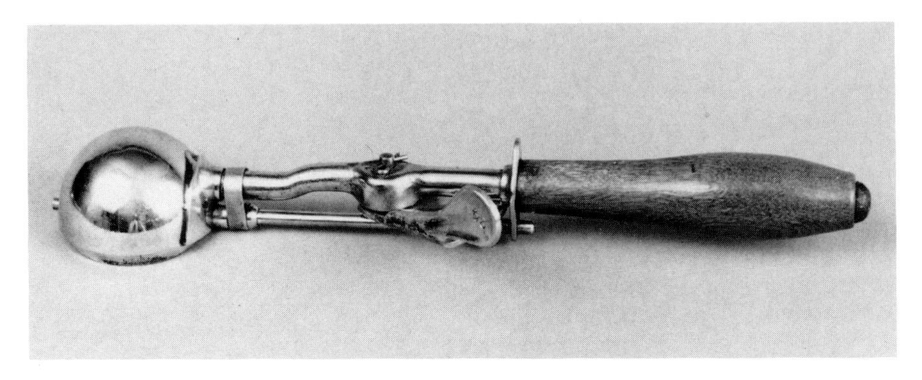

D-7. Fisher Motor Co., Orillia, Ont., Canada
**Material:** brass, nickel plated
**Handle:** wood
**Length:** 10¼″
**Bowl:** round
**Guide number:** 1
**Note:** thumb piece marked
"Fisher Made in Canada Orillia, On"

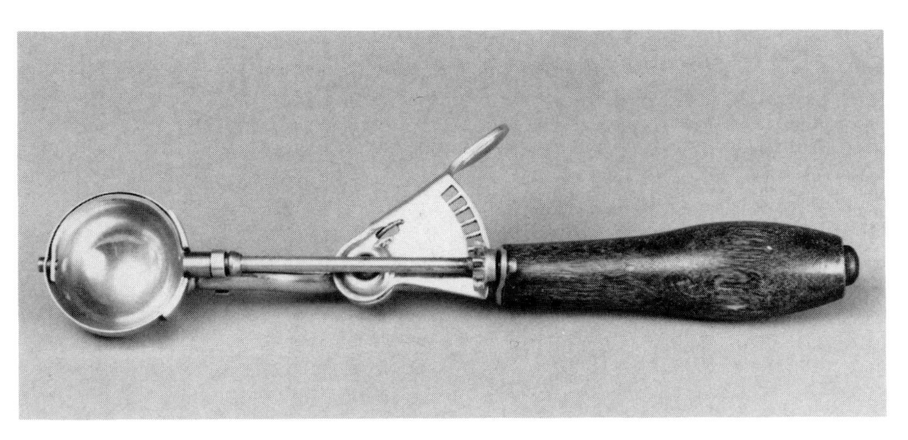

D-8. Caron Brothers, Inc., Montreal, Canada
**Material:** brass, nickel plated
**Handle:** wood
**Length:** 10″
**Bowl:** round
**Guide number:** 1
**Note:** front lever marked
"Caron Brothers, Inc. Montreal"

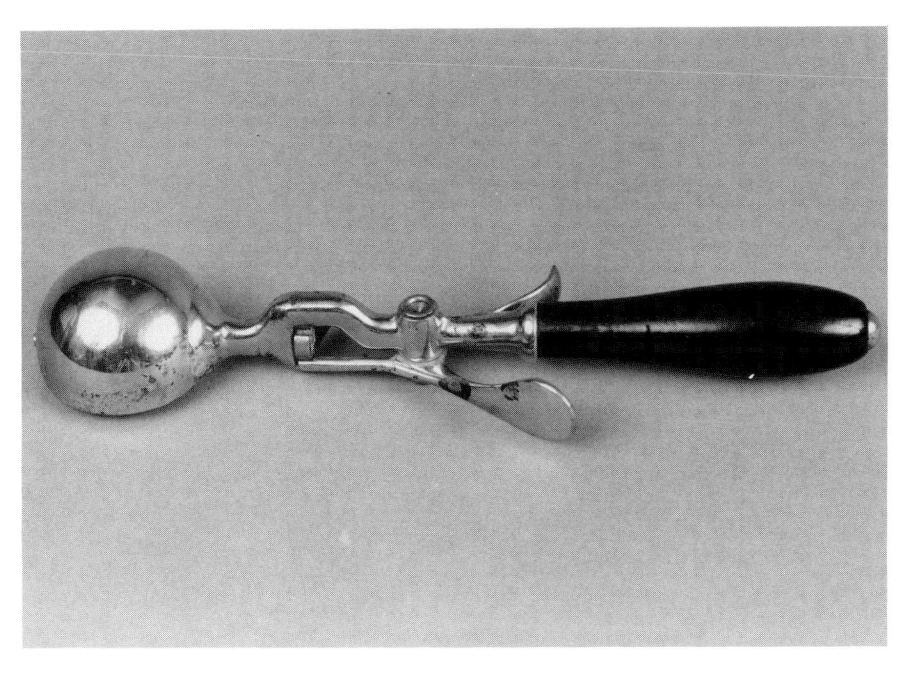

D-9. Dover Mfg. Co., Dover, N.H.
**Patent number:** 1712042
**Patent filed:** 20 Oct. 1927
**Patent issued:** 7 May 1929
**Inventor:** Charles H. Jockmus (Ansonia, Conn.)
**Material:** brass, nickel plated
**Handle:** wood
**Length:** 10″
**Bowl:** round
**Note:** 2
**Note:** thumb lever marked "Dover Mfg. Co. Pat. Appl'd For" does not require a spring to operate

*Allan Mellis*

*Soda Fountain* magazine—Feb., 1927

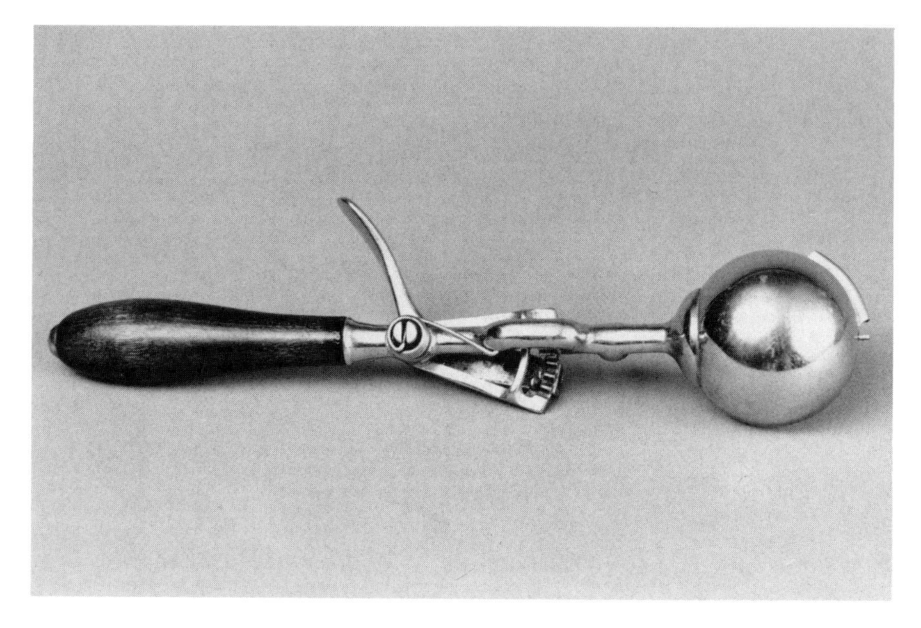

D-10. Dover Mfg Co., Dover, N.H.
**Patent number:** 1483938
**Patent filed:** 13 Nov. 1922
**Patent issued:** 19 Feb. 1924
**Inventors:** George E. Holmes
Frank W. Grant
(Dover, N.H.)
**Material:** brass, nickel plated
**Handle:** wood
**Length:** 11″
**Bowl:** round
**Guide number:** 5
**Note:** thumb lever marked
"Dover Mfg. Co. N.H. Pat. Feb. '24"
slicer cuts off excess ice cream

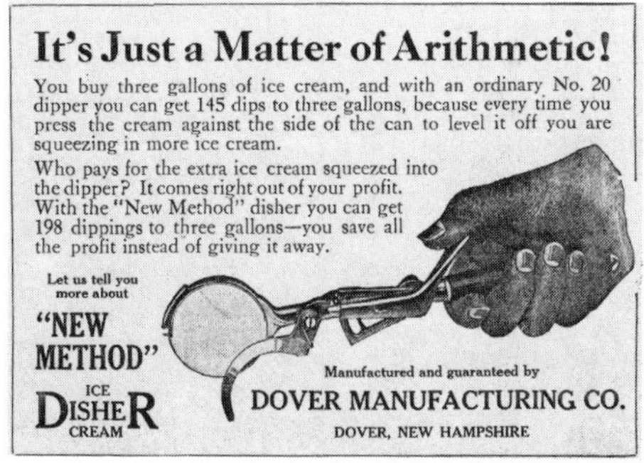


*Bob Bruce*

*Soda Fountain* magazine—Mar., 1925

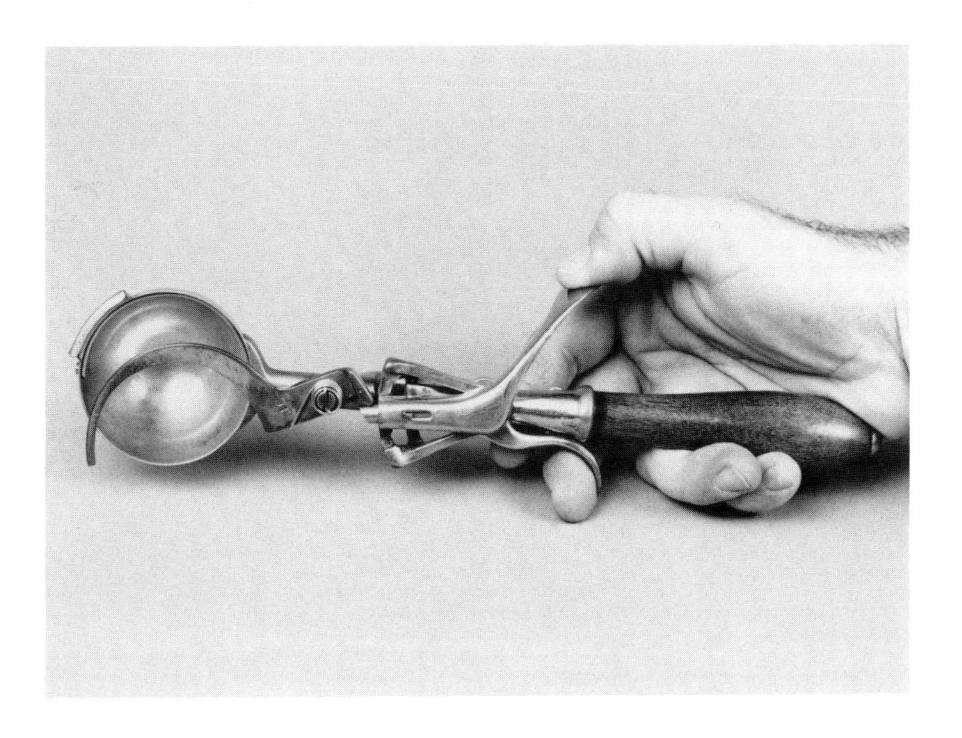

D-11. Dover Mfg. Co., Dover, N.H.
**Patent number:** 1657470?
**Patent filed:** 18 Sept. 1926
**Patent issued:** 31 Jan. 1928
**Inventors:** George E. Holmes
Frank W. Grant
(Dover, N.H.)
**Material:** brass, nickel plated
**Handle:** wood
**Length:** 11″
**Bowl:** round
**Guide number:** 5
**Note:** under thumb lever marked "Dover Mfg. Co. N.H. Pat. Feb. '24"
this slightly different model has a trigger to return the scraper
it was introduced in 1928, and was distributed by the Perfection Disher Co. of Boston, Mass.

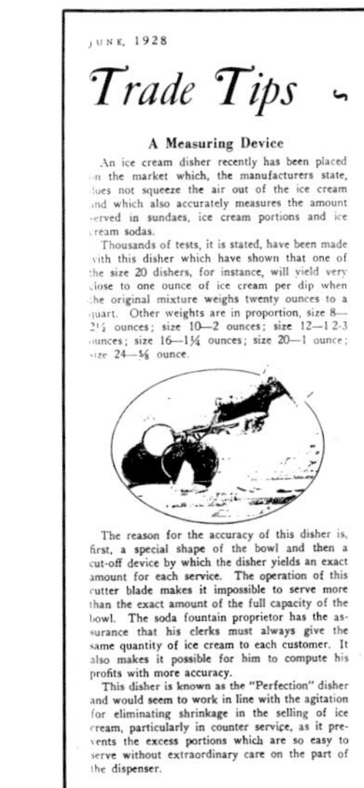

JUNE, 1928

*Trade Tips*

**A Measuring Device**

An ice cream disher recently has been placed on the market which, the manufacturers state, does not squeeze the air out of the ice cream and which also accurately measures the amount served in sundaes, ice cream portions and ice cream sodas.

Thousands of tests, it is stated, have been made with this disher which have shown that one of the size 20 dishers, for instance, will yield very close to one ounce of ice cream per dip when the original mixture weighs twenty ounces to a quart. Other weights are in proportion, size 8—2½ ounces; size 10—2 ounces; size 12—1 2-3 ounces; size 16—1¼ ounces; size 20—1 ounce; size 24—⅝ ounce.

The reason for the accuracy of this disher is, first, a special shape of the bowl and then a cut-off device by which the disher yields an exact amount for each service. The operation of this cutter blade makes it impossible to serve more than the exact amount of the full capacity of the bowl. The soda fountain proprietor has the assurance that his clerks must always give the same quantity of ice cream to each customer. It also makes it possible for him to compute his profits with more accuracy.

This disher is known as the "Perfection" disher and would seem to work in line with the agitation for eliminating shrinkage in the selling of ice cream, particularly in counter service, as it prevents the excess portions which are so easy to serve without extraordinary care on the part of the dispenser.

*Allan Mellis*

*Soda Fountain* magazine—June, 1928

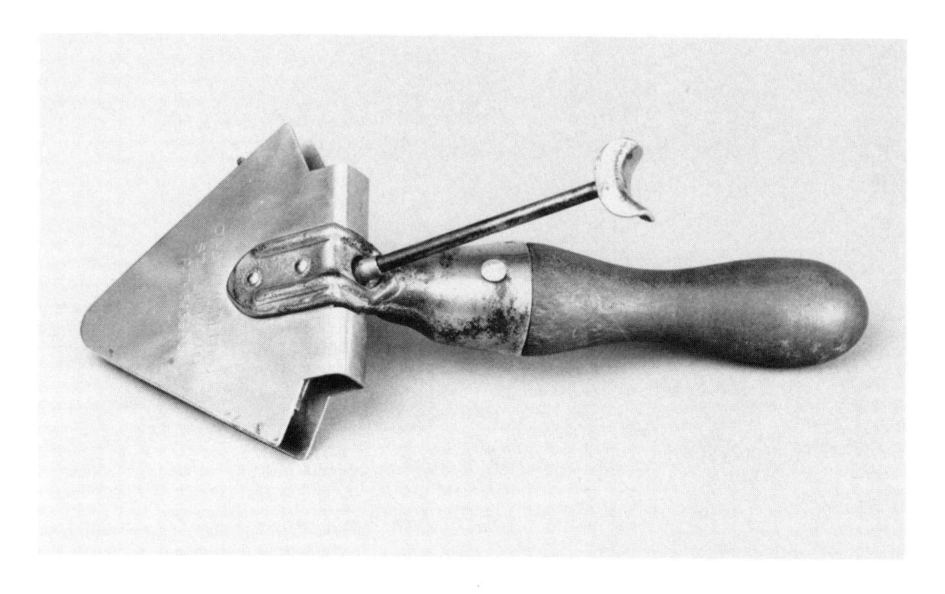

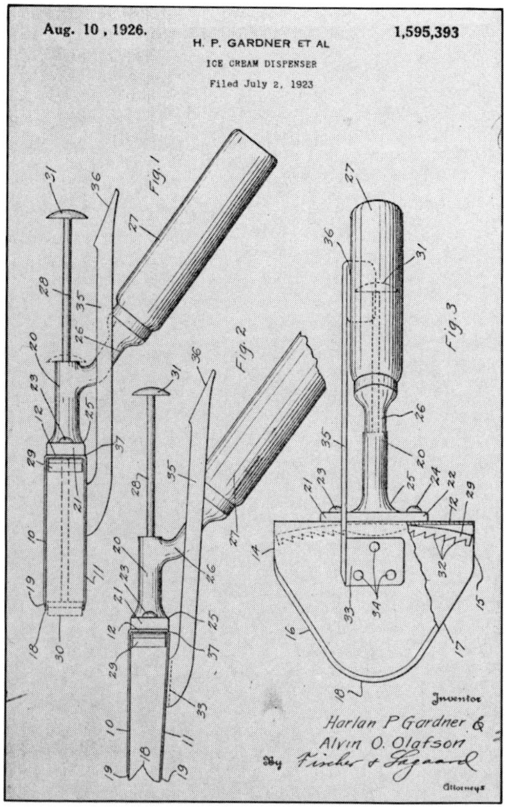


D-12. Pi-Alamoder, Inc., St. Louis, Mo.
**Patent number:** 1595393
**Patent filed:** 2 July 1923
**Patent issued:** 10 Aug. 1926
**Inventors:** Harlan P. Gardner
Alvin O. Olafson
(St. Louis, Mo.)
**Material:** aluminum
**Handle:** wood
**Length:** 4″ top 6″ handle
**Bowl:** triangular, flat
**Guide number:** 5
**Note:** top marked
"Pi-Alamoder, Inc.
St. Louis, Mo.
Pat-1595393"
used for pie-ala-mode
and special
triangular containers
handle offset at 45° angle

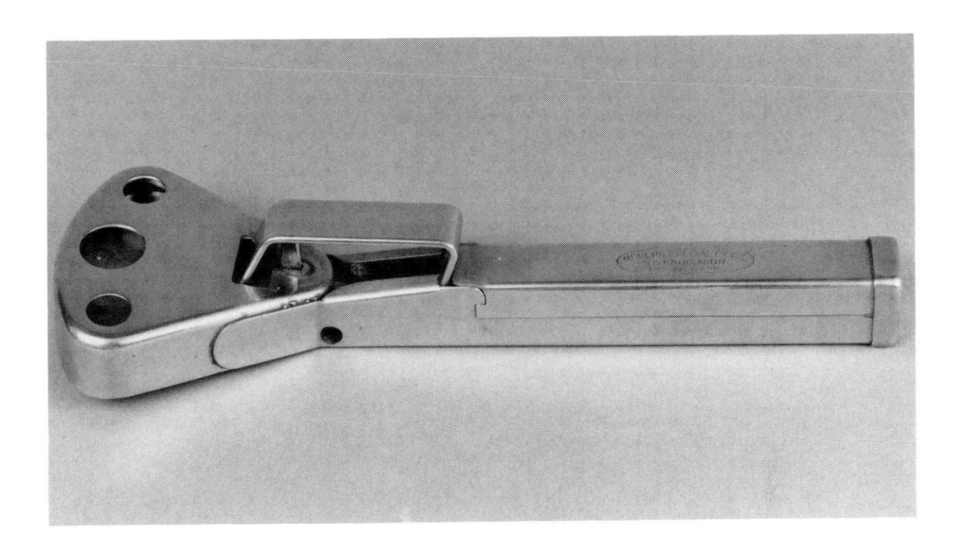

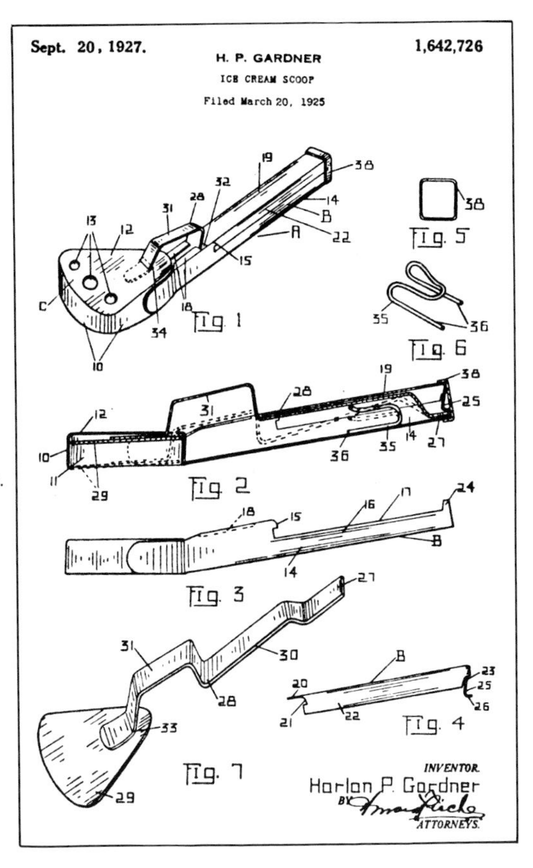


D-13. Modern Specialty Co., St. Paul Minn.
**Patent number:** 1642726
**Patent filed:** 20 Mar. 1925
**Patent issued:** 20 Sept. 1927
**Inventor:** Harlan P. Gardner (St. Paul, Minn.)
**Material:** stainless steel?
**Handle:** same
**Length:** 9½″
**Bowl:** triangular
**Guide number:** 5
**Note:** handle marked "Modern Specialty Co. St. Paul, Minn, Pat. Apld. For" used for pie-ala-mode

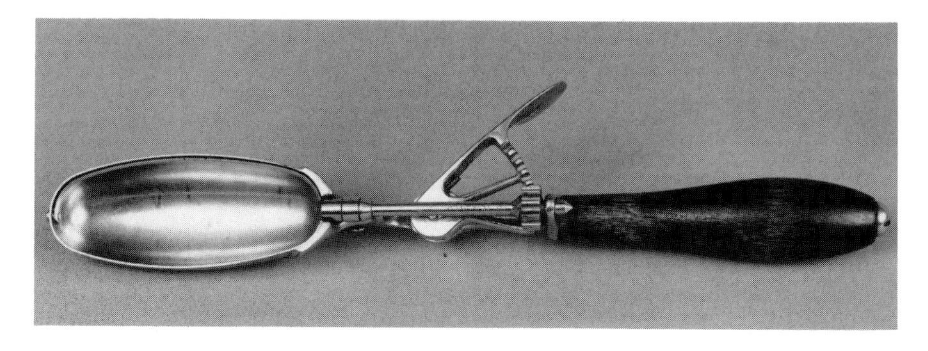

D-14. Gilchrist Co., Newark, N.J.
**Patent number:** 1132657
**Patent filed:** 3 Feb 1908
**Patent issued:** 23 Mar. 1915
**Inventor:** Raymond B. Gilchrist (Newark, N.J.)
**Material:** brass, nickel plated
**Handle:** wood
**Length:** 11½"
**Bowl:** oval
**Guide number:** 5
**Note:** scraper rod marked
"Gilchrist 31"
ca. 1920's
later model in 1930 was shorter and marked "Gilchrist 34"
used for banana splits

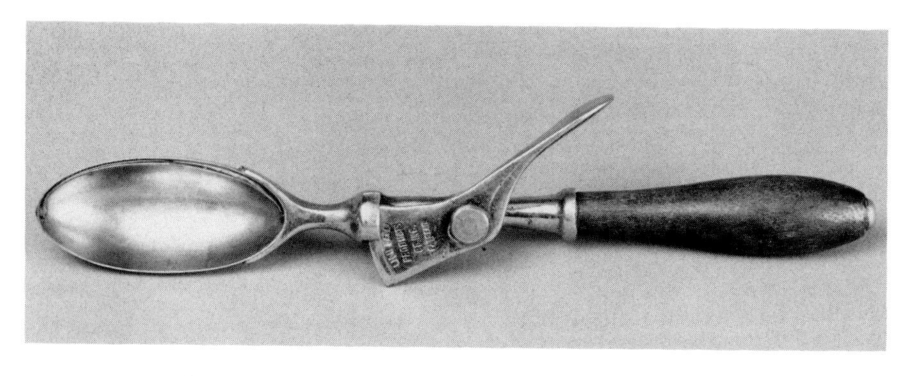

D-15. United Products Co., Chelsea, Mass.
**Material:** brass, nickel plated
**Handle:** wood
**Length:** 11½"
**Bowl:** oval
**Guide number:** 5
**Note:** lever marked
"United Products Co., Inc. Pat. Pend."
used for banana splits
ca. 1930

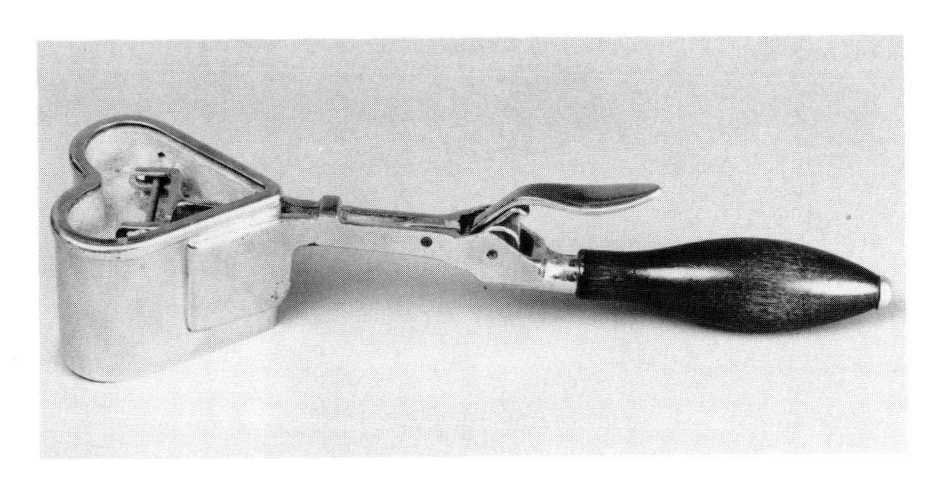

D-16. Manos Novelty Co., Toronto, Ohio
**Patent number:** 1561558
**Patent filed:** 3 Mar. 1925
**Patent issued:** 17 Nov. 1925
**Inventor:** John Manos
(Toronto, Ohio)
**Material:** brass, nickel plated
**Handle:** wood
**Length:** 11″
**Bowl:** heart
**Guide number:** 5
**Note:** inside plate on some marked
"Pat. Nov., 1925"
used to fill special heart shaped dishes
only 500 of this model produced, in addition to 500 of an earlier model
one of the rarest and most desirable of all dishers

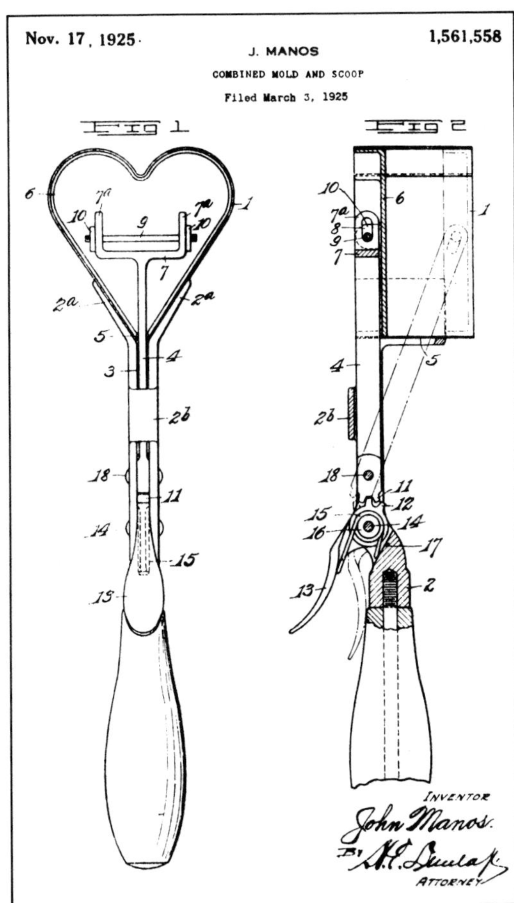

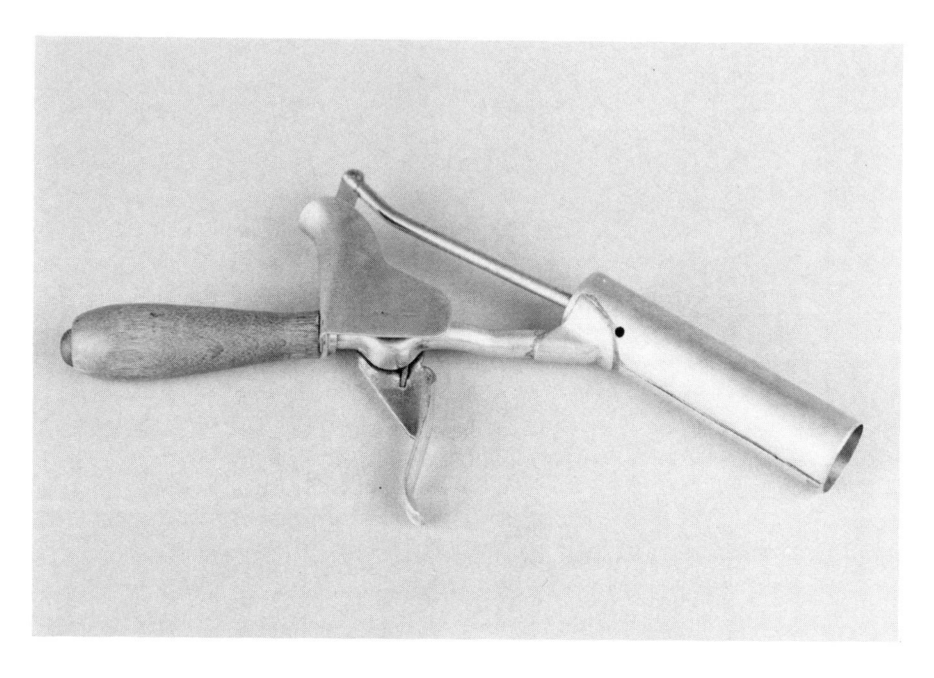

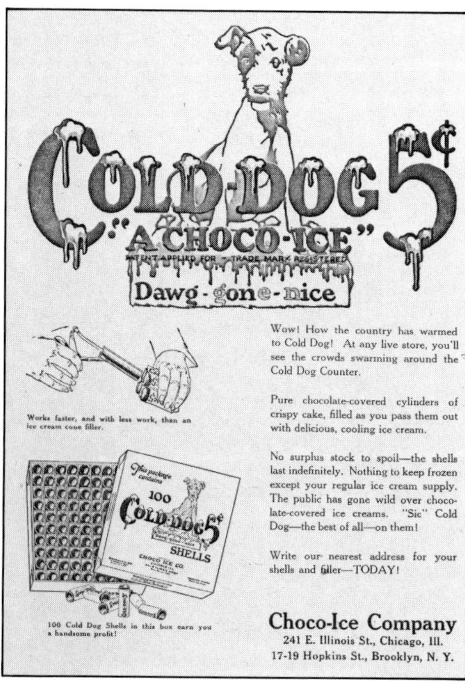


*Ed Marks*

*Candy and Ice Cream*—October, 1922

D-17. Fisher Motor Co., Ltd., Orillia, Ontario, Canada
**Patent number:** 1595635
**Patent filed:** 6 Dec. 1922
**Patent issued:** 10 Aug. 1926
**Inventor:** Frederick W. Vollans (Orillia, Canada)
**Material:** german silver
**Handle:** wood
**Length:** 9½″
**Bowl:** cylinder
**Guide number:** 5
**Note:** finger guard marked "Made in Canada" thumb lever marked "Pat. Appd. For" used for filling edible containers

D-18. Jack Frost
**Material:** steel
**Handle:** bakelite
**Length:** 6¼″
**Bowl:** cylinder
**Guide number:** 4
**Note:** handle marked
"Jack Frost Pat. Applied For"
ca. 1920's?

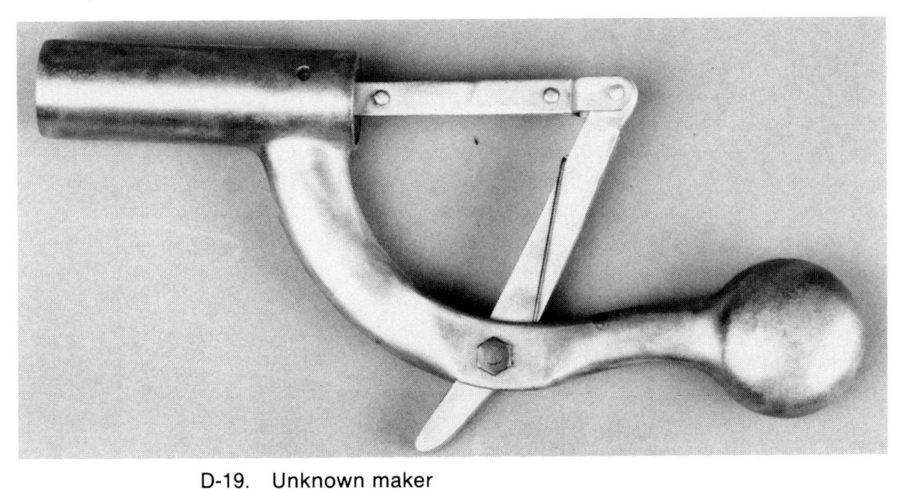

D-19. Unknown maker
**Material:** aluminum
**Handle:** same
**Length:** 9″
**Bowl:** cylindrical
**Guide number:** 5
**Note:** no markings
possibly used to fill edible containers
ca. late 1920's

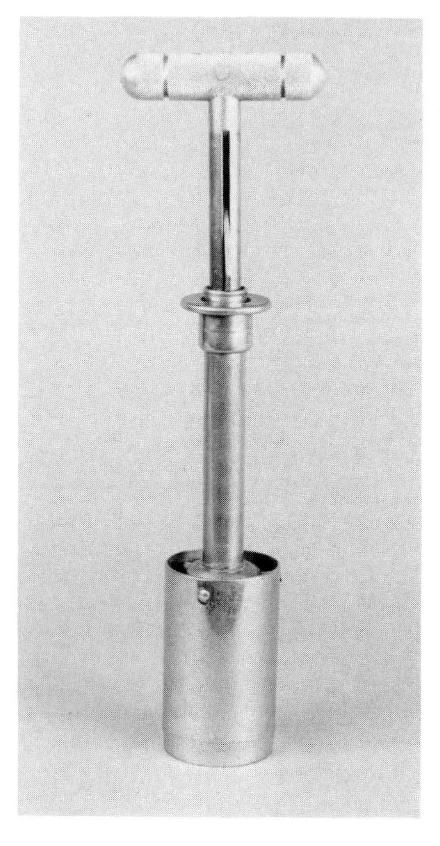

D-20. General Ice Cream Corp.,?
Schenectady, N.Y.
**Patent number:** 1531179
**Patent filed:** 13 Feb. 1922
**Patent issued:** 24 Mar. 1925
**Inventor:** William L. Daly
(Schenectady, N.Y.)
**Material:** brass, nickel plated
**Handle:** aluminum
**Length:** 8″ closed 11″ open
**Bowl:** cylinder
**Guide number:** 3
**Note:** inside plunger marked
"Property of Gen. Ice
Cream Corp.
Pat. 3-24-25"
used to transfer ice cream
from container to cone or
other receptacle

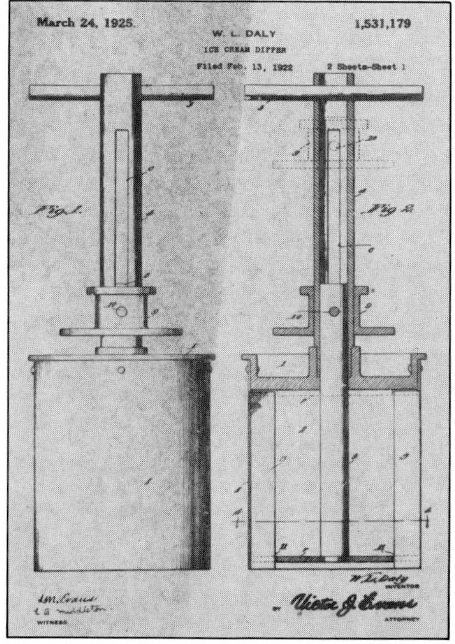

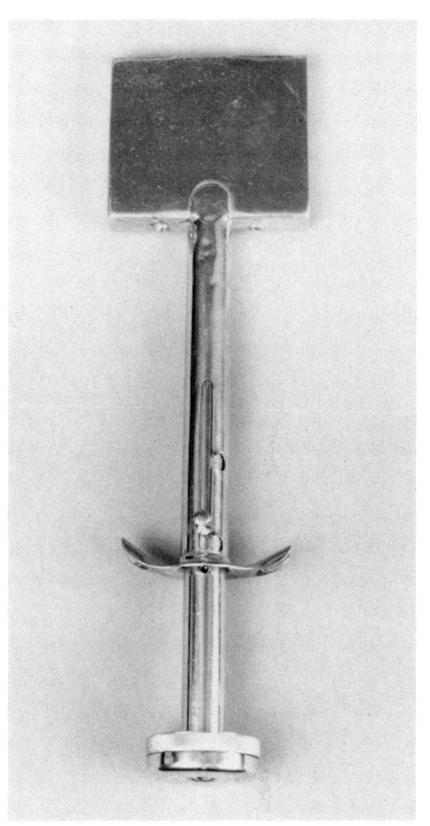

D-21. Dan Dee Dipper Co., Knoxville, Tenn.
**Patent number:** 1352756
**Patent filed:** 16 Sept. 1919
**Patent issued:** 14 Sept. 1920
**Inventor:** Samuel Levy (Knoxville, Tenn.)
**Material:** brass, nickel plated
**Handle:** same
**Length:** 11½″
**Bowl:** square
**Guide number:** 4
**Note:** end of plunger marked "The Dan Dee Dipper Co. Knoxville, Tenn. Pat'd Sep. 14–20 Two Pats." used for ice cream sandwiches

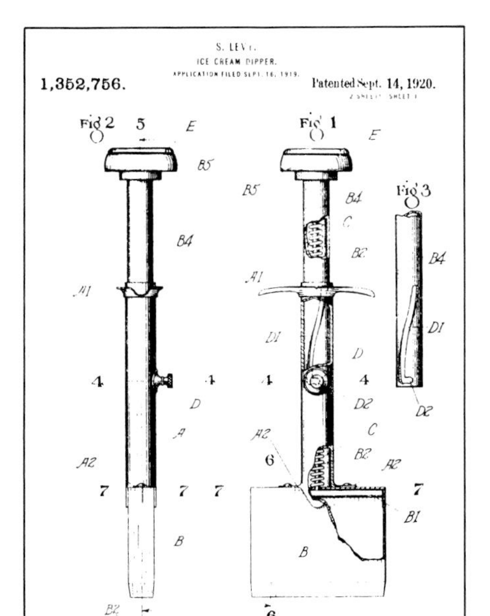

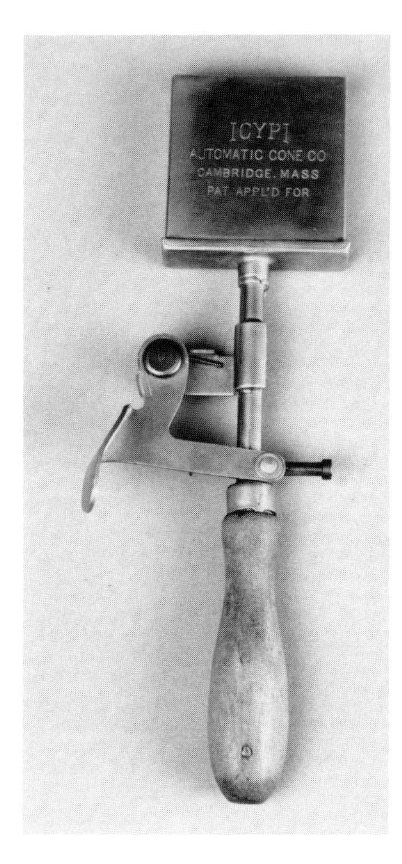


D-22. Automatic Cone Co., Cambridge, Mass.
**Inventor:** James Denaro (Cambridge, Mass.)
**Material:** german silver
**Handle:** wood
**Length:** 10″
**Bowl:** square
**Guide number:** 3
**Note:** front marked "Icypi Automatic Cone Co. Cambridge, Mass. Pat. Appl'd For"
used to fill square IcyPi containers
two slightly different models produced
ca. 1924–1930

*Allan Mellis*

*Soda Fountain* magazine—May, 1927

D-23. Automatic Cone Co., Cambridge, Mass.
**Inventor:** James Denaro (Cambridge, Mass.)
**Material:** german silver
**Handle:** wood
**Length:** 11″
**Bowl:** square
**Guide number:** 3
**Note:** front and back marked "Icypi Automatic Cone Co. Cambridge, Mass. Pat. Appl'd For"
used to fill square IcyPi containers
this springless model was possibly the first produced
ca. 1924–1930

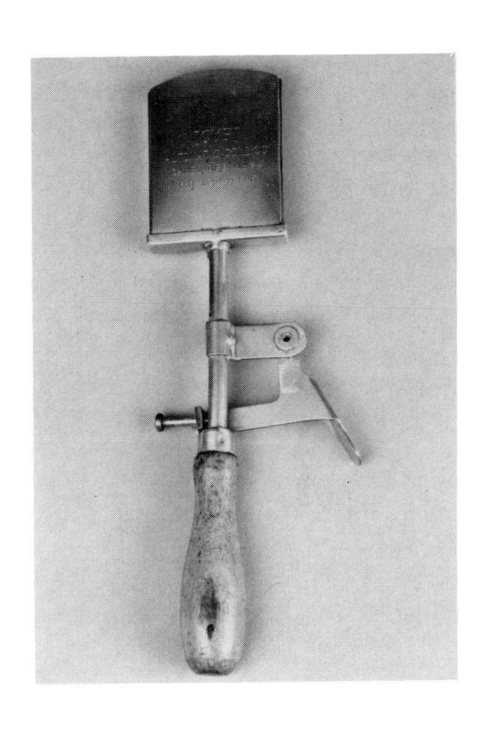

D-24. McLaren Cone Co., Dayton, Ohio
**Inventor:** James Denaro (Cambridge, Mass.)
**Material:** german silver
**Handle:** wood
**Length:** 10″
**Bowl:** square
**Guide number:** 3
**Note:** front marked "McLaren's ICYPI McLaren Consolidated Cone Corp'n Dayton, Ohio Pat. Appl'd For
manufactured by the Automatic Cone Co. for McLaren
used to fill IcyPi containers
ca. 1929

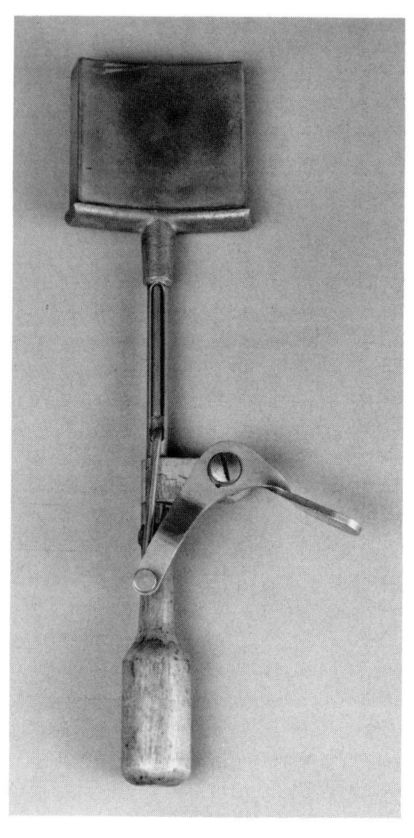

D-25. Jiffy Dispenser Co., Aurora, Ill.
**Patent number:** 1526753
**Patent filed:** 13 July 1923
**Patent issued:** 17 Feb. 1925
**Inventor:** Maurice L. Levene (Chicago, Ill.)
**Material:** german silver
**Handle:** wood
**Length:** 12½″
**Bowl:** square, curved
**Guide number:** 3
**Note:** front marked "Jiffy Dispenser Co. Aurora, Ill. Pat. Feb. 17, 1925"
curved to fit side of container
used for ice cream sandwiches

Ed Marks

*Soda Fountain* magazine—Sept., 1925

D-26. Mayer Mfg. Co., Chicago, Ill.
**Material:** german silver
**Handle:** wood
**Length:** 12″
**Bowl:** square
**Guide number:** 3
**Note:** front marked
"Mayer Mfg. Corp. Patent Pending 1606 S. Wabash Chicago"
extremely similar to pat. no. 1526753
shank has a 3 size adjusting ring
used for ice cream sandwiches

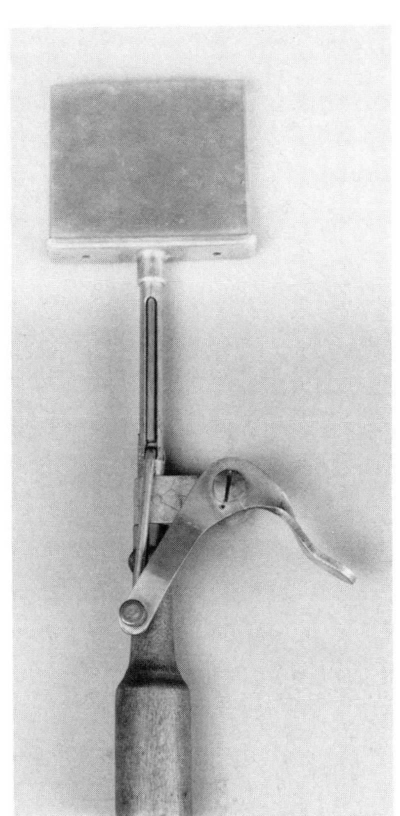

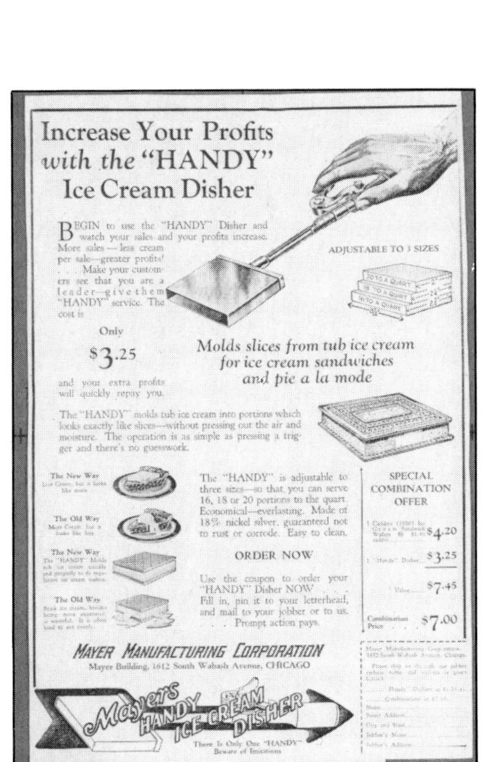

*Allan Mellis*

*Soda Fountain* magazine—May, 1927

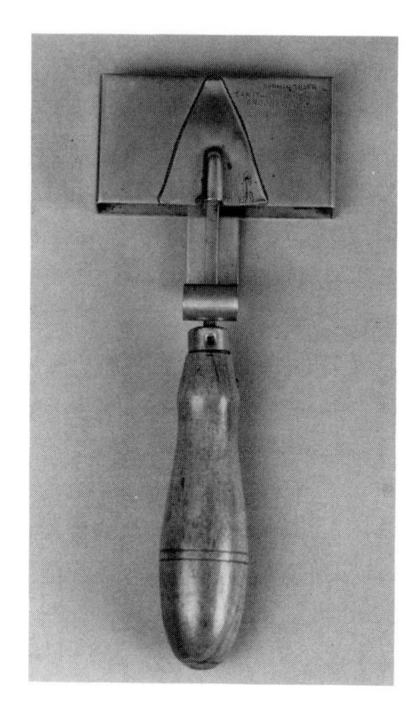

D-27. Sanitary Mould Co.,
Brooklyn, N.Y.
**Patent number:** 1529782
**Patent filed:** 18 June 1924
**Patent issued:** 17 Mar. 1925
**Inventor:** Barnett Gerstein
(College Point, N.Y.)
**Material:** german silver
**Handle:** wood
**Length:** 8¼″
**Bowl:** square
**Guide number:** 3
**Note:** front marked
"German silver Sanitary
Mould Co.
Brooklyn, N.Y."
push-up rod marked
"Pat'd. Mar. 17, 1925"
used for ice cream
sandwiches

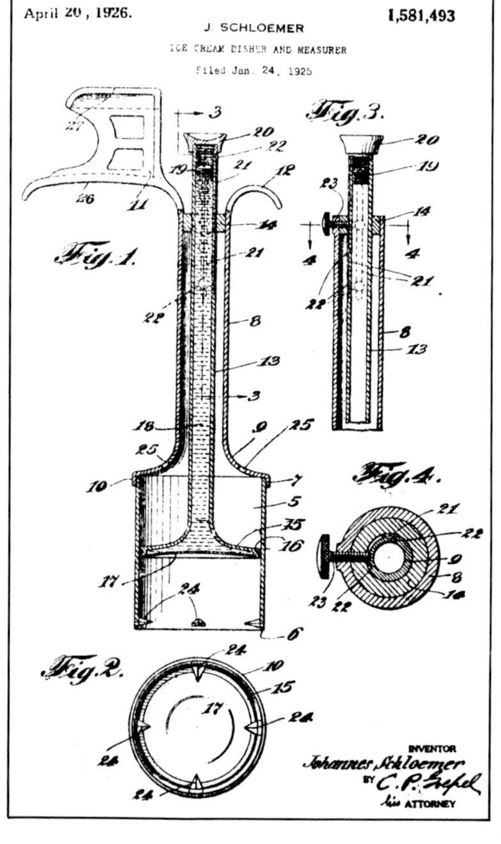

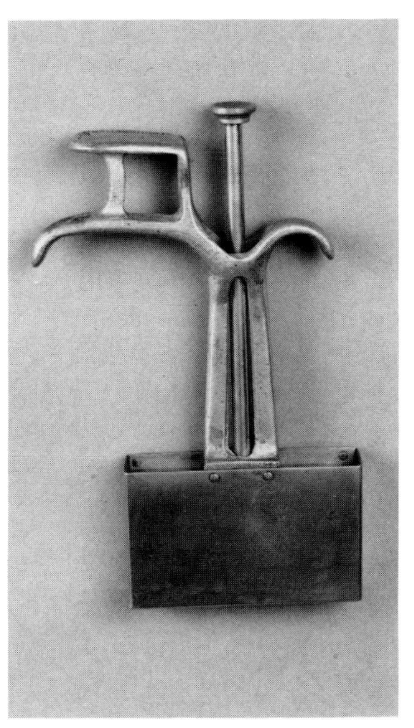

D-28. Johannes Schloemer, N.Y., N.Y.
**Patent number:** 1581493
**Patent filed:** 24 Jan. 1925
**Patent issued:** 20 April 1926
**Inventor:** Johannes Schloemer (N.Y., N.Y.)
**Material:** aluminum and stainless steel
**Handle:** aluminum
**Length:** 6½″
**Bowl:** square
**Guide number:** 3
**Note:** handle marked "J. Schloemer Pat." used for ice cream sandwiches

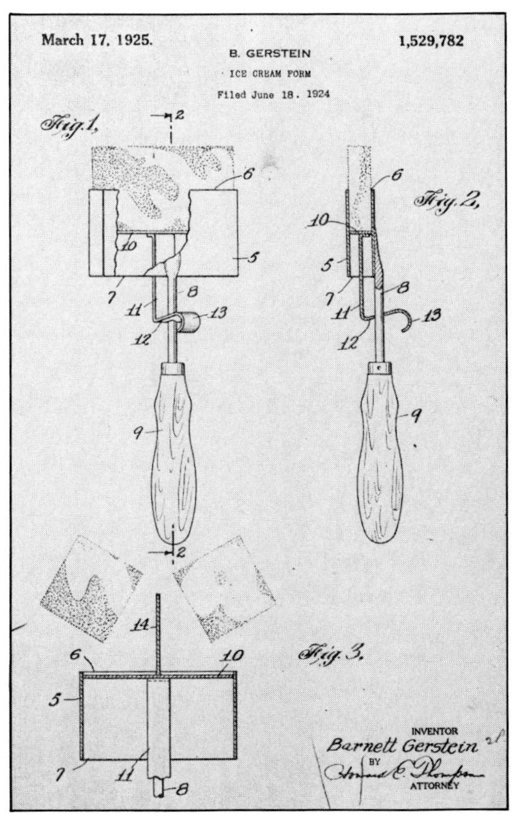

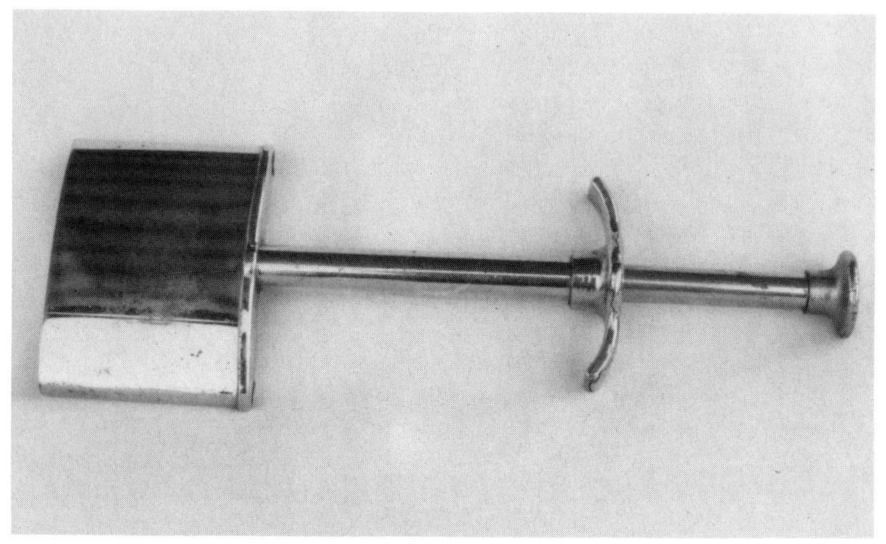

*Bob Cahn*

D-29. W. F. Wendel, Girard, Pa.
**Patent number:** 1627132
**Patent filed:** 25 June 1925
**Patent issued:** 3 May 1927
**Inventor:** William F. Wendel (Girard, Pa.)
**Material:** brass, nickel plated
**Handle:** same
**Bowl:** square, curved
**Guide number:** 4
**Note:** advertising literature marked patent pending
plunger mechanism
used for ice cream sandwiches

*Bob Cahn*

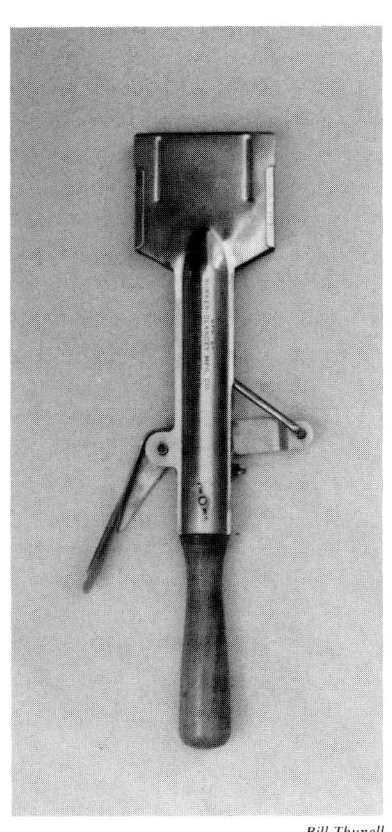
*Bill Thunell*

D-30. Bunker-Clancy Mfg. Co., Kansas City, Mo.
**Patent number:** 1620110
**Patent filed:** 8 Mar 1926
**Patent issued:** 8 Mar 1927
**Inventor:** Herman Landman (Kansas City, Mo.)
**Material:** white metal
**Handle:** wood
**Length:** 13¼″
**Bowl:** square
**Guide number:** 4
**Note:** shank marked "Mfd by Bunker-Clancy Mfg. Co.-B- Kansas City-Mo.-C Pat. 9-10-18, 5-4-26, 3-8-27"

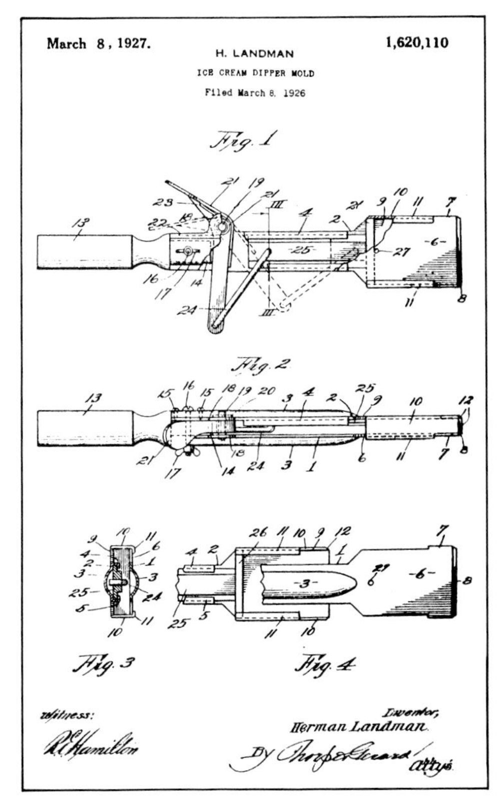

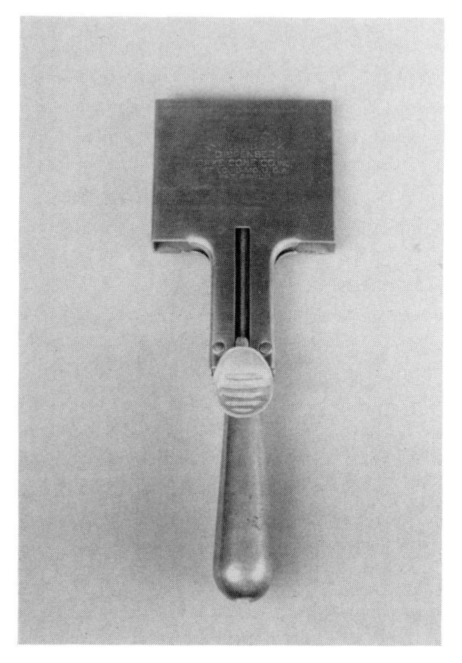

D-31. Cake Cone Co., St. Louis, Mo.
**Material:** german silver
**Handle:** aluminum
**Length:** 9″
**Bowl:** square
**Guide number:** 3
**Note:** front marked
"Rainbow Ice Cream Dispenser Cake Cone Co., Inc. St. Louis, Mo. Pat. Appl'd"
used for ice cream sandwiches

D-32. United Products Corp., Chelsea, Mass.
**Material:** brass, nickel plated
**Handle:** same
**Length:** 7½″
**Bowl:** square
**Guide number:** 4
**Note:** bowl marked
"Ice Cream Pie United Products Corp. Chelsea, Mass."
has push up mechanism
used for ice cream sandwiches
ca. late 1920's

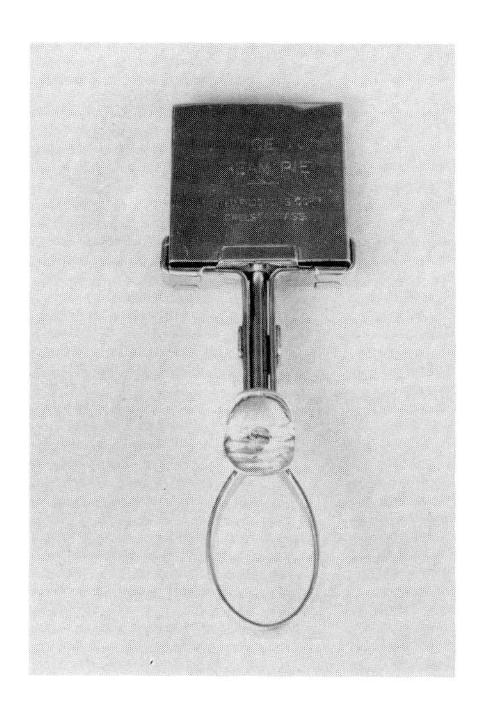

D-33. Unknown maker
**Material:** bronze
**Handle:** wood, offset
**Length:** 8½″
**Bowl:** rectangular
**Guide number:** 4
**Note:** has springless plunger and no markings
used for ice cream sandwiches

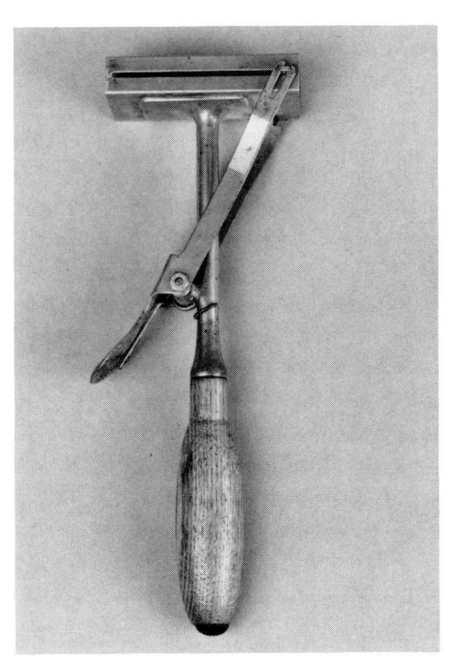

D-34. Unknown maker
**Material:** brass, nickel plated
**Handle:** wood
**Length:** 9½″
**Bowl:** rectangular
**Guide number:** 5
**Note:** thumb lever marked "Patent Applied For"
number stamped under scoop is possibly a production number.
used for ice cream sandwiches

# Chapter 10

## The Depression Era
## 1930–1940

The rise to the 1929 record levels of ice cream production was dramatic, but the decline in production after that year, was even more dramatic. As a direct result of the Depression, ice cream consumption dropped from 9.7 gallons per person, in 1929, to a low of 5.2 gallons, in 1933, a decrease of almost half. The state of the economy in the early 1930's was such that ice cream was a luxury that many just could not afford. In 1933, another great shock to the faltering ice cream industry came as the 18th Amendment repealed Prohibition. 13 million people were unemployed and the average wage was 60% of 1929 levels.

Many companies that produced scoops went out of business during these lean years. Some were acquired by larger companies. In 1931, for example, the Gilchrist Co. and the Arnold Co., were merged with the Hamilton Beach Co. Out of the 30, or so, companies that were manufacturing scoops in the 1920's, only 7 of these had survived into the 1930's. These were: Benedict, V. Clad, Keiner-Williams, Mills, New Gem, Philadelphia Ice Cream Cone Machinery Co., and United Products. To this list was added at least 7 new entries to the field; Economy, Hamilton Beach, Md. Baking Co., Myers, Perfection Equipment Co., Schupfer and Eaton, and Zeroll.

Characteristics of the scoops at this time generally reflected the era. The use of aluminum during the 1930's was much more prevalent than ever before. The round shaped bowl seemed to be the most popular. Gone were most of the novelty styles of the previous decade. Bakelite as a handle material, was more common, especially on the Benedict scoops.

Even the advertising was aimed at the soda fountain operator's desire to save money. Scoops had names like, "Economy" and "No-Pak." Hamilton Beach advertised its No-Pak disher, with the hole in the side, as giving 10–16% more servings per container. Zeroll claimed up to 20% more servings, when it's scoop was used. These features all translated to a little added profit for the soda fountain operator, at a time when it was much needed.

In 1935, a major change in ice cream scoop design took place, when Sherman Kelly introduced his Zeroll dipper. It's unique one piece design was more practical and sanitary, than any other previous dipper. As a result, sales were great and imitations began to appear, but none quite matched the Zeroll. The advent of mechanical refrigeration and the resulting hard ice cream, created a need for a sturdy and practical scoop, and Zeroll filled the bill. Mechanical dishers were still being made, but couldn't quite compete with the Zeroll.

By 1937, the worst was over for the country's economy and for the ice cream industry. Consumption soared to record levels once again. The ice cream scoop survived the era, but not without drastic changes. The complex mechanisms and exotic shapes began to disappear, to be replaced by the simple, economical and more practical styles. The evolution of scoop design had come almost full cycle by the 1930's. It began with the simple styles of the 1880's, evolving through the complex examples of the 1920's, and finally returning to the simple and practical styles of the 1930's.

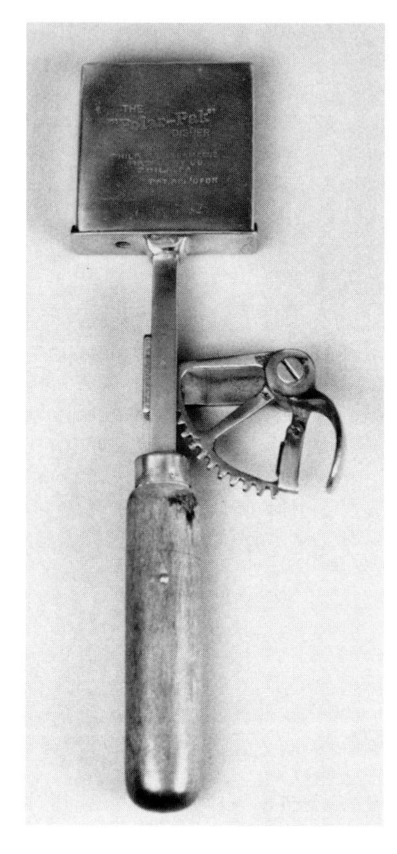


E-1. Philadelphia Ice Cream Cone Machinery Co., Philadelphia, Pa.
**Patent number:** 1868656
**Patent filed:** 24 Oct. 1928
**Patent issued:** 26 July 1932
**Inventor:** Joseph Brezin (Philadelphia, Pa.)
**Material:** brass, nickel plated
**Handle:** wood
**Length:** 10½″
**Bowl:** square
**Guide number:** 4
**Note:** front marked
"The 'Polar-Pak' Disher
Made by Phila. Ice Cream
Cone Machinery Co.
Phila, Pa. Pat. Apl'd For"
use for ice cream sandwiches

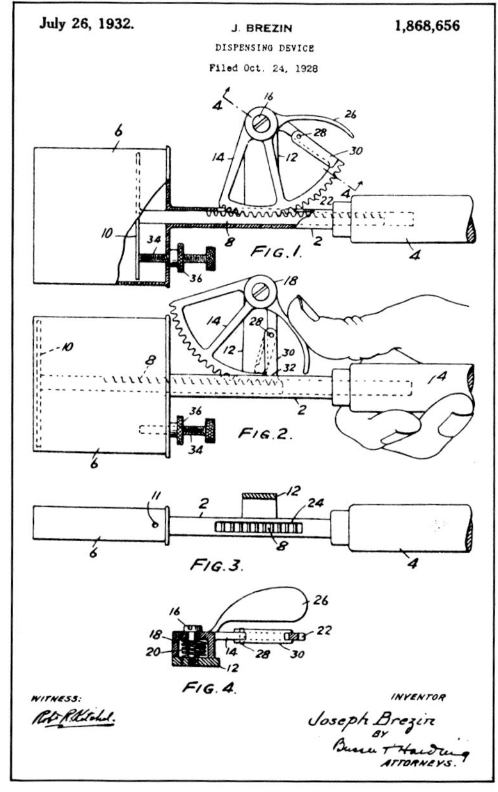

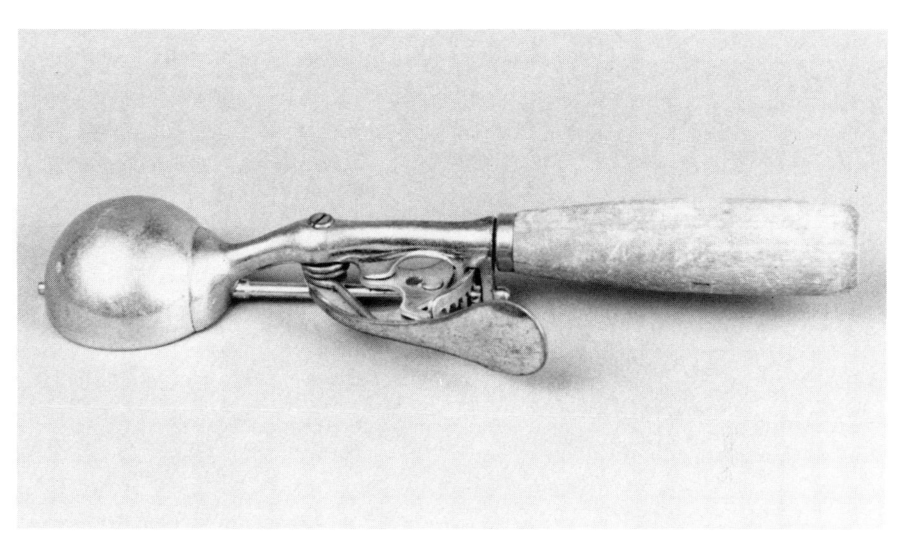

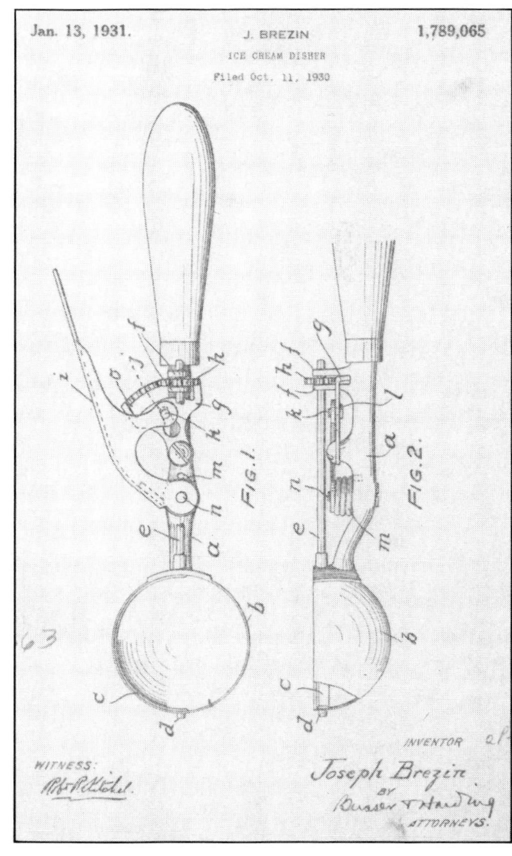


E-2. Philadelphia Ice Cream Cone Machinery Co., Phila., Pa.
**Patent number:** 1789065
**Patent filed:** 11 Oct 1930
**Patent issued:** 13 Jan 1931
**Inventor:** Joseph Brezin (Philadelphia, Pa)
**Material:** brass, nickel plated
**Handle:** wood
**Length:** 10″
**Bowl:** round
**Guide number:** 1
**Note:** thumb piece marked "Philcone Disher Pat. no. 1789065"

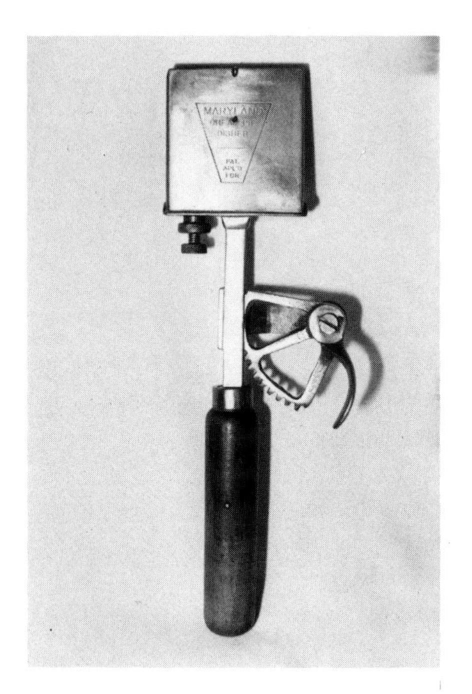


E-3. Philadelphia Ice Cream Cone Machinery Co., Philadelphia, Pa.
**Patent number:** 1868656
**Patent filed:** 24 Oct. 1928
**Patent issued:** 26 July 1932
**Inventor:** Joseph Brezin (Philadelphia, Pa.)
**Material:** brass, nickel plated
**Handle:** wood
**Length:** 10½″
**Bowl:** square, with wire divider across top
**Guide number:** 4
**Note:** front marked "Maryland Cream Pie Disher Pat. Apl'd For" used for making twin ice cream sandwiches

E-4. Maryland Baking Co., Baltimore, Md.
**Patent number:** 1789065?
**Patent filed:** 11 Oct 1930?
**Patent issued:** 13 Jan 1931?
**Inventor:** Joseph Brezin?
**Material:** brass, nickel plated
**Handle:** wood
**Length:** 10″
**Bowl:** round
**Guide number:** 1
**Note:** thumb piece marked "Maryland Baking Co. Baltimore, Md." possibly mfg. by the Phila. Ice Cream Cone Mach. Co.

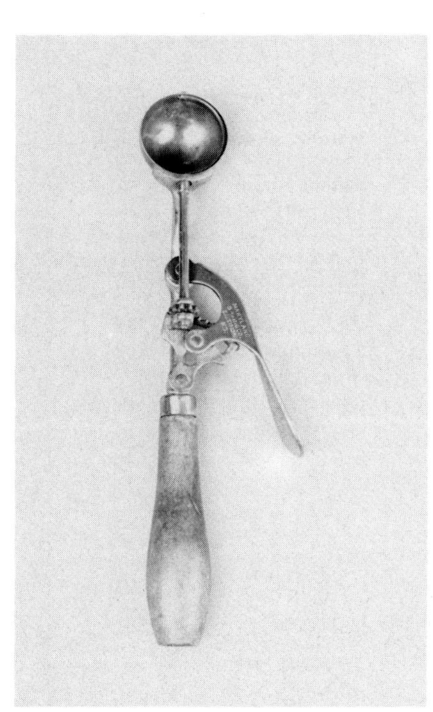

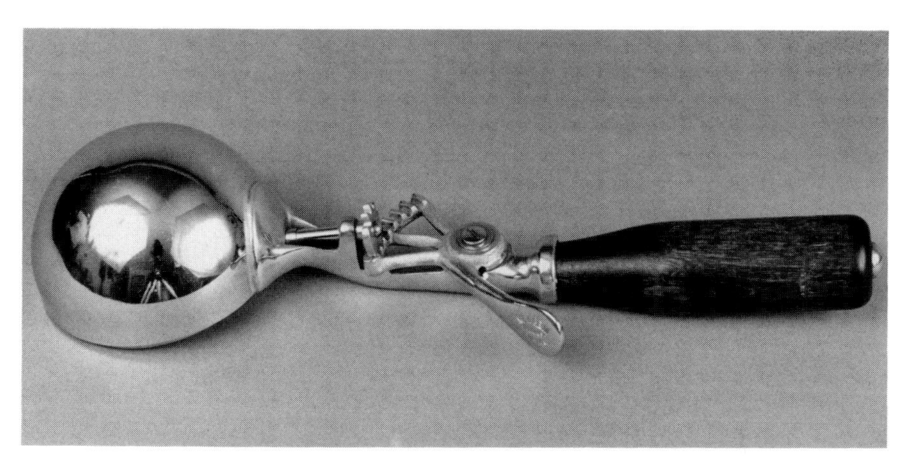

E-5. New Gem Manufacturing Co., Newark, N.J.
**Material:** brass, nickel plated
**Handle:** wood
**Length:** 10½″
**Bowl:** round
**Guide number:** 1
**Note:** thumb piece marked:
"New Gem Newark, N.J. Made in U.S.A."
this company was probably associated with the Gem Spoon Co. of Troy, N.Y.
ca. 1932–1940

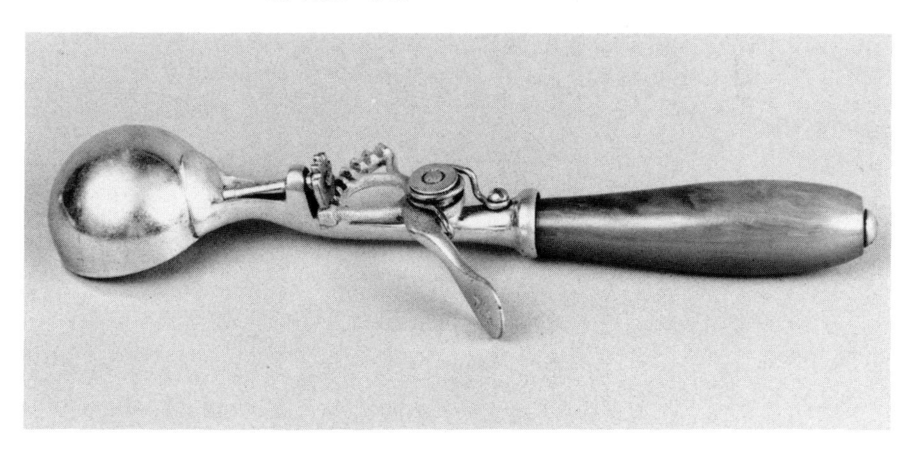

E-6. New Gem Manufacturing Co.,? Newark, N.J.
**Material:** brass, nickel plated
**Handle:** green, "marbleized" material
**Length:** 10″
**Bowl:** round
**Guide number:** 2
**Note:** thumb piece marked:
"Nu Gem Pat. Pend."
ca. 1930's

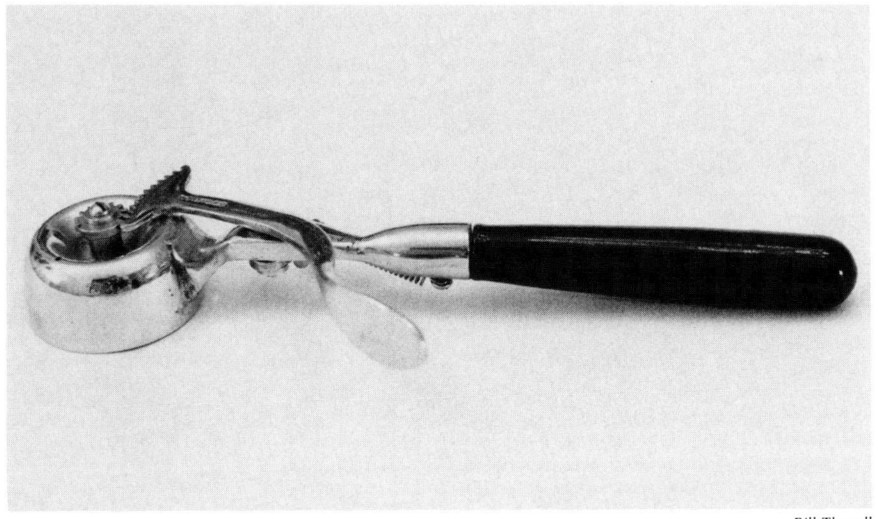

*Bill Thunell*

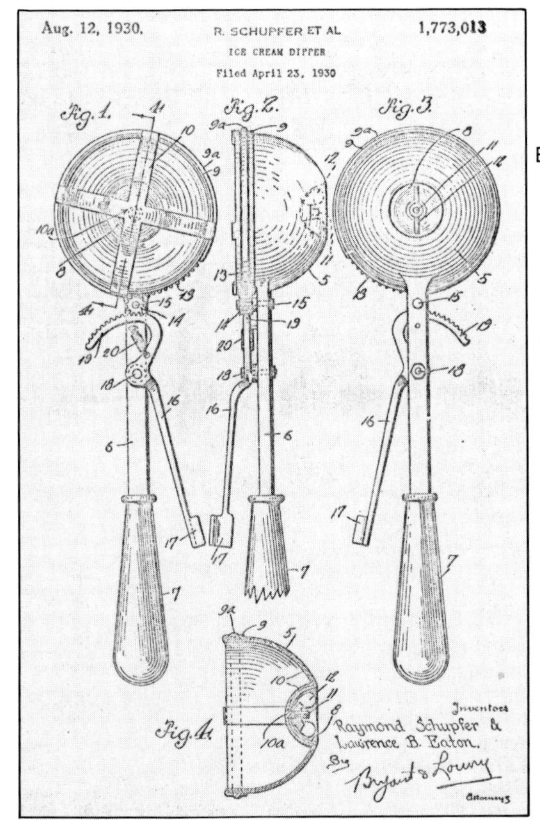


E-7. Schupfer and Eaton Co., Pawtucket, R.I.
**Patent number:** 1773013
**Patent filed:** 23 Apr 1930
**Patent issued:** 12 Aug 1930
**Inventors:** Raymond Schupfer (Pawtucket, R.I.)
Lawrence B. Eaton (Saylesville, R.I.)
**Material:** brass, nickel plated
**Handle:** wood
**Bowl:** round, cavity inside
**Guide number:** 4
**Note:** thumb lever marked "Pat. 1773013"
used for making "College Ice" cones, with a fruit on top

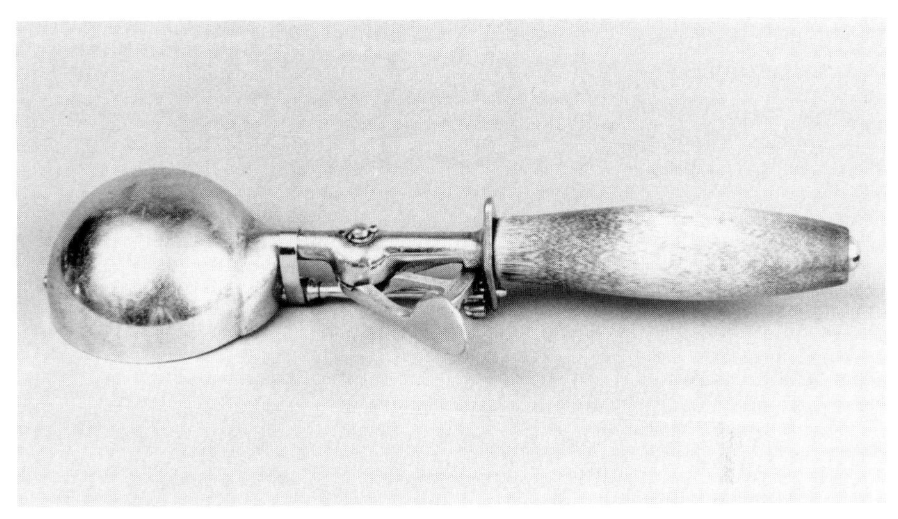

E-8. Gilchrist Co., Newark, N.J.
**Patent number:** 1862527
**Patent filed:** 31 Mar 1930
**Patent issued:** 14 Jun 1932
**Inventor:** John W. Cox
(Newark, N.J.)
**Material:** brass, chromium plated
**Handle:** wood, colored differently for each size
**Length:** 10″
**Bowl:** round
**Guide number:** 1
**Note:** scraper rod marked "Gilchrist 35"
this is the short shank version of the popular Gilchrist 31 model, introduced in 1930.

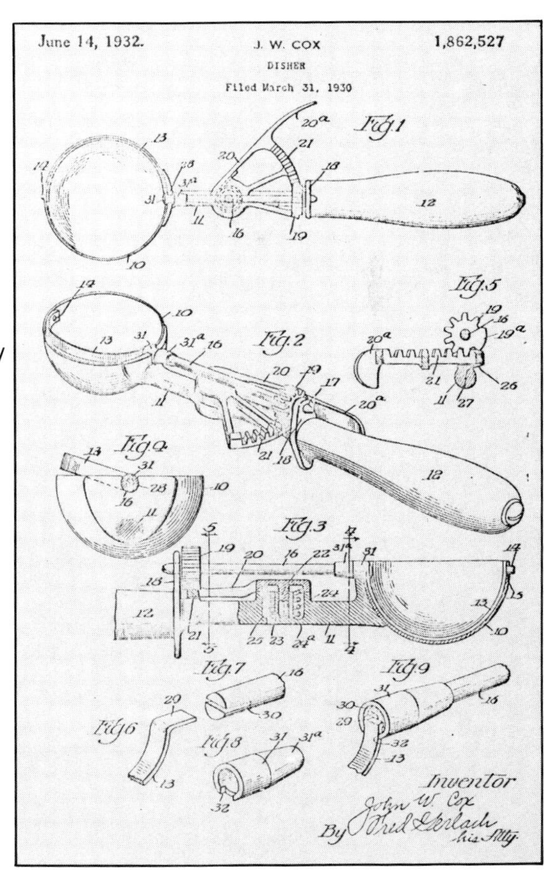

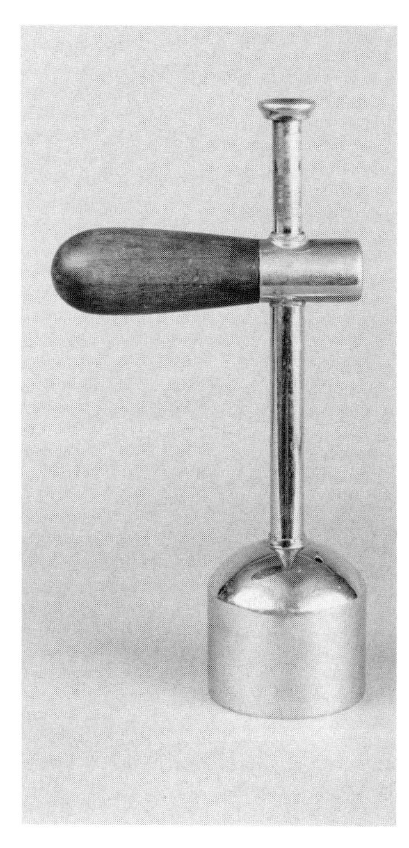

E-9. Unknown Maker
**Patent number:** 1826009
**Patent filed:** 14 June 1930
**Patent issued:** 6 Oct. 1931
**Inventor:** Edward J. Martineau (Seattle, Wash.)
**Material:** white metal?, nickel plated
**Handle:** wood
**Length:** 9″
**Bowl:** cylinder
**Guide number:** 4
**Note:** handle marked "Patented" plunger mechanism

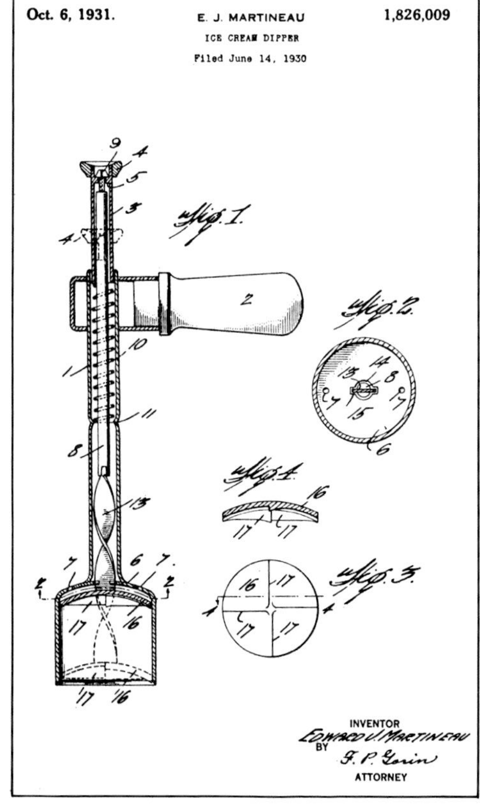

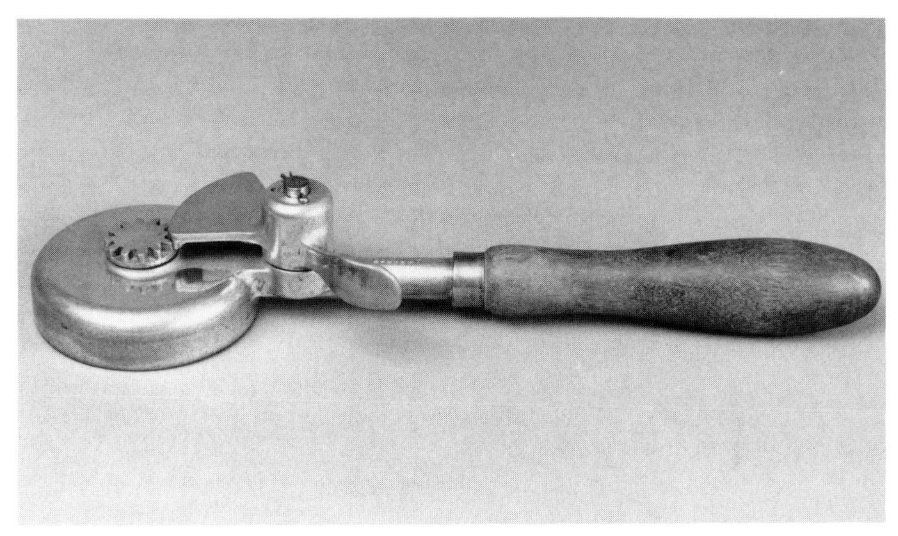

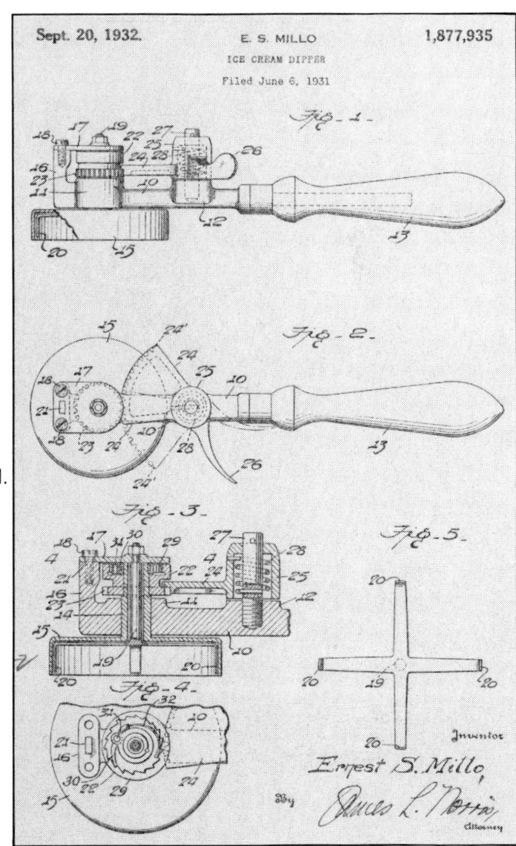


E-10. Unknown maker
**Patent number:** 1877935
**Patent filed:** 6 Jun. 1931
**Patent issued:** 20 Sept. 1932
**Inventor:** Ernest S. Millo (Bronx, N.Y.)
**Material:** aluminum
**Handle:** wood
**Length:** 10¼″
**Bowl:** disk shaped
**Guide number:** 5
**Note:** shank marked "Economy Patent Apld. For"
used to fill dixie cup type containers

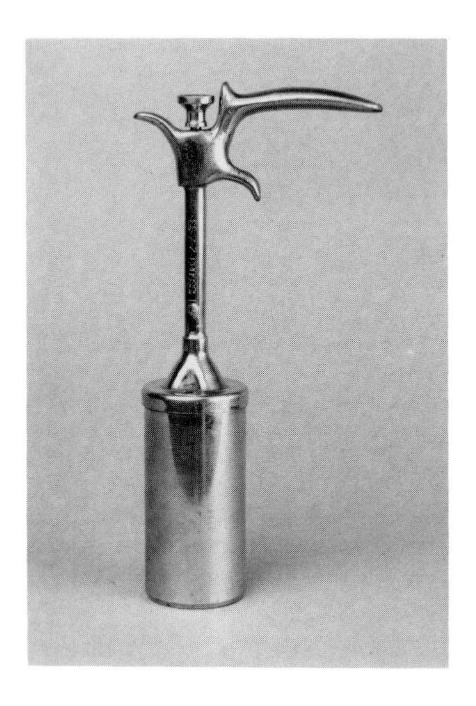

E-11. Perection Equipment Co., Kansas City, Mo.
**Patent number:** 1896083
**Patent filed:** 16 Oct. 1931
**Patent issued:** 7 Feb. 1933
**Inventor:** Ora E. Harris (Kearney, Neb.)
**Material:** brass, nickel plated
**Handle:** same
**Length:** 8½″
**Bowl:** cylinder (3½″)
**Guide number:** 3
**Note:** shank marked "Pat. 1896083 2-7-33" plunger mechanism used for making "Sky-Hi Cones"

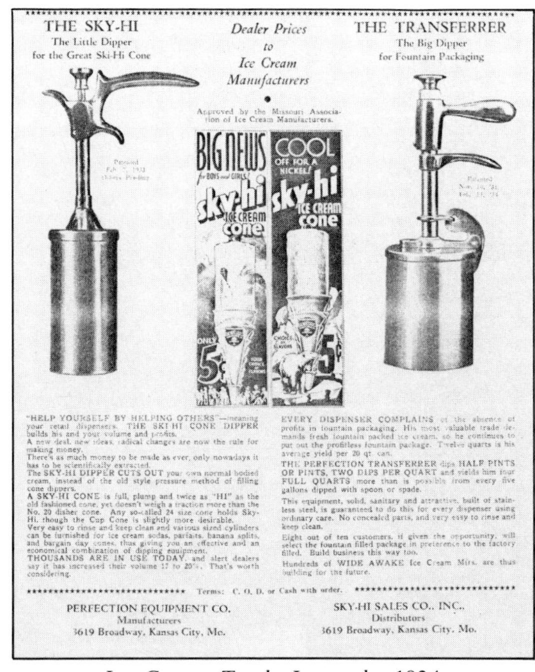


*Ice Cream Trade Journal*—1934

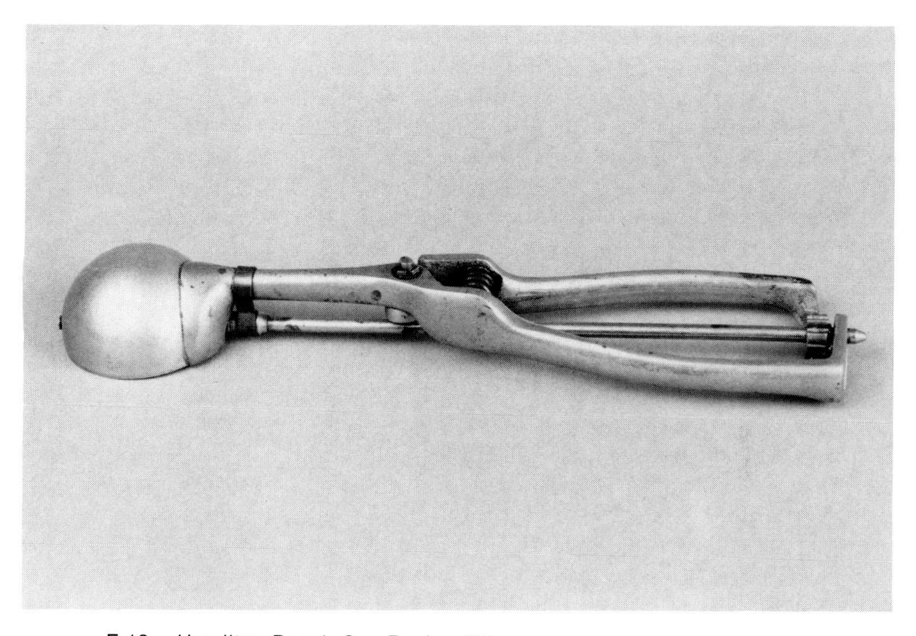

E-12. Hamilton Beach Co., Racine, Wisc.
**Patent number:** 1109576
**Patent filed:** 26 Sept. 1907
**Patent issued:** 1 Sept. 1914
**Inventor:** Raymond G. Gilchrist (Newark, N.J.)
**Material:** brass, chromium plated
**Handle:** same, squeeze type
**Length:** 10″
**Bowl:** round
**Guide number:** 1
**Note:** scraper rod marked
"Hamilton-Beach 30"
scraper marked
"Pat. No. 1961655"
this model was made after Ham. Beach acquired Gilchrist Co. in 1931

**Hamilton Beach Disher No. 30**
(GILCHRIST MODEL)

**Ideal for Left-Handed Dispensers**

A slight closing of the hand discharges the ice cream. The scraper is rotated by pressure of the hand on the metal handle. Can be taken apart for cleaning and put together quickly.

Bowl and scraper are made of 18% nickel silver, nickel plated. All other metal parts are of everlasting, rust-proof bronze, heavily nickel plated and beautifully polished.

Nine Sizes: 6, 8, 10, 12, 16, 20, 24, 30 and 40 to the quart. Shipping weight per dozen about 12 pounds.

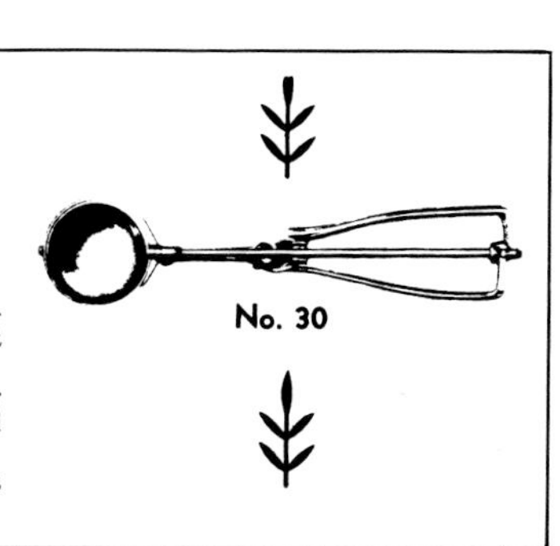


*Ed Marks*

Hamilton Beach Co. catalog—1934

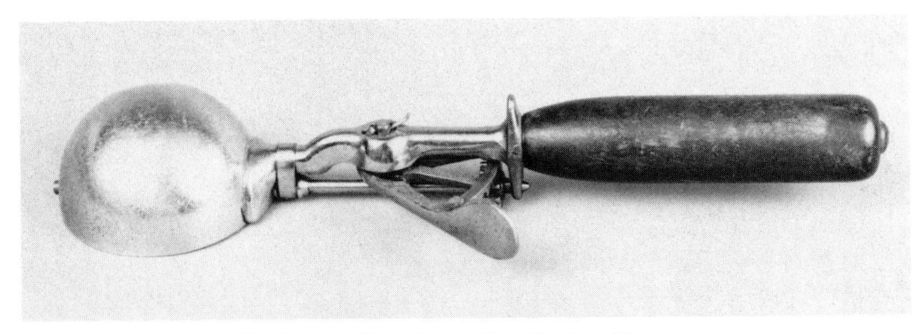

E-13. Hamilton Beach Co., Racine, Wisc.
**Patent number:** 1862527
**Patent filed:** 31 Mar. 1930
**Patent issued:** 14 June 1932
**Inventor:** John W. Cox (Newark, N.J.)
**Material:** brass, chromium plated
**Handle:** wood (also bakelite)
**Length:** 10″
**Bowl:** round
**Guide number:** 1
**Note:** scraper rod marked
"Hamilton-Beach 31"

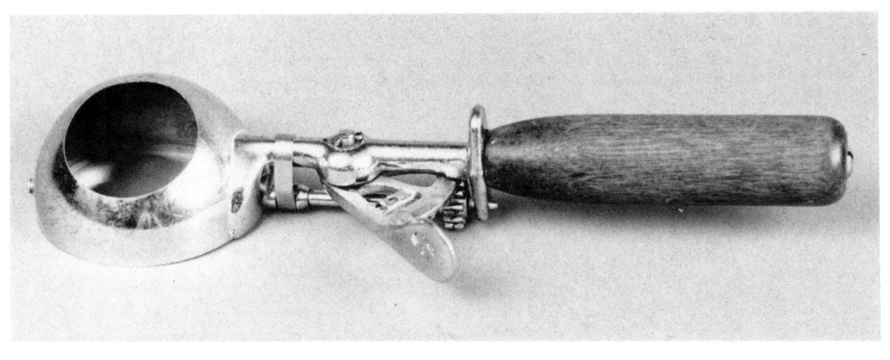

E-14. Hamilton Beach Co., Racine, Wisc.
**Patent number:** 1862527
**Patent filed:** 31 Mar. 1930
**Patent issued:** 14 June 1932
**Inventor:** John W. Cox (Newark, N.J.)
**Material:** brass, chromium plated
**Handle:** wood (also bakelite)
**Length:** 10″
**Bowl:** round, with hole cut in side
**Guide number:** 1
**Note:** scraper rod marked
"Hamilton Beach Pat. No. 1862527"
thumb piece marked
"NO-PAK 31"
the No-Pak feature was designed to give 10–16% more servings per gallon, because it didn't compress the ice cream. It was available on all models.

5. Hamilton Beach Co., Racine, Wisc.
**Patent number:** 1615939
**Patent filed:** 17 June 1925
**Patent issued:** 1 Feb. 1927
**Inventor:** Harrison D. Flegel (Racine, Wisc.)
**Material:** brass, chromium plated
**Handle:** bakelite
**Length:** 8½″
**Bowl:** round
**Guide number:** 1
**Note:** thumb piece marked "Hamilton Beach Mfg. Co. Racine, Wis. Patent Nos. 1615939-1829442"
scraper marked "Pat. No. 1961655"
this model was made after Ham. Beach acquired Arnold Electric Co. in 1931

YOUR CUSTOMERS SAY . . . . . "A DISHER

*Your customers DO notice your dishers. Bright, new dishers look clean and inviting.*

Take an old disher and sterilize it. But it still looks unclean if it's old and shabby and dull. You can't afford to take a chance on old dishers. Your customers form an immediate impression of your service and sanitation from the way you serve their ice cream.

New dishers are a vast improvement over the old kind. They are designed especially to handle hard ice cream easier and faster. Their heavy chromium plate stays brilliant . . . looks clean and appetizing.

**Hamilton Beach Disher No. 51**
(ARNOLD MODEL)

**The Most Remarkable Disher on the Market**

New dishers represent such a small investment, when compared with what they do to build business, that every fountain can afford the best. This No. 51 Disher, leader of the Hamilton Beach line, has every feature needed in a disher.

**Bakelite Handle**—Black, with a different colored tip for each size. Strong and tight; never loosens nor breaks.

**Hamilton Beach Disher No. 50-A**
(ARNOLD MODEL)

This is exactly the same as the Arnold Model No. 51 except the No. 50-A has a hardwood handle and therefore the price is slightly lower. All other specifications are the same as for the No. 51, viz: chromium finish; edge-sharpened bowl; short shank; color marker. Made in seven sizes: 8, 10, 12, 16, 20, 24 and 30 to the quart. Shipping weight per dozen about 12 lbs.

**Edge-Sharpened Bowl**—Made of heavy gauge 18% nickel silver; retains its shape under the most severe use; bowl is electrically welded to the shank. The edge of the bowl is sharpened. The Disher cuts through hard ice cream without compressing it. You get more servings per gallon.

**Chromium Finish**—The extra thick chromium plated finish is always bright and appetizing.

**Short Shank**—The patented thumb piece design makes possible a very short shank, giving greater leverage and requiring a minimum of wrist pressure.

Seven Sizes: 8, 10, 12, 16, 20, 24 and 30 to the quart. Shipping weight per dozen about 12 lbs.

*Ed Marks*

Hamilton Beach Co. catalog—1934

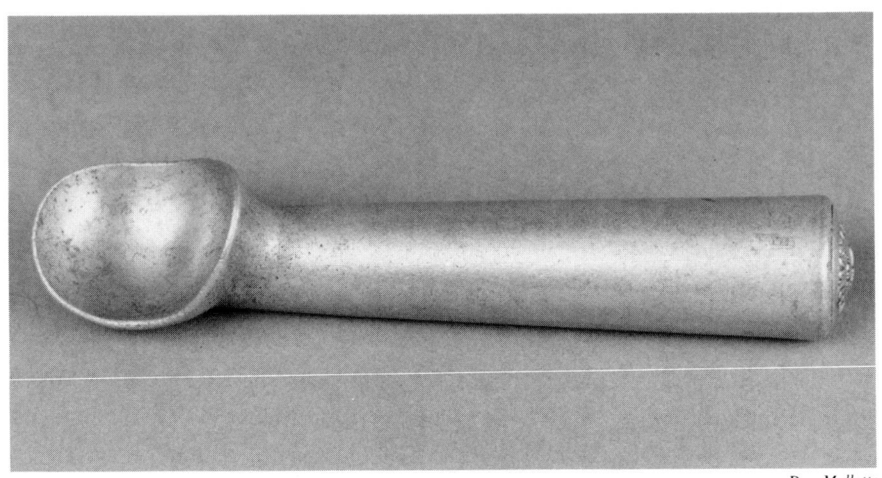

*Dan Mallette*

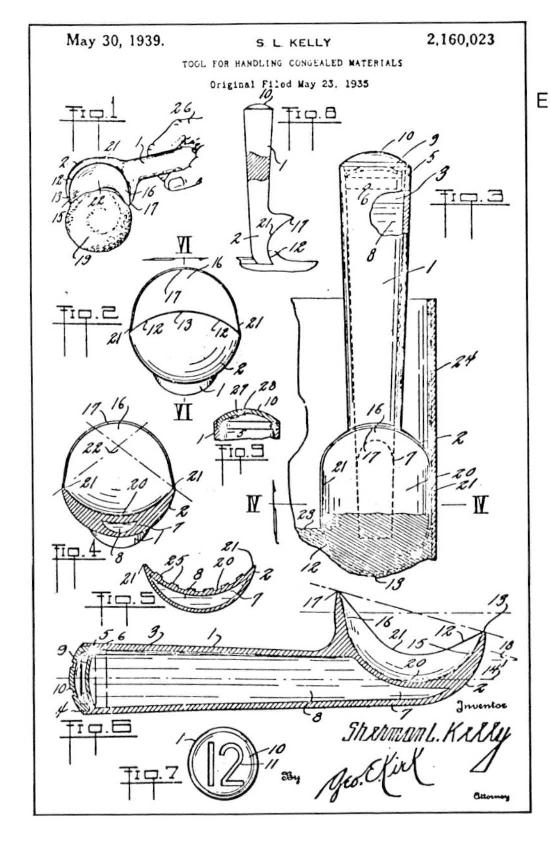


E-16. Zeroll Co., Toledo, Ohio
**Patent number:** 1974051
**Patent filed:** 14 Apr 1933
**Patent issued:** 18 Sept 1934
**Inventor:** Sherman L. Kelly (Toledo, Ohio)
**Material:** aluminum
**Handle:** same
**Length:** 7″
**Bowl:** half round
**Guide number:** 1
**Note:** plug on end of handle marked "The Zeroll Co. Toledo, Ohio Pats. Pend."
handle marked "Zeroll"
handle filled with a self-defrosting liquid

# THE ZEROLL COMPANY

**Toledo, Ohio**

**PRODUCTS**
**Zeroll Non-Mechanical Self-Defrosting Ice Cream Dipper**

The Zeroll Non-Mechanical Dipper completely revolutionizes the old conventional oftentimes wasteful method of dipping ice cream.

Zeroll **rolls** up a big-looking uniform portion of ice cream with rapid ease. It eliminates compression losses and definitely increases retail profits from 10% to 20%. More servings per gallon can be made with Zeroll because Zeroll **rolls up** the serving instead of scraping or squeezing it together. And yet in spite of the larger looking portion served with Zeroll, it actually weighs less than a compressed serving made with a conventional dipper.

Patented and patents pending

With Zeroll it is unnecessary to soften up hard ice cream to "dipping temperature." Zeroll is designed to serve any ice cream with speed and ease. Very little muscular effort is required to dip even very hard ice cream. This advantage enables attendants to speed up service and does away with any straining and fatigue.

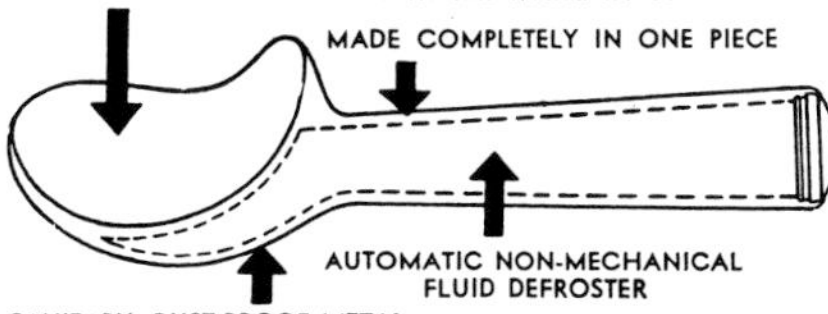


## AUTOMATIC NON-MECHANICAL DEFROSTING ELIMINATES ICE PELLETS IN ICE CREAM

Ice cream cannot freeze or stick to Zeroll because of an automatic defrosting element sealed within the handle. As soon as the ball of ice cream has been rolled up the heat transmitted from the handle of Zeroll by the fluid releases the ice cream to cone or dish. This defrosting arrangement

**ZEROLL** is trouble-free and is entirely automatic. It does not depreciate or wear out nor lose its defrosting power. It also eliminates the necessity of placing Zeroll in water when not in use. Zeroll slides or cuts into the ice cream without dripping water into the cream.

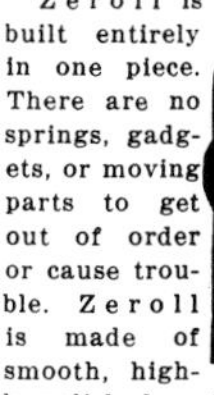

Proper method for rolling portion

## ONE PIECE NON-MECHANICAL CONSTRUCTION

Zeroll is built entirely in one piece. There are no springs, gadgets, or moving parts to get out of order or cause trouble. Zeroll is made of smooth, highly polished sanitary metal. Cleaning and polishing is easy and simple because there are no crevices, holes, fittings or corners in a Zeroll Dipper.

## DEALERS ENTHUSIASTIC WHEREVER ZEROLLS ARE USED

Even a day's trial of Zeroll quickly convinces any dealer that these new dippers will make more money for him— in more servings per gallon and in reduced labor. Zerolls are also trade stimulators because of the larger-looking portions they serve.

Finished portion ready to serve

## SIZES

Nos. 12-16-20-24-30. Price, $2.25 each in aluminum. The price of each is the same for all sizes. Special discounts are allowed on dozen orders.

*Reprint of advertisement from the 1936 issue of Dairy Industries Catalog File.*

*Carl Abel*

Dairy Industries Catalog File—1936

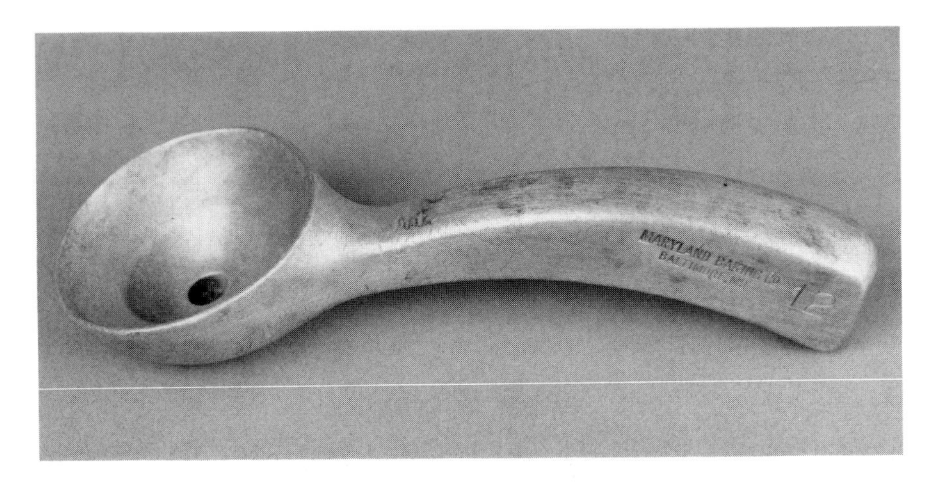


E-17. Maryland Baking Co., Baltimore, Md.
**Material:** aluminum
**Length:** 6½″
**Guide number:** 1
**Note:** handle marked
"Maryland Baking Co., Baltimore, Md."
ca. 1930–1940

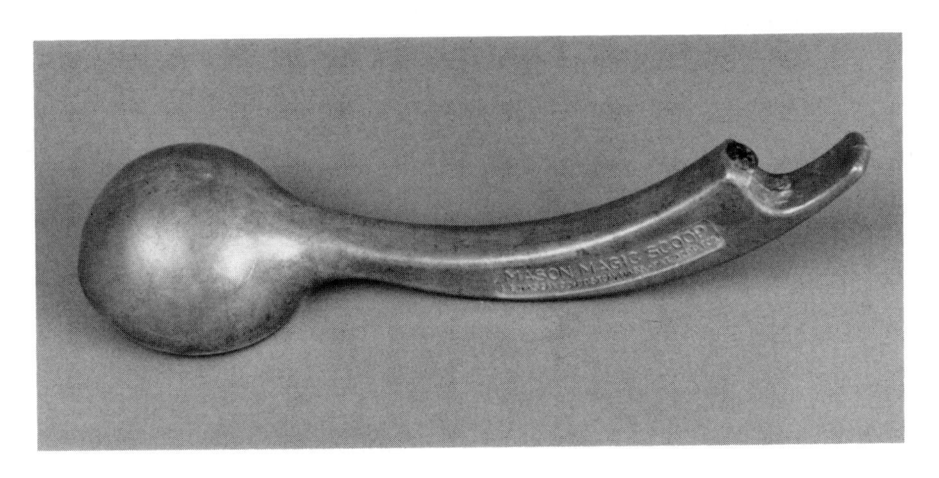


E-18. L. E. Mason Co., Boston, Mass.
**Material:** aluminum
**Length:** 8″
**Guide number:** 1
**Note:** handle marked
"Mason Magic Scoop L. E. Mason Co. Boston, Mass.
Pat. App'd. For"
ca. 1930's?

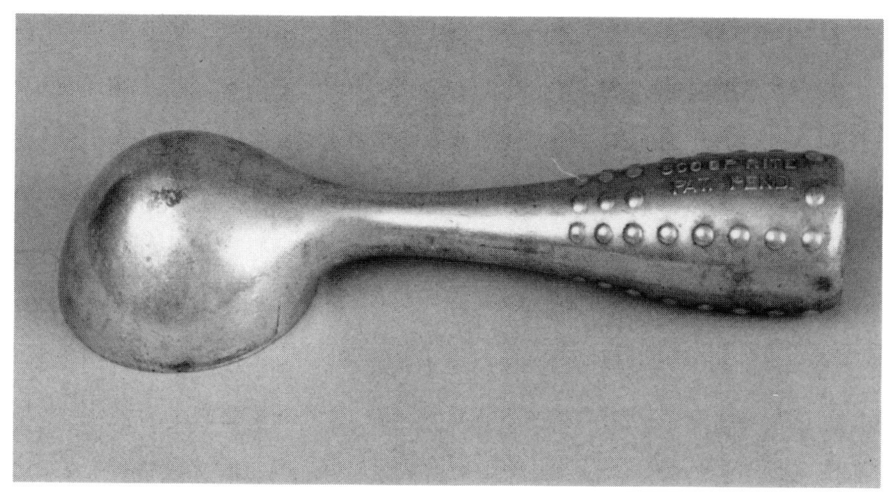


E-19. Scoop Rite
**Material:** aluminum
**Length:** 6½″
**Guide number:** 1
**Note:** handle marked
"Scoop Rite Pat. Pend."
ca. 1930's?

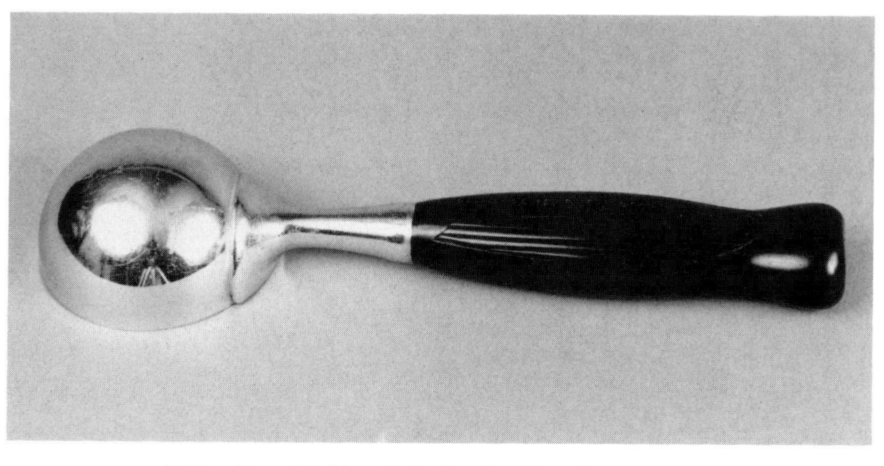

E-20. Benedict Manufacturing Co., East Syracuse, N.Y.
**Material:** brass, nickel plated
**Handle:** bakelite
**Length:** 8″
**Bowl:** round
**Guide number:** 1
**Note:** handle marked
"Benedict Indestructo"
has no operating mechanism
ca. 1930–1940

E-21. Benedict Manufacturing Co., East Syracuse, N.Y.
**Material:** brass, nickel plated
**Handle:** bakelite
**Length:** 9½″
**Guide number:** 1
**Note:** end of handle marked
"Benedict Indestructo"
used to pack ice cream into cartons
ca. 1930–1940

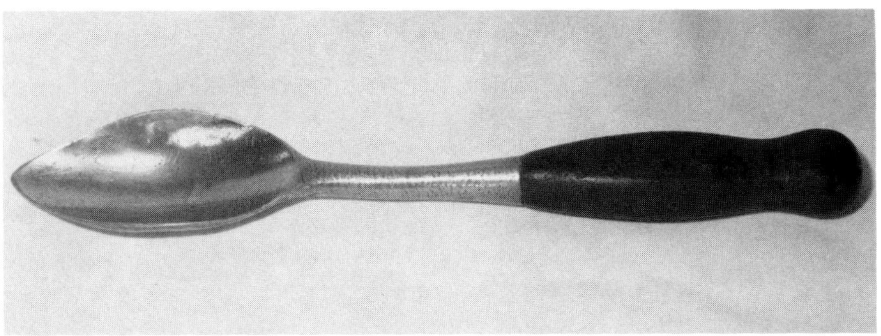

*Bill Burg*

E-22. Rainbow
**Material:** brass, nickel plated
**Handle:** bakelite
**Length:** 11″
**Bowl:** spade with curved sides
**Guide number:** 1
**Note:** handle marked
"Rainbow"
used to make multi-flavored "rainbow" cones
ca. 1935

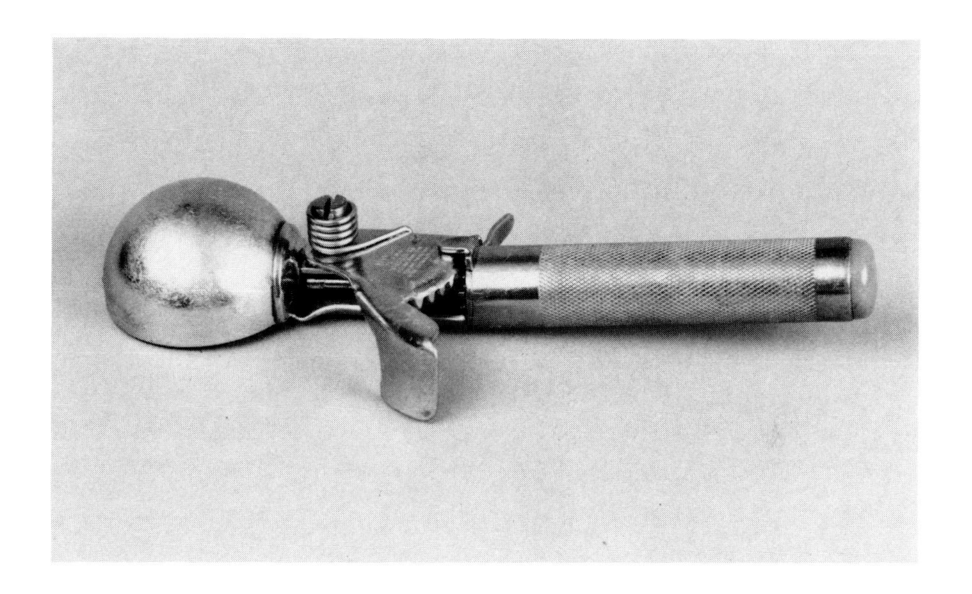

E-23. Myers Manufacturing Co., Galesburg, Ill.
**Patent number:** 2041200
**Patent filed:** 16 Feb. 1934
**Patent issued:** 19 May 1936
**Inventor:** Louis Myers (Chicago, Ill.)
**Material:** brass, nickel plated
**Handle:** same
**Length:** 8½″
**Bowl:** round
**Guide number:** 1
**Note:** thumb piece marked "Myers DeLuxe Disher Pat. no. 1903791 Pat. no. 2041200"

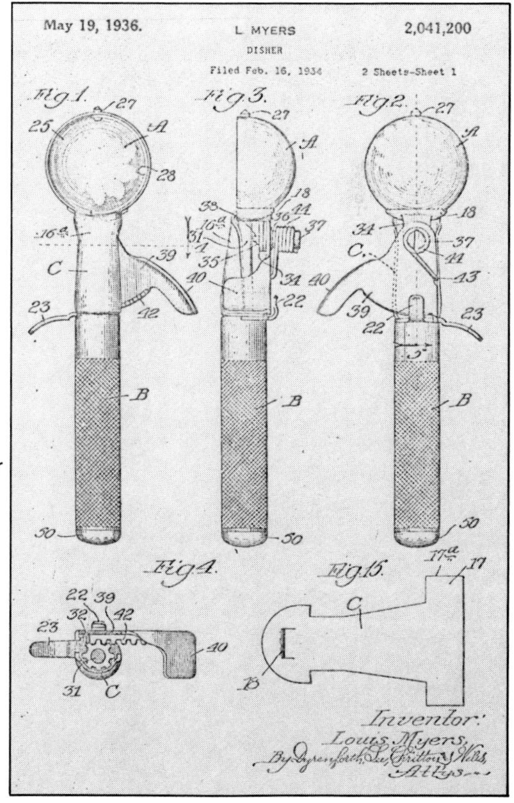

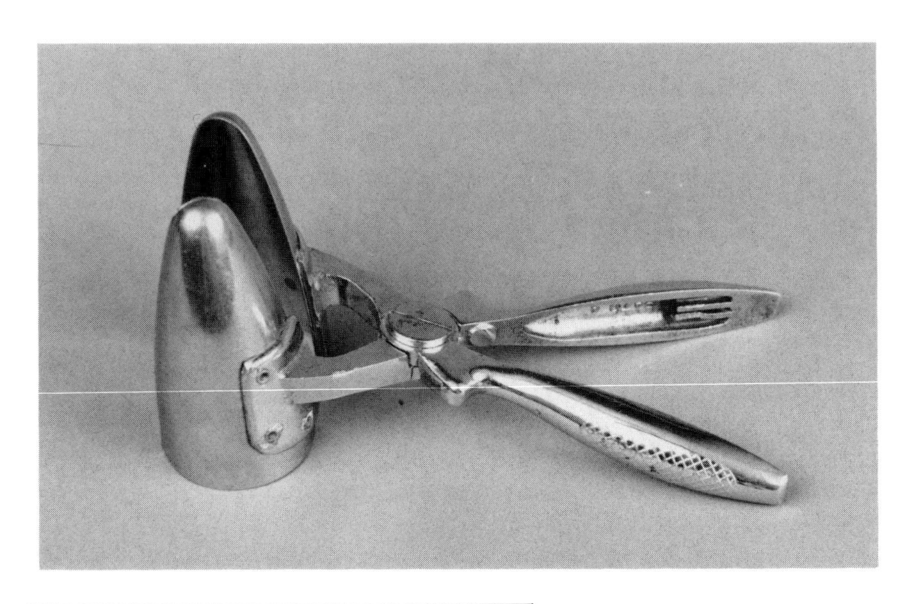

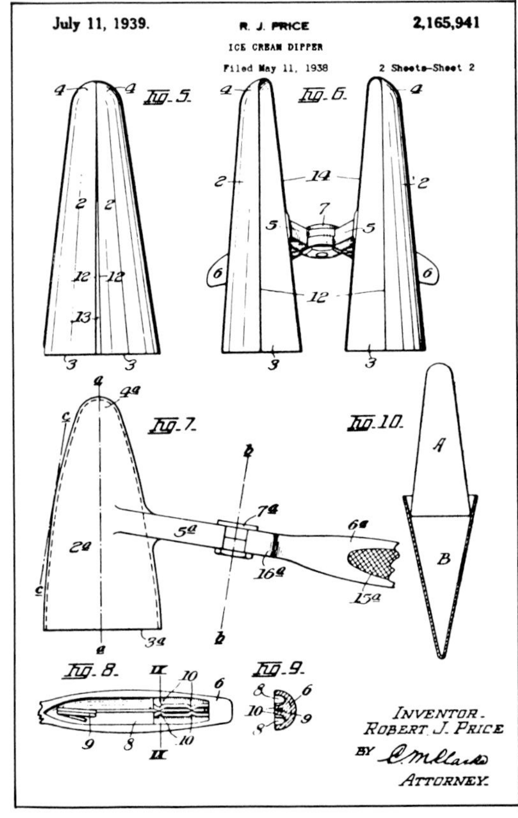


E-24. Unknown maker
**Patent number:** 2165941
**Patent filed:** 11 May 1938
**Patent issued:** 11 July 1939
**Inventor:** Robert J. Price (Uniontown, Pa.)
**Material:** white metal, chromium plated
**Handle:** same, squeeze type
**Length:** 7½"
**Bowl:** cone (3½")
**Guide number:** 3
**Note:** inside handle marked "PATD"
used to fill cones (point on top)
this example missing spring

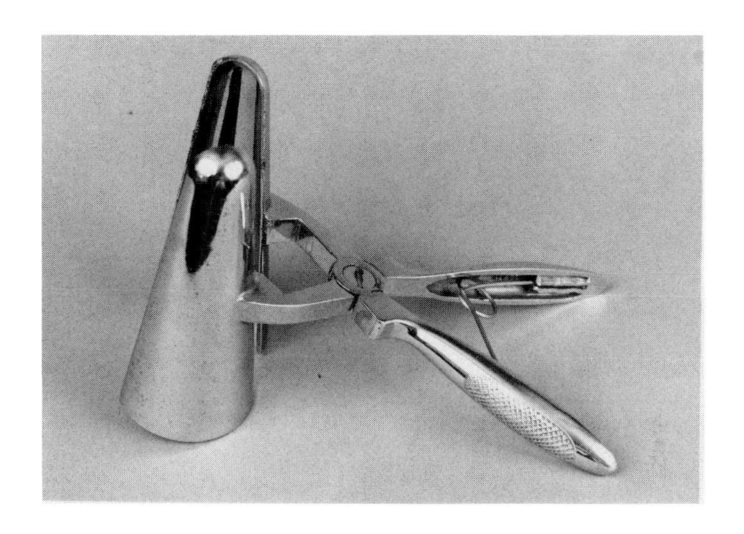

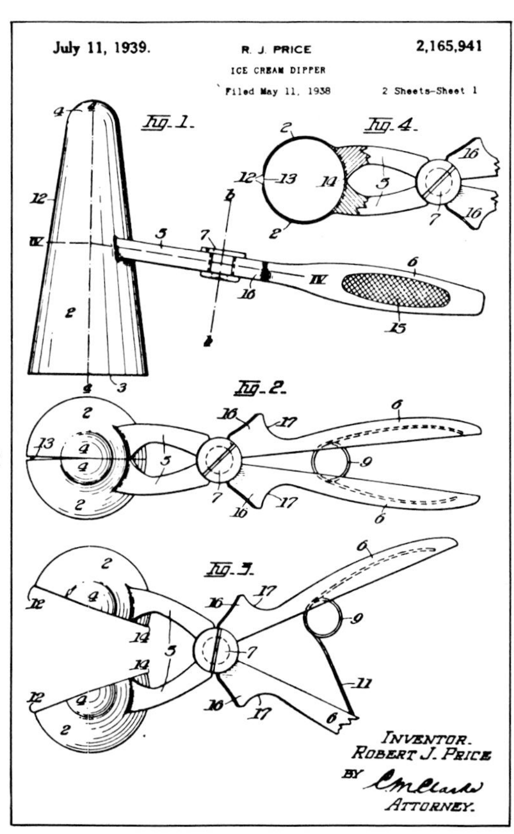


E-25. Unknown maker
**Patent number:** 2165941
**Patent filed:** 11 May 1938
**Patent issued:** 11 July 1939
**Inventor:** Robert J. Price (Uniontown, Pa.)
**Material:** white metal, chromium plated
**Handle:** same, squeeze type
**Length:** 8″
**Bowl:** cone (4½″)
**Guide number:** 3
**Note:** inside handle marked "PATD"
used to fill cones (point on top)

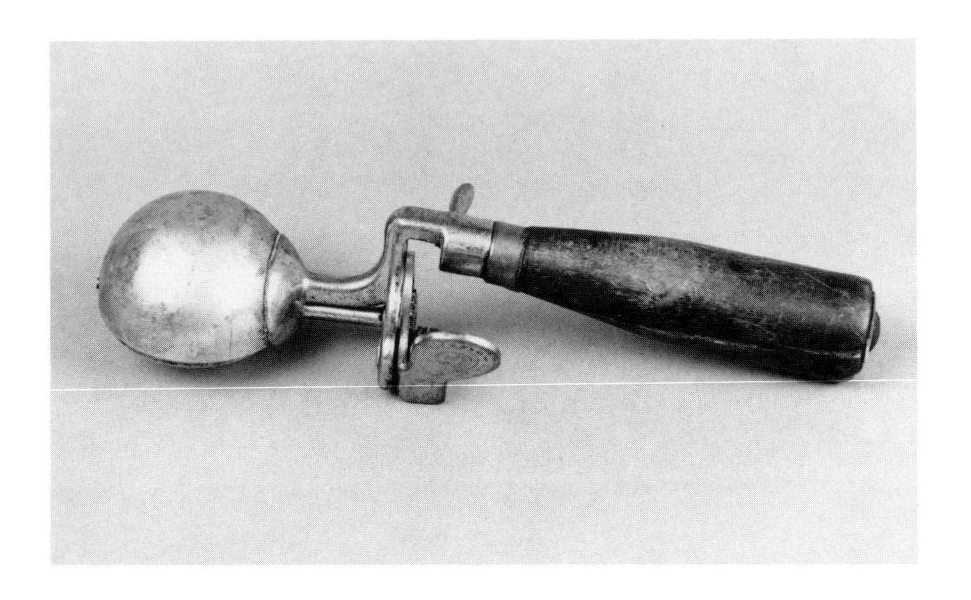

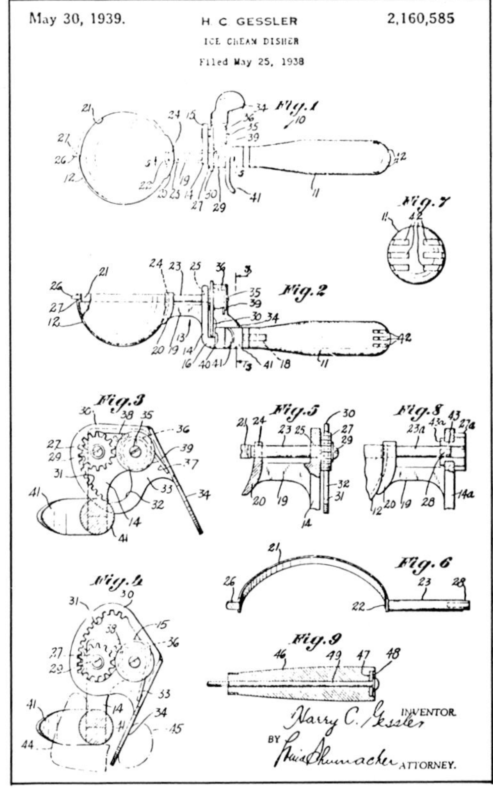


E-26. Measuring Device Corporation, New York, N.Y.
**Patent number:** 2160585
**Patent filed:** 25 May 1938
**Patent issued:** 30 May 1939
**Inventor:** Harry C. Gessler (Brooklyn, N.Y.)
**Material:** brass, nickel plated
**Handle:** wood
**Length:** 8½″
**Bowl:** round
**Guide number:** 1
**Note:** thumb piece marked "Medco-NYC-Pat. Pend. U.S. Pat Off. Pat. no. 2160585"

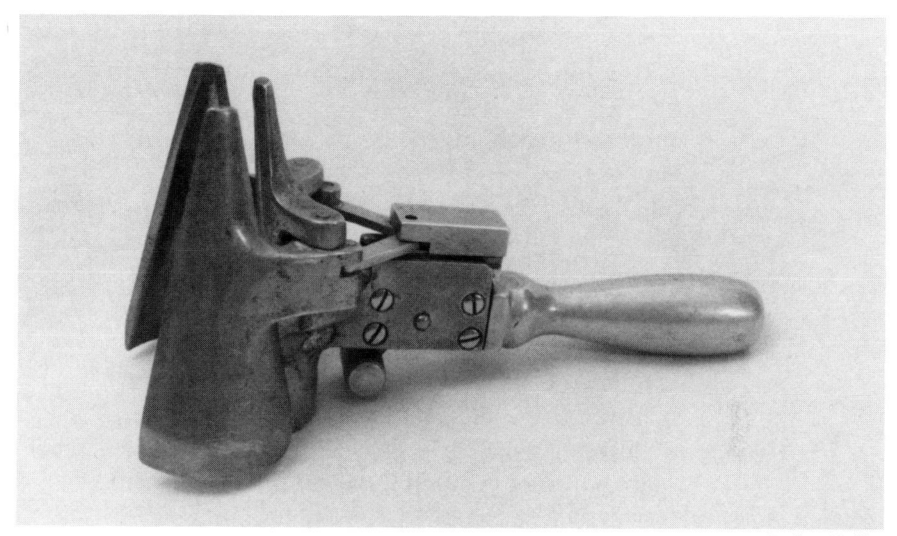

*Barbara Hadden*

E-27. Feller Cone Scoop Co., Canton, Ohio
**Patent number:** 2,259,337
**Patent filed:** 9 Apr. 1940
**Patent issued:** 14 Oct. 1941
**Inventor:** John E. O. Feller (Canton, Ohio)
**Material:** aluminum
**Handle:** same
**Length:** 7½"
**Bowl:** conical
**Guide number:** 5
**Note:** handle marked "Feller Pat. Pend." when thumb lever is pushed, bowl divides into three sections dropping ice cream into cone.

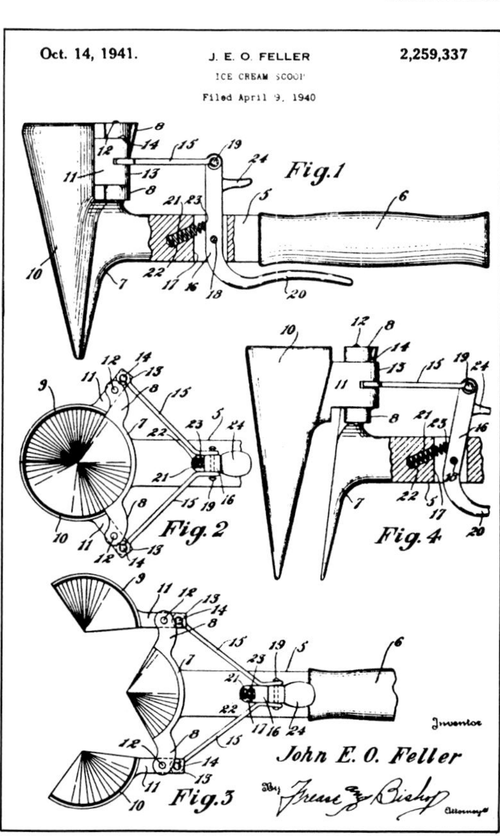

# Chapter 11

# More Scoop on Scoops

## Part Terminology

Each part of an ice cream disher has a specific name. It is not practical here to list every part on every disher, because of the great variety. For general purposes, however, we will list the parts of the Gilchrist #31 disher. The terminology can be adapted to fit most other dishers. From the *Gilchrist Catalog No. 20,* the parts are as follows:

| | |
|---|---|
| (1) handle | (6) scraper rod |
| (2) shank | (7) spring clip |
| (3) bowl | (8) thumb piece |
| (4) trunnion | (9) cog |
| (5) scraper | not shown: spring, cotter pin |

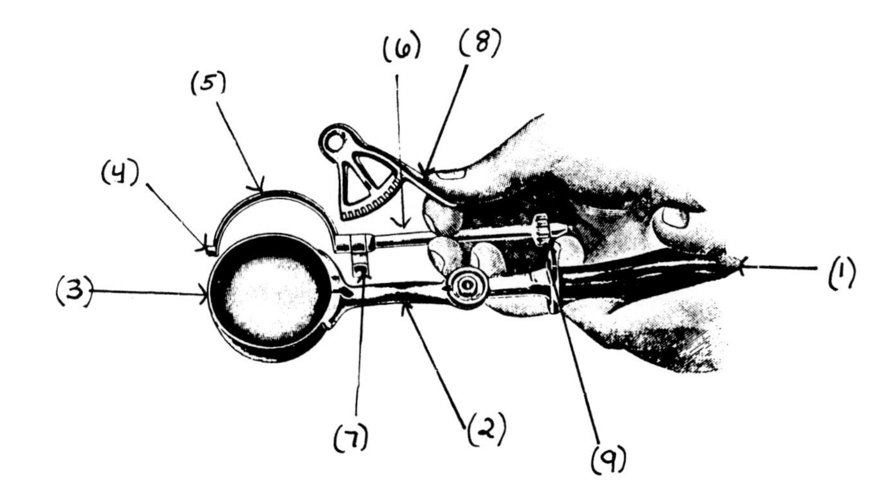

## Cleaning

After you purchase that special disher, and before you add it to your collection, it should be thoroughly cleaned. This is especially true if you intend to use it. Many dishers haven't been cleaned since the last time they were used, some 50 or 60 years ago.

The first step is to take the disher completely apart. Most come apart quite easily, but pay close attention to this step, because you will have to reassemble it when you are finished. Be careful not to break or lose any pieces. The cotter pin can be removed with needle nose pliers, in a cloth, to prevent scratches. Next, clean the brass thoroughly, especially around the spring, with hot soapy water. An old toothbrush works great to get in the crevices. After drying, polish with a soft cloth and a fine polish, such as Simichrome. The polish residue can then be washed off with hot water, dried, then reassembled.

For the early steel and tin dishers, #0000 steel wool can be used to remove light rust. Then, a very light coat of oil can be rubbed on for protection. I would not recommend using these dishers for ice cream, for sanitary reasons.

Once you have cleaned your disher, it's appearance has generally improved 100%, and it is much more attractive in a display.

## Displaying Your Collection

I would guess that there are almost as many methods of displaying ice cream dishers, as there are collectors. Each collector has his personal favorite, based in part upon the amount of space available. Some collectors simply line them on shelves, while others use glass cabinets or display cases, which can run into some money. Some mount them directly on the wall, in arrangements, and still others tie them with fish line onto wall racks. Whatever method you choose, depends upon how much time and creativity you want to put into it. Let me offer one suggestion. If you have any dishers that are lacquered, don't put them near a source of heat. The lacquer will discolor and crack.

I will describe the method I have chosen for my collection. It consists of a wooden rack with hanging pegs, hung across the top of the wall. This has the obvious advantages of being inexpensive, utilizes seldom used wall space, keeps scoops out of the reach of ever curious small children, and displays everything at a glance.

The wood I use is a pine 1 × 4″, stained, and cut to the proper length to fit across the top of the wall. Each disher is hung with the bowl up, on two ¼″ dowels, placed in holes drilled at a slightly upward angle, near the bottom of the board. The dowels should be 1–1½″ apart, with each disher about 4″ apart. Some odd shaped dishers may require special placement of

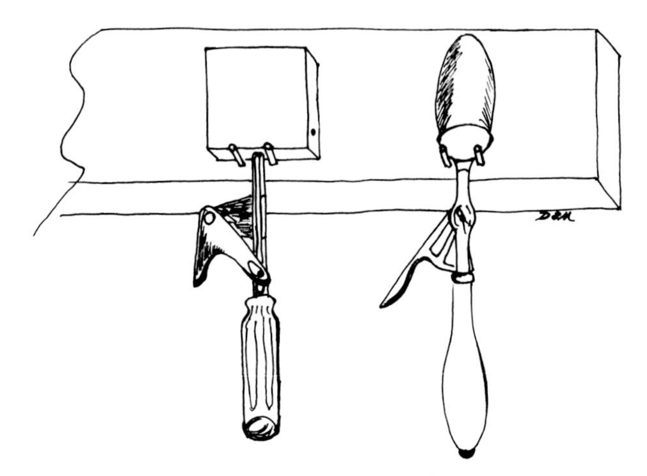

Ice cream scoop display rack.

the dowels. The whole rack can then be hung with serrated picture hangers. Each disher can be lifted off easily for examination. They can be grouped according to manufacturers, years, sizes, types, or any number of ways. Use your imagination!

## Original Boxes

An item of particular interest to ice cream scoop collectors, is the box that they were packaged in. Very few of these boxes have survived through the years. The reason being, that once the disher was unpacked, for use at the fountain, the box had no further use, and was discarded. Probably only 5–10% of the original boxes are still around.

Some of the boxes, of course, are much nicer than others. The Dover disher box is very plain, except for the end flap, which has the name and address of the company. On the other hand, the IcyPi box has a full illustration of the scoop on top. The other sides of the box tell of it's advantages,

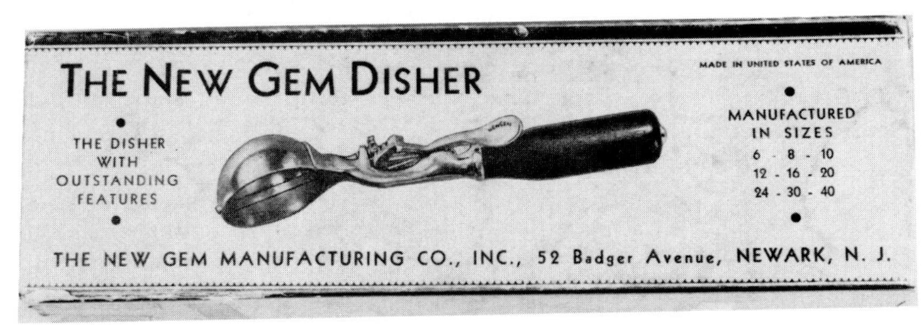


Gem Spoon Co. box.

how to use it, and how to clean it. The package is very attractive. The Gilchrist #31 box shows a dis-assembly diagram, for ease in cleaning. Hamilton Beach advertised their other fountain product lines on the box, as well as a picture of their chromium plated disher. The New Gem Co. also had attractive boxes.

If you find one of the original boxes, by all means, don't throw it away, even though it may be damaged. A lucky collector can add 10–20% to the value of his disher, if it has the original box!

## Reproductions

As with anything of value, one should always be cautious of reproductions. At the time of this writing, I know of no intentional reproductions of early ice cream dishers. *However,* there are several recent dishers that are being mistakenly sold for the earlier Gilchrist #30 model.

One such disher is marked, "Standard Made in Germany", on the bottom, and "D.R.G.M." on the scraper. It is a good quality imitation of the squeeze handle Gilchrist, except that under the nickel plating, the bowl is brass, unlike the early model. It was made in the 1950's or 1960's.

The second imitation is marked, "Dairy Fresh" on the handle. A paper label states that it was "Made in Taiwan", but this is easily removed. The giveaway is the inferior quality workmanship and the rough marks on the brass. This scoop sells for $10–12 at various import stores.

Beware of these scoops when you are buying for your collection. Also, watch for alterations in the older ones; new or replaced handles, springs, scrapers, etc.

## Size

Ice cream dishers came in a wide variety of sizes. The size of a disher is usually found expressed as a number on the scraper or the shank. The number indicates the number of level scoops to a quart of ice cream. Most dishers were made in a number of different sizes. The Gilchrist #31, for example was made in 9 sizes: 6, 8, 10, 12, 16, 20, 24, 30, and 40 scoops to the quart. Size 6 was the largest and size 40 was the smallest. Some of the earlier conical dishers were made in sizes 5 and 10. Mosteller made a tiny size 60 disher.

The size is related to the use of the disher. Generally, the larger sizes were used for sundaes, while the smaller sizes were used for cones, sodas, and samples.

The following concoctions are taken from the 1915 edition of *The Dispensers Formulary or Soda Water Guide*. They illustrate some of the fancy soda fountain creations of the period, and how the different sizes of dippers were actually used.

### High School

Take three portions of chocolate ice cream (No. 16 disher) and place them in triangular form on a flat ice cream saucer; then place some whipped cream in the center and dust over with finely chopped walnuts, or, if preferred, a Maraschino cherry may be used. Price 15 cents.

### Sorority

Into a tall goblet put one No. 12 dipperful of chocolate ice cream, then add a small quantity of chopped nuts and a small ladleful of maple syrup. Put a No. 16 dipperful of vanilla ice cream on top of this and over it put a spoonful of thick bitter-sweet chocolate. Top off with whipped cream and a chocolate-dipped maraschino cherry. Charge 15 cents. (A. F. Perkins.)

## Related Ice Cream Collectables

The field of ice cream and soda fountain collectables is broad. Many collectors of ice cream dishers, also collect related items. Virtually any piece of equipment or advertising used in a soda fountain, falls into this category. Included, are such items as glassware, serving pieces, milkshake machines, cone holders, syrup bottles and dispensers, strawholders, signs, trays, molds, furniture, and even backbars. *Anything* used in the making or serving of ice cream is collected.

One field of interest, to ice cream collectors, is in the area of paper and advertising pieces. Most of these were disposed of after they were used, consequently, they represent a great challenge for the collector to find. Cartons, counter signs, window signs, wrappers, dixie lids, fans, and postcards, to mention a few, fall into this category. Also included are trade magazines and catalogs. Some of the early advertising is very beautiful and well done. The Menasha Printing Co., the Wolf Co., and the Mulholland Co. produced some of the nicest material.

A rapidly growing collectable, is the ice cream related postcard. The "heyday" of the penny postcard roughly coincided with that of the soda fountain, in the first quarter of this century. So, logically, some of the postcards reflected America's love for ice cream. There were well over 500 dif-

Cast iron mold from the machine used to bake the IcyPi wafers.

ferent ones produced. That doesn't mean they are easy to find, though. The main categories of cards are; soda fountain interior and exterior views, ice cream factories, comic cards, and advertising. Probably the most desirable, are the actual photo views of soda fountains. Prices of cards have increased, as collector awareness increases. An example is the photo card of a soda fountain that sold 5 years ago, for $2–3, now sells in the $10–20 range.

In conclusion, whatever you decide to collect, whether specialized or generalized, ice cream collecting is a fun and exciting hobby.

*Bill Burg*

Ergos ice cream wafer holder, with original box. It was used to mold and serve ice cream sandwiches.

Bob Cahn

Pan-American ice cream sandwich mold.

FOR ALL THOSE WHO STUDY THE HISTORY OF THE ICE CREAM INDUSTRY AND ENJOY THE COLLECTING OF ITS MEMORABILIA

As this book comes to a conclusion, one might ask, is there an organization for collectors of ice cream dishers and other ice cream memorabilia? The answer is . . . there is! It's title is appropriately, the ICE SCREAMERS. It's members are dedicated to the preservation and study of ice cream and soda fountain memorabilia.

For years, the ice cream collector had to be content with meeting other collectors by chance. In the summer of 1982, two enthusiastic collectors, Ed Marks, of Lancaster, Pa., and Bob Bruce, of San Diego, Ca., decided the time had come to do something about the situation. They saw that ice cream collectors around the country needed a common focal point. That focal point was to become a publication called, *THE ICE SCREAMER*. Using a nucleus of a mailing list compiled by Allan "Mr. Ice Cream" Mellis, of Chicago, Ill., and additional names gathered from other collectors, the first issue of *THE ICE SCREAMER* was mailed to 42 hopeful subscribers. This publication features various articles of collector interest, reprints of early soda fountain trade magazine items, current happenings in the field, buy, sell, and swap ads, and much more.

As word of the new organization spread, the membership increased. The first get-together for members was a modest one, in terms of numbers. It was held Oct. 1983, in conjunction with the 50th Anniversary Convention of the National Ice Cream Retailers Association, at the Drake Hotel, in Chicago. Several members displayed their collections in the NICRA meeting room, and many new members were recruited. The following year, in August, a separate ICE SCREAMER get-together was held in Gettysburg, Pa. This second meeting, a two day affair, brought together 42 collectors, from 12 different states. The third annual Ice Screamer Social, in Lancaster, Pa., was a tremendous success, with 72 members, from 16 states, present. The current membership numbers around 400.

Interested collectors and ice cream lovers can obtain further information on membership in the ICE SCREAMERS, by writing to: Ed Marks, P.O. Box 5387, Lancaster, Pa. 17601.

# Price Guide

To use this price guide, first find the category that fits the most obvious feature of the ice cream disher. It is usually the shape of the bowl. Under each category is the description of, or wording on the disher, listed alphabetically, by manufacturer. Refer to the page number listed to find complete information and a photo of the disher. These prices assume that the scoop is in good condition.

Remember that prices are relative and the final price is determined in negotiations between the buyer and seller. For more information on value determining factors, refer to Chap. 2.

## Round

| Manufacturer | Description | Page | Price |
|---|---|---|---|
| Arnold | no. 50 | (p. 121) | $20–40 |
| Benedict | Indestructo no. 3 | (p. 117) | $20–40 |
| | Indestructo no. 4 | (p. 118) | $20–40 |
| | Indestructo no. 16 | | $20–40 |
| Caron | Montreal | (p. 122) | $20–40 |
| Dover | springless | (p. 123) | $40–75 |
| Erie Specialty Co. | Quick and Easy | | $40–75 |
| F.S. Co | Clipper, pat. 1915 | (p. 112) | $20–40 |
| Fisher | Made in Canada | (p. 122) | $20–40 |
| Geer Mfg. Co. | Clipper Disher, pat. 1905 | (p. 81) | $75–125 |
| H. S. Geer Co. | Trojan Disher | (p. 99) | $40–75 |
| Gem Spoon Co. | pat. 1895 | (p. 74) | $40–75 |
| | Trojan | (p. 107) | $20–40 |
| Gilchrist Co. | no. 30 | (p. 108) | $40–75 |
| | no. 31 | (p. 109) | $20–40 |
| | no. 35 | (p. 151) | $20–40 |
| Giles and Nielsen | Clipper Spoon | (p. 81) | $75–125 |
| Guaranteed Disher Co. | pat. 1926 | (p. 120) | $40–75 |
| Hamilton Beach Co. | no. 30 | (p. 155) | $20–40 |
| | no. 31 | (p. 156) | $20–40 |
| | NO-PAK 31 | (p. 156) | $40–75 |
| | no. 51 | (p. 157) | $20–40 |
| Kingery | Victor, pat. 1908 | (p. 87) | $40–75 |

| | | | |
|---|---|---|---|
| Maryland Baking Co. | | (p. 148) | $20–40 |
| Medco | pat. 2160585 | (p. 166) | $20–40 |
| Myers Mfg. Co. | Myers Deluxe Disher, brass handle | (p. 163) | $20–40 |
| New Gem Mfg. Co. | New Gem | (p. 149) | $20–40 |
| | Nu Gem, marbelized handle | (p. 149) | $40–75 |
| Phila. Ice Cream Cone Mach. Co. | Philcone Disher | (p. 147) | $20–40 |
| Quick and Easy | "sundae cream" disher | (p. 100) | $75–125 |
| Shore Craft | brass, wood handle, ca. 1950 | | $20–40 |

## Conical

| | | | |
|---|---|---|---|
| Benedict | Indestructo no. 5 | (p. 119) | $40–75 |
| V. Clad | pat. May 3, 1876 | (p. 68) | $20–40 |
| | pat. May 3, 1878 | (p. 68) | $20–40 |
| | pat. Nov. 12, 1878 | (p. 69) | $20–40 |
| | copper plated | (p. 71) | $20–40 |
| Erie Specialty Co. | key release | (p. 89) | $40–75 |
| | pat. 1908 | (p. 85) | $125–200 |
| | Quick and Easy | (p. 103) | $40–75 |
| | "sundae cream" disher | (p. 101) | $75–125 |
| F.S. Co. | Clipper, pat. 1914 | (p. 113) | $40–75 |
| Geer Mfg. Co. | Cone Clipper, pat 1906 | (p. 82) | $75–125 |
| H. S. Geer Co. | pat. 1906 | (p. 83) | $75–125 |
| Gilchrist Co. | key release, "G" | (p. 111) | $20–40 |
| | no. 33 | (p. 110) | $40–75 |
| Kingery | key release | (p. 71) | $20–40 |
| | squeeze handle, pat. 1894 | (p. 73) | $75–125 |
| K-W | key release, pat. 1905 | (p. 80) | $20–40 |
| Thos. Mills and Bro. | tin, key release | | $20–40 |
| Mosteller | | (p. 88) | $40–75 |
| N. and Co. | Delmonico | (p. 90) | $40–75 |
| Naylor | pat. June 19, 1888 | (p. 70) | $20–40 |
| Quick and Easy Specialty Co. | pat. 1908 | (p. 88) | $40–75 |
| John W. Wallace Co. | key release, "W" | (p. 93) | $20–40 |
| Unknown maker | squeeze handle, pat. 1901 | (p. 79) | $125–200 |
| | key release, Royal | (p. 92) | $20–40 |
| | any steel or tin, key release | (p. 72,92) | $20–40 |

## Square or Rectangular

| | | | |
|---|---|---|---|
| Automatic Cone Co. | ICY-PI | (p. 134) | $75–125 |
| | ICY-PI, plastic handle, ca. 1950 | | $40–75 |
| Bunker-Clancy Mfg. Co. | pat. 1927 | (p. 141) | $125–200 |
| Cake Cone Co. | Rainbow Ice Cream Dispenser | (p. 142) | $75–125 |
| Dan Dee Dipper Co. | pat. 1920 | (p. 133) | $125–200 |
| Jiffy Dispenser Co. | pat. 1925, curved | (p. 136) | $75–125 |
| McLaren Cone Co. | ICY-PI | (p. 135) | $75–125 |
| Maryland Cream Pie Disher | | (p. 148) | $125–200 |
| Mayer Mfg. Co. | | (p. 137) | $75–125 |
| Phila. Ice Cream Cone Mach. Co. | Polar-Pak disher | (p. 146) | $125–200 |
| Sanitary Mould Co. | pat. 1925 | (p. 138) | $75–125 |
| J. Schloemer | | (p. 139) | $75–125 |
| United Products | Ice Cream Pie | (p. 142) | $125–200 |
| Unknown maker | horizontal | (p. 143) | $200+ |
| | offset handle | (p. 143) | $125–200 |
| W. F. Wendel | plunger mechanism | (p. 140) | $125–200 |

## Novelty

| | | | |
|---|---|---|---|
| The Best | cone holder | (p. 97) | $200+ |
| Bohlig Mfg Co. | pat. 1908, bowl divides | (p. 86) | $200+ |
| C+G Co. | cylindrical | (p. 78) | $200+ |
| Dover Mfg. Co. | slicer, pat. 1924 | (p. 124) | $200+ |
| Economy | disk shaped | (p. 153) | $200+ |
| Feller | aluminum cone filler | (p. 167) | $200+ |
| Fisher Motor Co. | cylinder, made in Canada | (p. 130) | $200+ |
| Fletcher Mfg. Co. | egg shaped | | $200+ |
| Jack Frost | cylinder | (p. 131) | $125–200 |
| H. S. Geer Co. | cone holder | (p. 98) | $200+ |
| General Ice Cream Corp. | cylinder | (p. 132) | $75–125 |
| Gilchrist Co. | no. 31, banana split | (p. 128) | $200+ |
| | no. 34, banana split | | $200+ |
| Hamilton Beach | no. 34, banana split | | $200+ |
| Manos Novelty Co. | heart shaped, pat. 1925 | (p. 129) | $200+ |
| Modern Specialty Co. | triangular | (p. 127) | $200+ |

| | | | |
|---|---|---|---|
| Mosteller | bowl flips over, pat. 1906 | (p. 84) | $200+ |
| Perfection Equip. Co. | cylinder, pat. 1896083 | (p. 154) | $75–125 |
| Pi-Alamoder | triangular | (p. 126) | $200+ |
| Prince Castle | PC Server, cube, ca. 1950 | | $40–75 |
| Quick and Easy | cone disher | (p. 106) | $125–200 |
| Schupfer and Eaton Co. | pat. 1773013 | (p. 150) | $125–200 |
| United Products Co. | banana split | (p. 128) | $200+ |
| Unknown maker | cone filler | (p. 96) | $200+ |
| | cylinder | (p. 131) | $200+ |
| | cylinder, plunger mechanism | (p. 152) | $125–200 |
| | point on bowl | (p. 97) | $75–125 |
| | squeeze handle, cone filler | (p. 164) | $75–125 |
| Veeder Mfg. Co. | with counter, pat. 1899 | (p. 75) | $200+ |

## Non-mechanical

| | | | |
|---|---|---|---|
| Benedict | Benedict Indestructo | (p. 161) | $5–15 |
| | ice cream spade | (p. 162) | $5–15 |
| Gilchrist Co. | ice cream space | (p. 111) | $5–15 |
| Maryland Baking Co. | | (p. 160) | $5–15 |
| L. E. Mason Co. | Mason Magic Scoop | (p. 160) | $5–15 |
| Rainbow | curved spade | (p. 162) | $20–40 |
| Scoop Rite | | (p. 161) | $5–15 |
| Zeroll | | (p. 158) | $5–15 |

# Selected Bibliography

## Books

Albright, Raymond W. *Two Centuries of Reading, Pa., 1748–1948*. Reading: Historical Society of Berks County, 1948.
*Census, United States*. Pennsylvania (1870, 1880, 1900). New Jersey (1910).
Dickson, Paul. *The Great American Ice Cream Book*. N.Y.: Atheneum, 1978.
*Dispenser's Formulary or Soda Water Guide, The*. N.Y.: D. O. Haynes and Co., 1915.
*Erie, Pa., An Historical and Descriptive Sketch*. ca. 1889.
*Erie, Pa. City Directories*. (1882–1902).
Fisk, Walter W. *The Book of Ice Cream*. 1921.
*Industrial Directories of Pennsylvania*. Harrisburg: (1916–1942).
Lorant, S. *Pittsburgh*.
*Memoirs of Allegheny County, Pa*. Madison, Wisc.: Northwestern Historical Association, 1904.
Miller, John. *A Twentieth Century History of Erie County, Pa*. Chicago: Lewis, 1909.
*Newark, N.J. City Directories*. Price and Lee, (1902–1943).
Patent and Trademarks Commission. *Patent Records*.
*Pennsylvania Annual Report of the Factory Inspector*. Harrisburg, (1900–1902).
*Pittsburgh and Allegheny City Directories*. Diffenbacher, (1896–1897).
Pomeroy, Ralph. *The Ice Cream Connection*. N.Y.: Paddington Press, 1975.
*Reading, Pa. City Directories*. Boyds, Brooks, and Owens. (1856–1903).
Reed, John E. *History of Erie County, Pa*. Indianapolis: Historical Publishing Co., 1925.
Selitzer, Ralph. *The Dairy Industry in America*. N.Y.: Dairy and Ice Cream Field, 1976.
Sommer, Hugo. *Theory and Practice of Ice Cream Making*. 1932.
Turnbow and Raffetto. *Ice Cream*. N.Y.: Wiley, 1928.
Weymouth, Lally. *America in 1876*. N.Y.: Vintage Books, 1976.

## Periodicals

*Confectioners Journal*. Philadelphia: 1930.
*Ice Cream Field*. D. Loyless, 1927.
*Ice Cream Review*. Milwaukee: Olsen Pub. Co., 1951.
*Ice Cream Trade Journal*. N.Y.: R. H. Donnelly, 1905–    .
*Ice Screamer*. Lancaster: Ed Marks, editor, 1982–    .
*Pharmaceutical Era*. N.Y.: D. O. Haynes.
*Soda Fountain, The*. N.Y.: D. O. Haynes, 1902–    .

## Catalogs

Antiques Research Publications. *Soda Fountain Supplies and Furnishings of the Early 1900's*. Chattanooga: 1968.

Beach, Hamilton and Co. *Catalog no. 4*. Racine, Wisc.: 1934.
Bishop-Babcock-Becker. *Blue Book of Soda Water Supplies*. Cleveland: ca. 1915.
Clad, V. *Clad's Ice Cream Machinery,* Philadelphia: 1905.
Creamery Package Manufacturing Co. *Catalog 830*. Chicago: 1917.
Curtis and Moore. *Soda Water Supplies Catalog*. Boston: 1904, 1905.
*Dairy Industries Catalog File*. Milwaukee: Olsen Pub. Co., 1935.
Dairyman's Supply Co. *Catalog 24*. Lansdowne, Pa.
Erie Specialty Co. *Erie Specialty Co. Catalog*. Erie: 1909.
Gilchrist Co. *Catalog No. 20*. Newark: ca. 1928.
Kingery Mfg. Co. *Catalog*. Cinn.: 1901.
Mills, Thomas and Bro. *Ice Cream Manufacturers Equipment Catalog 31*. Philadelphia: ca. 1931.
Pick, Albert and Co. *Catalog*. Chicago: 1925.

## Articles

Clewell, Wm. obituary in *Reading Eagle*. (Nov. 27, 1903): 5.
Gale, David M. and Charlotte. "The Drugstore Soda Fountain, A Study and Catalog of Nineteenth Century Soda Tokens." *The Numismatist,* (Jan., 1983).
Hall, Norman S. "Evolution of the Soda Fountain" *America, An Illustrated Diary of it's Most Exciting Years*. Valencia, Ca.: 1973. 41–45.
Mellis, Allan. "Ice Cream, Anyone? Post Cards That Is!" *Barr's Post Card News*. (Oct. 6, 1983): 97.
———. "Ice Cream Serving Trays." *Collector's Showcase*. (July/Aug., 1983): 7–11.
Smith, Wayne. "Evolution of the Ice Cream Dipper, 1876–1940" *Antique Trader Weekly*. (Sept. 22, 1982): 62–65.
Spiller, Dr. Burton. "A Double Scoop, Please!" *Spinning Wheel*. (June, 1973): 22–24.

## Interviews

Denaro, James. June, 1984. (grandson of inventor James Denaro).
Funka, Thomas. April, 1985. (President, Zeroll Co.).
Manos, John. June, 1983. (inventor of heart shaped ice cream scoop).

# Index